The Reel Thrilling Events of Bank Robber Henry Starr

Figure 1 Henry Starr, glamor photo for *A Debtor to the Law*, 1920. Author's collection.

The Reel Thrilling Events of Bank Robber Henry Starr

From Gentleman Bandit to Movie Star and Back Again

Mark Archuleta

University of North Texas Press
Denton, Texas

© 2025 Mark Archuleta

All rights reserved.
Printed in the United States of America..

10 9 8 7 6 5 4 3 2 1

Permissions:
University of North Texas Press
1155 Union Circle #311336
Denton, TX 76203-5017

The paper used in this book meets the minimum requirements of the
American National Standard for Permanence of Paper for Printed Library
Materials, z39.48.1984. Binding materials have been chosen for durability.

Library of Congress Cataloging-in-Publication Data

Names: Archuleta, Mark, 1964- author
Title: The reel thrilling events of bank robber Henry Starr : from gentleman
  bandit to movie star and back again / Mark Archuleta.
Description: Denton, Texas : University of North Texas Press, [2025] |
  Includes bibliographical references and index.
Identifiers: LCCN 2025019201 (print) | LCCN 2025019202 (ebook) |
  ISBN 9781574419788 cloth | ISBN 9781574419863 ebook
Subjects: LCSH: Starr, Henry, 1873-1921 | Starr, Henry, 1873-1921--
  In motion pictures | Frontier and pioneer life--Oklahoma | Bank
  robbers--Southwestern States--Biography | Motion picture actors and
  actresses--Southwestern States--Biography | Cherokee Indians--Mixed
  descent--Oklahoma--Biography | Outlaws in motion pictures | Silent
  films--United States--History | LCGFT: Biographies
Classification: LCC F700 .A73 2025 (print) | LCC F700 (ebook) |
  DDC 973.04/975570092 $a B--dc23/eng/20250430
LC record available at https://lccn.loc.gov/2025019201
LC ebook record available at https://lccn.loc.gov/2025019202

The electronic edition of this book was made possible by the support of the
Vick Family Foundation.

Typeset by vPrompt eServices.

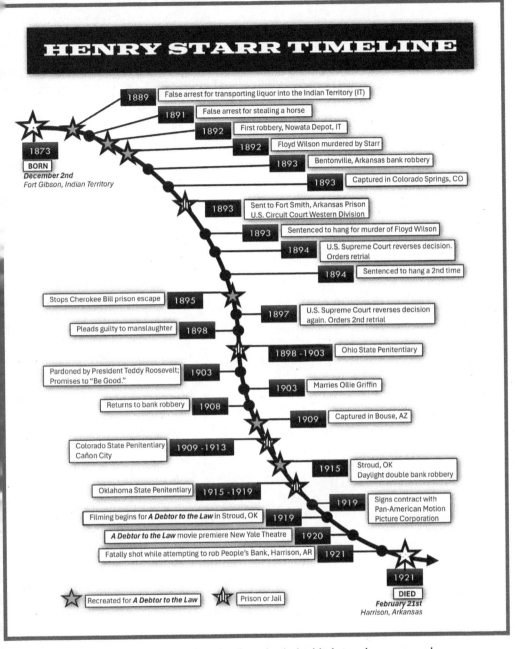

Figure 2 Starr timeline from birth to death, highlighting the moments he re-created and reimagined for his filmed biography, *A Debtor to the Law*, 1920. Infographic by Artxie Media.

Contents

Preface   ix

Prologue   xiii

Reel One	I'm on the Road Called Straight Now	1
Reel Two	The Stroud Doubleheader	41
Intermission	Starr's in Stripes Forever	83
Reel Three	Henry Movie Starr	89
Reel Four	Start Picture	139
Reel Five	Pushed to the Brink	183
Reel Six	Post-Credit Scenes	211

Epilogue   221

Endnotes   223

Bibliography   267

Index   279

Preface

The Reel Thrilling Events of Bank Robber Henry Starr is both a hunt for lost treasure and a detective story. In 1921 the star of the silent film *A Debtor to the Law*, Henry Starr, was gunned down in Harrison, Arkansas, while attempting to rob a bank. Starr was a classically handsome movie star, rivaling John Barrymore and Douglas Fairbanks. He was tall and raven haired and had the strong facial features that affirmed his Cherokee heritage.[1]

Starr was also the greatest bank robber of his era. His "blood and thunder" escapades mirrored dime novels, except his story was all true. As a teenager Starr had been condemned to hang on the notorious gallows of Fort Smith, Arkansas—twice—and lived. At 25 Starr was sentenced to serve fifteen years in the Ohio State Penitentiary, but President Theodore Roosevelt pardoned him for heroism; he had foiled a deadly prison revolt.[2] Roosevelt asked Starr, "Will you be good if I set you free?"[3] Starr promised he would go straight, and he kept that vow—for roughly five years. In 1915, at age 42, Starr pulled off the most extraordinary feat in bank robbing history, robbing two banks in Stroud, Oklahoma, at the same time in broad daylight.[4] Starr had bested the likes of Jesse James and the Dalton Gang and earned the moniker of "the King of Bank Robbers."[5] In 1919, at 47, Starr was paroled from the Oklahoma State Penitentiary. When the prison gates swung open, Starr entered a new world swept up in a mania for motion pictures. A decade earlier Starr had written his autobiography *Thrilling Events: Life of Henry Starr, by Himself.*[6] Little could he have imagined it would serve as the template for a screenplay—known in 1919 as a "scenario"—in a medium that was barely in his consciousness in 1913.

The Reel Thrilling Events of Bank Robber Henry Starr begins in 1913 when the jailer's keys unlocked the prison doors and Starr was released from the Colorado State Penitentiary in Cañon City, Colorado.[7] The book focuses on the last eight years of his life, examining how a unique quirk of cinematic fate turned a notorious outlaw into a glamorous motion picture star—and what drove him back to bank robbery. Starr's biographical film, *A Debtor to the Law*, is lost to history, but this biography leverages surviving posters, lobby cards, interviews, and on-set photos to re-create the film as audiences saw it shimmering on the silver screen in 1920. Newspaper accounts provide clues to Starr's mindset as forces lined up in opposition to prevent him from bringing his life story to the screen. Ministerial religious organizations, the Women's Christian Temperance Union, and state and federal legislators feared *A Debtor to the Law* would corrupt America's youth, and they fought hard to stop the public from seeing it.

To add context, *The Reel Thrilling Events of Bank Robber Henry Starr* compares the experiences of two contemporaneous outlaws who also became moving picture stars: Al Jennings and Emmett Dalton. Outlaws from the era shortly before Starr, like Frank James and Cole Younger, came too early to capitalize on motion pictures, although they did have their own traveling Wild West show.[8] Outlaws after Starr, Dillinger,[9] Bonnie (Parker) and Clyde (Barrow),[10] and Charles "Pretty Boy" Floyd[11] died violent deaths, so there was no second act. Even so, if they had lived, by the 1930s motion pictures had evolved to the point where a real outlaw would not be hired as an actor. Case in point: on the evening of July 22, 1934, Dillinger was gunned down outside Chicago's Biograph Theater, where he'd just finished watching Clark Gable play a gangster in the film *Manhattan Melodrama*.[12]

Only Starr, Jennings, and Dalton lived in that window where a horseback outlaw bridged the invention of motion pictures. While all three received scorn for capitalizing on their infamy, only Starr suffered the stereotypical racist language and whitewashing of his image. Starr's life began in 1873 with the invasion of white settlers on Cherokee lands in the Indian Territory and ended with the bubbling racial tensions that led to the Tulsa Race Massacre in 1921. This biography exposes how racial tensions sparked Starr's outlaw career and influenced the filming of his life story.

Motion pictures were the siren call for people from all walks of life—like US Deputy Marshal William Tilghman, who, as producer/director, first put Starr on film, and Vivian Woodcock Kay, a college actress who would become an independent film producer and write the screenplay for *A Debtor to the Law*. This book shows how moving picture professionals

Preface

fell into Starr's orbit and how the biographical film compromised the real versus reel facts.

Like an alchemist, Starr hoped to turn infamy into fame via moving pictures and live the American myth of reinvention, where one could "fashion a future liberated from the past."[13] Starr realized that *Thrilling Events* didn't sufficiently explain his story of lost innocence and the futility of crime. Only through the power of cinema could Starr redeem himself in the eyes of the public, his family, and the Cherokee Nation.

The Reel Thrilling Events of Bank Robber Henry Starr would not be possible without Glenn Shirley, a member of the Oklahoma Journalism Hall of Fame.[14] His knowledge of Western history was unmatched, and his works are cited throughout. Another influential historian, Michael Wallis, provided an excellent summation of Starr's life: "Henry Starr's story was pure Hollywood. It was pure Oklahoma. And like the lives of so many other cowboys, it was the stuff of movies."[15]

Henry Starr was a horseback gunslinger who robbed more banks than any man in America, but in 1919 motion pictures were the new Wild West.

Saddle up! You're in for a wild ride!

Prologue

William J. "Bill" Myers felt powerless standing in the counting room with his hands in the air. On February 18, 1921, the People's Bank in Harrison, Arkansas, was under siege. Moments earlier three armed bandits had banged through the front door and swiftly descended on the cashier windows, pointing their rifles and barking orders.

Two bandits held the cashiers at gunpoint, while the third—a swarthy man in his late 40s—breached the threshold. Myers and the rest of the bank staff threw up their hands as ordered. The older outlaw demanded the head cashier open the safe.

Sixty-nine-year-old Myers watched with silent anger as the bandit began scooping handfuls of currency into a pillowcase. He scoured his mind, thinking of what he could do to stop the vile marauders. Then he had a moment of startling clarity: a rifle was hidden in the bank vault behind him. While the robbers were distracted, Myers slipped into the vault unnoticed.

Inside, he found the Winchester Model 1873 rifle he had hidden there twelve years earlier for just such a moment. Was it still loaded? Quietly, Myers eased the lever action downward, opening the chamber window. The light caught the brass casing, and it winked at him.

Myers stepped to the vault proscenium and brought the steel-cased Winchester to his shoulder. His small, round spectacles and white, hangdog mustache gave some people the impression that he was a doddering old man. But age had not diminished Myers's grit. He sighted down the barrel and found his target—Cherokee outlaw Henry Starr on one knee in front of the safe. Starr was stylishly dressed in a luxurious overcoat topped by a homburg with a silk hatband. In any other situation, Myers would have mistaken him for one of the bank's wealthier and distinguished clients. If Myers recognized Starr from his movie posters or his wanted posters, he never said. All Myers cared about was keeping his depositors' money safe.

He squeezed the trigger.

Bang!

Across the counting room, Starr spun and hit the wall. The .38 bullet had cut the air at 1,235 feet per second, dropping with a parabolic trajectory. The force pierced Starr's clothing and flesh and struck bone, sending him flying.

A bank clerk shrieked and quickly ran to the fallen bandit. She gently cradled Starr's head in her lap as he lay bleeding.

Starr's eyes lost their focus.

Where is the director?

Why did the effects man use so much blood—and why is it warm?

Something wasn't right.

He'd vowed to go straight.

I'm an actor now.

Where is the scenarist?

The scene needed a rewrite.

Starr would insist on a rewrite.

Reel One

I'm on the Road Called Straight Now

In November 1913 40-year-old career bank robber Henry Starr was released from the Colorado State Penitentiary in Cañon City. He had just completed four years at his third prison in twenty years. If Starr had been told that in seven years he would be a matinee idol, he would have found it just as likely as his jumping into a bullet-shaped rocket ship and crashing into the eye of the man on the moon—imagery he might have seen from the 1902 French science-fiction film *Le voyage dans la lune* by George Méliès.[1]

Now, as the prison gates swung open,[2] Starr was focused on repairing his relationship with his wife, Olive, who went by Ollie, and their boy, Teddy, who was 5 when he was locked up. Starr and Ollie met in 1903, shortly after President Theodore Roosevelt commuted his sentence and he was released from the Ohio State Penitentiary.[3] He was 30 and she was 21. Like Starr, Ollie was part-Cherokee, and he described her as "a girl of much refinement and culture."[4] Blinded by love, Ollie ignored the bank-robbing past of her dashing young man. It would be an understatement to say they fell in love at first sight. They met on a Tuesday and were married by Friday.[5] Starr promised Ollie his life as a bank robber was over, and he would "beat back"—slang for going straight. At first Starr made good on his promise. He became a land

Figure 3 Henry Starr and his wife Olive "Ollie" Griffin, holding their son Theodore "Teddy" Quay Roosevelt Starr. After his pardon from President Theodore Roosevelt, Starr left the Ohio State Penitentiary to begin a new life in Guthrie, Oklahoma. Globe Studio, 1910. Courtesy of the Oklahoma Historical Society.

I'm on the Road Called Straight Now

agent in Guthrie, and with the birth of Teddy Quay Roosevelt Starr a year later, they'd formed a picture-perfect family.[6] The outlaw—sometimes called the Bearcat because he was stealthy, swift of foot, and would fight like a wild animal if ever cornered—had become a domesticated tabby.[7]

Then, in December 1907, Starr's criminal past came back to haunt him. Arkansas acting Governor Xenophon Pindall seethed when he heard Starr was now a free man despite never facing justice for the June 6, 1893, heist of the People's Bank in Bentonville, Arkansas.[8] Governor Pindall demanded that Oklahoma Governor Charles Haskell turn Starr over immediately to stand trial.[9]

When Starr heard the news, he was livid. He had been only 19 years old when he orchestrated the Bentonville robbery and felt he'd already paid his debt to society, having spent the last decade behind bars—although not for Bentonville. Since then Starr had made an honest man of himself and was now a 35-year-old husband and father of two children. Ollie had recently given birth to a second child.

Starr sent a friend to the Oklahoma state capitol, then in Guthrie, to find out Governor Haskell's intentions. The friend misreported that the governor had granted the extradition. Starr broke the news to Ollie. He said he wasn't going to wait around to be dragged to an Arkansas prison, so he fled to the Osage Hills west of Bartlesville. Being forced to flee his home and family ate at him. He grew increasingly embittered at the injustice of his having to hide like a hunted animal. Driven by rage and hostility toward fate, Starr and one of his old gang from the 1893 Bentonville, Arkansas, heist, John "Kid" Wilson, robbed the Tyro Bank in Kansas, just north of the Oklahoma border.[10] "I can see now what a foolish thing it was to do," Starr said. "But at the time, all the past wrongs seemed to rise up and cloud my better judgment. My reason left me, and I simply went to pieces."[11]

There was no turning back. Starr was an outlaw again and would have to live life on the lam. In March 1908 a family friend from Dewey arrived at Starr's hideout along the Hominy and Bird Creek confluence outside Skiatook.

"Ollie sent me," the man said. "I've got bad news."

Their infant had died. Starr felt like his heart had been ripped out, and all he wanted to do was ride to Dewey and collapse in the arms of Ollie.

The friend held him back, trying to reason with him. Dewey's chief of police chirped to the newspapers that if Starr showed up to the funeral, he'd be arrested—even if it required a bloody shootout. "He might get some of us fellows," Chief Brown boasted. "But we are sure to get him."[12]

Instead, Starr mounted his horse and rode incognito into Bixby, where he wired a telegram to Ollie. He dispatched friends and family to be by her side, but it was cold comfort. Two miles north of downtown Dewey, a grave was dug for a child-sized casket in the city cemetery. Later, a miniature gravestone would be placed in the lawn reading, "Baby Starr," with the "S" engraved backward. Henry was not there.

Following the burial, Ollie, lost in grief and depression, fell ill. Starr knew he had made an unforgivable mistake by allowing himself to be so hot-headed and selfish. He had brought disaster upon his perfect family life, and Ollie, without his knowledge, started slowly drifting out of love with him.[13]

Starr was on the lam from 1907 to 1909, robbing banks and living in Mexico. When "Kid" Wilson began to act strangely, and Starr feared violence at his hands, they separated. Low on funds, Starr asked a Tulsa friend, S.W. Fenton, to wire him money he was owed. The wily Fenton, thinking he could both renege on his debt and collect reward money, alerted authorities. In May 1909, when Starr arrived at the post office in Bouse, Arizona, to pick up his wired money, lawmen got the drop on him.[14]

Starr was transported under armed guard from Bouse to Lamar, Colorado, to stand trial for the July 6, 1908, Amity bank robbery. Colorado authorities considered Starr so dangerous that they placed him in solitary confinement for six months before his trial. The isolation wore on Starr, and when he appeared before the court, he confessed. In November 1909 the judge sentenced Starr to serve between seven to twenty-five years at the Colorado State Penitentiary in Cañon City. Ollie was in the courtroom, with little Teddy in her arms, when the verdict was read. She burst into tears.[15]

Once again Starr was hustled onto a train in handcuffs and shackles, this time steaming for Cañon City. Fortunately for Starr the Colorado State Penitentiary had recently hired a new warden, Thomas J. Tynan. Previous wardens were small-minded, harsh disciplinarians who punished prisoners by strapping them across a pommel horse called the Old Gray Mare and paddling them violently until the seat

I'm on the Road Called Straight Now 5

Figure 4 Henry Starr (age 36), booking photo taken November 28, 1909, Colorado Penitentiary, Cañon City, Colorado. Courtesy of the Museum of Colorado Prisons.

of their pants split.[16] Warden Tynan, a personable former traveling salesman, was a reformer. He wanted to return prisoners to society as "restored mended men" rather than as broken and revenge-minded individuals.[17] Among Tynan's innovations was placing birdhouses in the trees, starting a sports program, and instituting vocational training. In the new woodshop, prisoners like Starr built handcrafted, inlaid wood gift boxes to sell in town.[18]

Starr thrived under Tynan's progressive policies and earned enough trust that the warden selected him to pilot an innovative work-release concept. Under the program a trustee would be placed in charge of a work camp, sometimes two hundred miles from the prison, to supervise roadbuilding crews made up of fellow prisoners. Astonishingly, Starr was provided with a rifle and a horse and could have fled at any opportunity. Yet he never tried to escape.[19] "To the average person who has gleaned opinion of me from newspaper writers, it would mean murder, bank robbery, and every crime in the calendar. Truth is, I stayed it out," Starr wrote.[20]

Believing Starr was a changed man, Warden Tynan approved Starr's early release in 1913. Declaring himself fully reformed, Starr walked out of the Colorado State Penitentiary full of optimism. His heart swelled with emotion as he laid eyes on his aging mother, Mary Gordon, and his now 9-year-old son, Teddy. Starr kneeled, and the boy raced into his father's arms. After a long hug, Starr looked at his mother and asked, "Where's Ollie?"

Gordon wrung her hands; she had been dreading this moment.

Two Gut Punches

Sixty-four-year-old Mary Gordon was born in 1849 in Fort Gibson, Indian Territory, and was one-quarter Cherokee. A devout Methodist, she wore her hair tied up neat and high.[21] She shared her son's piercing black eyes and plainspokenness.

"She's divorced you, Henry."

Gordon handed him a document. His eyes raced down the page.

"It became final on February 14th," Starr observed. "Some Valentine."

The news hit Starr hard. His eyes watered. Starr couldn't blame her for leaving him.[22]

As they stood on the steps outside Colorado State Penitentiary, a question from Teddy broke Starr's reverie.

"When can we leave?"

The innocent question hung in the air as Starr knuckled away the tears from the corners of his eyes. Warden had just informed him that the State Board of Pardons had insisted that as a condition of his release, he wouldn't be allowed to leave the borders of Colorado. Starr attempted to clear his throat but answered huskily, "They're not going to let me return to Tulsa just yet, son."[23]

The parole conditions were a bitter pill for Starr to swallow, but he was determined not to let his previous impetuousness cloud his judgment. He would have to make it work and find someplace to live. Gordon suggested Starr contact Arthur Dodge, an uncle by marriage who ran a large horse and cattle ranch in Granada, Colorado, near the Kansas border.[24] Starr agreed. "All I want is a chance to make good," Starr told his mother. "For Teddy's sake."[25]

I'm on the Road Called Straight Now 7

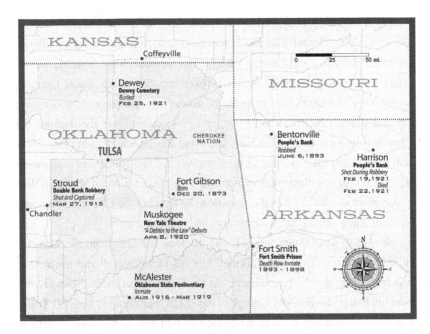

Figure 5 The Oklahoma and Arkansas border where Starr roamed as a bandit, prisoner, and actor from 1873 to 1921. Map by Artxie Media.

Starr made himself useful on Dodge's Granada ranch. When he arrived, the Colorado air already had a snap to it. Starr spent the next few weeks repairing fences, building livestock shelters, and storing feed. He had been a broncobuster in his youth and knew all aspects of ranching. But at 41 Starr had to be realistic. He knew riding, roping, and sleeping under the stars was a young man's game. Starr needed to find work that didn't require manual labor.

A disheartening obstacle was his lack of formal education. Born in 1873, Starr had been raised in a cabin at Fort Gibson, Indian Territory, and attended the Tahlequah Male Indian Seminary. Unlike the Carlisle Indian Industrial School, in Carlisle, Pennsylvania—a federally funded, off-reservation boarding school founded by a white US Army Lieutenant, Richard Henry Pratt, who preached cultural assimilation of the Indians through mental and physical abuse—Tahlequah was established and funded by the Cherokee government. In 1851 the Cherokee built a Male Seminary southwest of Tahlequah and a Female Seminary a few miles away, north of Park Hill. The three-story brick structures were influenced by classic Greek architecture, with massive Doric columns along three sides. Initially the instructors were Eastern educated, recruited from Yale, Mt. Holyoke, and Newton Theological Seminary (Newton, Massachusetts). The curriculum for the male Cherokee included Greek, Latin, German, and French; chemistry, botany, geology, astronomy, and zoology; geography; US and English history; economics; and philosophy. Over the decades the Cherokee became trained teachers and were the principal instructors. Both seminaries were shuttered during the Civil War and had only recently reopened when Starr began elementary school. The original vision of the Cherokee government was for the boarding school to be free, but the Cherokee economy was still recuperating, and students now had to pay tuition.[26]

In 1884, when Starr was 11, the Tahlequah Male Seminary director called him to his office and informed him his father was ill and his mother was requesting that he return home. At the Fort Gibson cabin, Starr discovered his father, 41-year-old George "Hop" Starr, curled up in bed, his health rapidly deteriorating. George whispered to him that if the family were to survive financially, Starr would have to quit the seminary to run their walnut timber business and farm their land. Starr recalled, "My father's ill health made it necessary for me to stay at home, and I can honestly say that it was with regret that I gave up my books to help win our daily bread."[27]

To his credit Starr later used his time in the Colorado State Penitentiary to buttress his lack of education. He was an autodidact who always set a little money aside to buy newspapers and borrow books on history and the law. Starr even claimed he was admitted to the Colorado bar.[28]

A longtime friend of Starr's offered a glimmer of hope, giving him the money to purchase a cafe in the small town of Holly, ten miles west of Granada. Starr sparked to the idea. He had even developed a secret chili recipe in prison that he hoped would become his signature dish. Starr's excitement was palpable as he bid farewell to Arthur Dodge and boarded the Atcheson, Topeka, and Santa Fe for Holly. In the 1890s Holly was a ranching boomtown located along the Santa Fe Trail and catering to cattlemen. When sugar beets sprouted into the new cash crop, the economy shifted to agriculture. In 1912 the Santa Fe railroad replaced the old wooden depot with a sturdy brick building in the Spanish colonial mission style.[29]

I'm on the Road Called Straight Now

When Starr arrived at the new Holly depot a year later, his spirit was filled with optimism. He tipped his hat to a passing lady who smiled at the confident newcomer. She was taken by the gaunt six-footer with the eye of an eagle and hair black as coal. It was written at the time, "But for the lines of care on his swarthy face, he retained a rather youthful expression."[30]

Starr took a room at a boardinghouse, then jumped in with both boots and started getting his new business, the Star Cafe—star with one *R*—in order. He cleaned up, replaced broken crockery, and replenished staples such as salt, sugar, and coffee from the local market. Starr read in the newspaper about a diner in nearby Ordway that had installed new stools and footrails at the luncheon counter and had an electric sign in the window. Renovations like those would have to wait until the Star Cafe started to turn a profit, which Starr expected to happen quickly.

When Starr was ready for his grand opening, he went to the Holly print shop to place his order. While he was there, Starr met a Kansas man who stuck out his hand and introduced himself. Starr said, "I'm Henry Starr." The man's eyes widened, and Starr could see the man looked dyspeptic. The Kansas man remembered Starr as a "fine figure straight as an arrow, with a kindly look out of his eye," yet he was relieved that the former bandit who "shows his Indian blood unmistakably" didn't rob him.[31] Starr was despondent after the encounter, realizing how difficult it would be to change people's perceptions.

In retrospect Holly wasn't the ideal spot for Starr to make a new start. The town was only a few miles from Amity, whose bank he and "Kid" Wilson had robbed in 1908. At the time the Amity townsfolk were on the brink of financial disaster. The city had a high water table that failed to drain effectively. The standing water leached alkali to the surface, making it useless for crops. The economy was dead when Starr and Wilson arrived to steal what little the Amity residents had saved. Starr didn't endear himself when sharing a story at the Star Cafe about how he and Wilson had hidden in a tree and snickered to themselves as the Amity posse rested on the ground below them.[32]

Starr was treated with suspicion. "The people expected me all the time to go out some night and rob the bank," Starr said. "I didn't even have a gun. But it was no use trying to make a good impression."[33] Despite his claim of being unarmed,

Starr was known to take walks to the Arkansas River south of town and fire his .32-caliber pistol—perhaps to keep his marksmanship skills sharp.[34]

The Star Cafe quickly made a name for itself with its popular chili. But unfortunately it also became infamous for something far less appetizing. One evening a boy named Ray Jones left the Electric Theatre after watching a silent picture and strolled down Holly's main business district. As he passed Starr's cafe, he peeked in the window and saw a giant cockroach crawling in and out of the sugar bowl.[35]

One of Starr's first hires was Carl Suedekum, a 19-year-old semipro shortstop for the local baseball team. Suedekum didn't share Holly's irrational fear of his new boss. He described Starr as one of the nicest guys he had ever known, and the former outlaw was "constantly being chased by women."[36] One of the cafe's most frequent customers was 36-year-old Loretta "Retta" Elwick, who had enchanting bedroom eyes and a pert, impish nose. Unfortunately, Retta was already married to an auto mechanic named Guy Elwick, and they had two children.[37]

The ensuing love triangle was akin to F. Scott Fitzgerald's *The Great Gatsby*, with Guy as George B. Wilson, the "sad sack" gas station owner, and Retta as his wife Myrtle, trapped in the Valley of Ashes and yearning for excitement.[38] Starr was Tom Buchanan, but instead of tantalizing Retta with wealth and privilege, he was tall, dark, and handsome and represented danger and adventure. Their romance also had the heat of James M. Cain's *The Postman Always Rings Twice*, which was also set in a diner.[39] Starr was the charismatic drifter Frank Chambers, and Retta was Cora, the voluptuous young woman trapped in a loveless marriage. Starr and Retta would not conspire to kill the husband like in Cain's novel, but they would take a bold risk to remain together.

After less than six months outside of prison, Starr's attempt to run a restaurant had failed. His famous Star Cafe chili, while popular, could not overcome his notorious reputation as an outlaw. Although to be fair, with the prevalence of cockroaches, perhaps people were less afraid of Starr's past and more fearful of contracting dysentery. He needed a change of scenery.

Starr asked the State Board of Pardons for permission to leave Colorado, hoping they would allow him to return to Oklahoma, where he had the emotional

Figure 6 Loretta "Retta" Elwick abandoned her husband and children and moved from Holly, Colorado, to live as Starr's common-law wife in Tulsa, Oklahoma. Photo: *Tacoma Times*, April 8, 1915.

and financial support of family and friends. The board hesitated to let him go too far from their watchful eye but eventually approved a move to Wyoming under the condition that he keep his real name. With only ten dollars in his pocket, Starr headed north. He worked odd jobs selling furniture and working on a railroad crew for a measly dollar a day. Although Starr had never robbed a bank or a train in Wyoming, his notorious reputation preceded him. "Every time I got a job, someone would point me out as the 'bad man from Oklahoma,' and they kicked me out," Starr explained. "I couldn't light anywhere. I couldn't 'beat back.'"[40]

Once again, Starr felt cornered and desperate. Would bank robbery provide an easy solution once again?

Dear Son, Forgive Me

By June 1914 Starr's life had hit rock bottom. He was jobless and longing for his family in Oklahoma. He believed the State Board of Pardons restrictions had once again doomed him to failure. Starr decided to break his parole. "I promised not to leave Colorado, but the desire to take my boy into my arms became so strong that I beat my way back to Oklahoma."[41]

The fastest way home was by rail, but Starr only had thirty cents to his name. So he snuck aboard the Union Pacific to Ellsworth, Kansas, and the Missouri Pacific southeast to Wichita, picked up the St. Louis & San Francisco to Cherryvale, then took the Missouri Pacific south, through Coffeyville into Tulsa. Along the route Starr "bummed [his] chuck" by knocking on the back doors of prairie folks who understood what it was like to hit a rough patch. On June 11 Starr arrived in Tulsa "dirty, ragged, hungry, determined again to start over and be good."[42]

Starr had one last idea for making honest money. He entered the office of R. D. Gordon, a Tulsa publisher, and presented his handwritten memoir, *Thrilling Events: Life of Henry Starr, Famous Cherokee Indian Outlaw Narrates His Many Adventures from Boyhood to Date*. Gordon jumped on the idea. He knew the public craved "blood and thunder stories," and he suggested adding to the cover that the autobiography was written behind the walls of the Colorado Penitentiary to bolster its gritty authenticity.

Soon, a modest advertisement appeared in the *Tulsa World Daily:*

> For Sale Miscellaneous:
> Life of Henry Starr in book form. 50c.
> —Orpheum News Stand or Black Printing Co.[43]

Starr's goal for writing his autobiography was to expose the corrupt US deputy marshal system and how sworn lawmen enriched themselves at the expense of the innocent. Starr detailed how he was railroaded at 17 with a false charge of horse thievery. The truth was, Starr found an unbranded horse in a gully and brought it home to care for it. He asked people in the Nowata area who the horse belonged to, and a few days later, a rancher, Charles Eaton, claimed the stray horse. Starr wrote that Eaton "seemed so

I'm on the Road Called Straight Now   13

pleased to find him in such good condition, even offering to pay me for my trouble."[44] Starr considered his actions just a part of being a good neighbor and refused the money.

However, two months later, Eaton returned with Deputy US Marshal Jasper Exendine with a signed writ accusing Starr of horse theft. The deputy marshal placed Starr in handcuffs and put him in a wagon bound for the 150-mile ride to the jail at Fort Smith, Arkansas.[45] At the time deputy marshals weren't paid a salary. They made their money by running errands for the court, such as executing warrants.[46] However, unscrupulous deputy marshals could make additional money by arresting innocent people and transporting them to the court at Fort Smith. Later, Starr learned that the court paid Deputy Marshal Exendine and Eaton a per diem plus meals to escort him to Arkansas.

The experience at Fort Smith "chilled my heart," wrote Starr.[47] He was an innocent thrown in among horse thieves, highwaymen, and killers. The screams and curses of two hundred prisoners echoed across the three tiers of metal cages—a cacophony of madness. The stench reminded Starr of the animal section of the circus. He was assigned a cell on the second floor and given bedclothes reeking of filth and teeming with lice. Once inside the two-person cell, he saw bedbugs and mites hopping on his stained mattress. Starr's gorge rose in his throat as the odor of feces and urine rose from the chamber pot in the corner. He'd hardly gotten settled when a prison gang jumped him and tried to remove a ring from his finger—a gift from his girl-friend May Morrison. Starr was young, but he had moxie. He successfully fought off the grown ruffians with his flying fists.

Starr languished in jail for several weeks, awaiting trial. "I became a soured, sullen man, brooding over this great wrong that had been done to me," he wrote. When his case finally went before the court, Eaton folded and admitted lying. The judge reprimanded Eaton and Deputy Marshal Exendine, and Starr was set free.

When Starr returned to Nowata, people noticed his "rollicking boyish-ness" was gone.[48] Even though the charge of larceny was proven false, towns-folk looked at him differently, believing he was the latest in a long line of Starr outlaws. Reporters often wrote erroneously that he was either the husband, son,

Figure 7 Henry Starr (age 17) was an innocent thrown in among horse thieves, highwaymen, and killers at Fort Smith prison when he was falsely accused of horse thievery. Afterward, his "rollicking boyishness" was gone. Courtesy of the Pawnee Bill Ranch and Museum, Oklahoma Historical Society Site.

or brother of the notorious cattle rustler Belle Starr. Starr often had to correct the record. "She came from Missouri and married Sam Starr, a distant cousin of mine," Starr said. "She was not a bad woman. I knew her well."[49] However, his great uncle was Tom Starr, a convicted whiskey peddler, cattle rustler, and sociopath who boasted of killing nearly thirty men in the Cherokee Civil War. He allegedly wore a necklace made from the ears of his enemies. Tom's ranch, named Younger's Bend, became a refuge for outlaws like the Youngers (Cole, Jim, and Bob) and James (Frank and Jesse).[50]

Figure 8 Five year's before filming *A Debtor to the Law*, Starr wrote *Thrilling Events: Life of Henry Starr* (published July 1914) to explain what led him to bank robbery and how he was now completely reformed. Courtesy of the Princeton University Library.

Starr's father, George, was nothing like Tom. He made an honest living and raised his children, Elizabeth, Adna, and Henry, to be good citizens. "My father was a splendid man, and my mother was one of nature's noblewomen," Starr said.[51] George Starr's early death at 41 meant he couldn't protect his boy from opportunists who sought revenge on anyone from the Tom Starr lineage. Teenage Starr was an easy mark, and his false arrest for horse thievery altered his outlook forever: "When they let me out I was bitter against the world. I decided that if they sent people to jail when they had violated no law they couldn't do more to a criminal. Having been branded a criminal, I thought I might as well be one in fact."[52]

Thus, Starr's outlaw career was set in motion.

In *Thrilling Events* Starr didn't just wallow in hurt and outrage. He also wrote humorous anecdotes about his life on the lam, including helping a preacher by shooting the vermin (prairie dogs) on his property, only to be served their greasy pan-fried carcasses for breakfast the following day, and being cajoled by pushy women at a tent revival to testify to God's glory despite his lack of religion.[53] His picaresque journey emphasized the kindness of people and their simpler pleasures. Starr's autobiography concluded with the upbeat message that he had reformed entirely.

By the summer of 1914, Starr's hastily printed booklet *Thrilling Events* appeared at newsstands and hotel gift shops.[54] The striking salmon-colored cover featured a black-and-white photograph of Starr in a dapper suit and tie. Starr claimed his print run of ten thousand copies sold out in months.[55]

However, Starr's hope that telling his life story would allow him to make a fresh start in the minds of the public was dashed when a string of bank robberies occurred across Oklahoma and Kansas in the early fall of 1914. Newspaper editors were quick to point the finger at Starr. "They blamed them all on me," Starr told journalist A. B. MacDonald. "So help me God, I didn't have a hand in any one of them." Although Starr was often cagey about his involvement in bank robberies in the past, in this instance he was telling the truth. The real culprit for the slew of bank heists was 23-year-old Joe Davis, a part-Cherokee outlaw from Porum, Oklahoma, sixty miles west of Fort Smith, Arkansas.[56]

Starr had to admit that Davis reminded him of himself at that age.

The Gentleman Bandit Returns

By the late summer of 1914, Starr finally had enough of trying to go straight. "They got after me and chased me hard, and last September I broke over," Starr said. The nation's most notorious bank robber was back on the prowl.[57]

Starr tapped Davis to become his new partner, and the bold, young outlaw jumped at the chance to work with the old-timer. Davis biographer Jerry Thompson wrote, "There is little doubt that Starr was one of Davis's role models and someone Joe emulated—a bandit who robbed banks and got away with it."[58] Starr and Davis had a lot in common. Both were members of the Cherokee Nation and swore off alcohol and tobacco. However, their upbringing differed greatly. Davis came from a family of cattle barons and grew up wealthy, entitled, and lethal. His family made their money stealing cattle, altering the brands, and selling the livestock to buyers willing to look the other way. The Davis family evaded justice by having enough money to tie up the courts with delays and buy off witnesses and jurors. Knowing this, Davis acted with impunity, strutting like a peacock, although his prominent facial features made him look more akin to an Oklahoma crow.

The most significant difference between Starr and Davis was their regard for human life. "To take something that cannot be replaced has always been my horror," Starr said. "To never shoot until absolutely necessary has been my motto."[59] Over his entire career, Starr never fatally shot anyone in the commission of a crime. Conversely, Davis had no qualms about cold-blooded murder. During the Porum Range War, Davis shot the horse from under 18-year-old Clifford Hester, somersaulting him into the tall grass. As the young man stood up, Davis cold-bloodedly fired two fatal bullets through his stomach.[60] If he was managed tightly, Starr thought Davis was the perfect cocky, gritty sidekick he could rely on if a heist turned sour.

Despite being 41, Starr seemed less revengeful and more playful as a bank robber in 1914. When he and Davis burst into Arkansas's Cove Bank for their first joint venture, they wore matching Old West costumes—riding chaps and spurs, blue shirts, and wide-brimmed Stetsons. The bank employees, however, weren't impressed by their antics. After emptying the cash drawers, Starr ordered the cashier, W. C. Martin, and a customer, Joe Hilton, into the vault.

Figure 9 Starr's new sidekicks after his failure to once again "beat back." *Left*: Joe Davis booking photo taken April 13, 1917, Leavenworth Penitentiary, Kansas; Identifier: 571125, National Archives at Kansas City, MO. *Right*: Elijah "Lige" Higgins, booking photo taken March 3, 1916, Colorado Penitentiary, Cañon City, Colorado. Courtesy of the Museum of Colorado Prisons.

When Hilton heard the spoke wheel turn and the bolts engage, he began to hyperventilate. Martin, a cool customer, retrieved a satchel of tools and started working on the door's hinges. After fifteen minutes Martin and Hilton were free, but the Old West cowboys had long disappeared with $1,300.[61]

Next up was the Keystone Bank. This time the cashier was a timid man with the comical name Mr. Duck. The cashier filled their grain sacks with $1,600 in silver, $100 in gold, and $1,000 in currency. Since the sacks were so heavy, they ordered Mr. Duck to help them carry them to their horses. As they mounted up and rode off, Mr. Duck waddled away and took cover. He easily identified Starr and Davis since neither wore masks.[62]

Starr and Davis returned to wearing costumes when they robbed the First National Bank in Baxter Springs, Kansas. Frank Brewster, the assistant

I'm on the Road Called Straight Now

cashier, said two of the robbers wore "false chin whiskers," while a third man covered his upper lip with a deerskin mustache dyed black.[63] Starr had added a new member—Elijah "Lige" Higgins. The 43-year-old Higgins was tall with an intimidating glower. He liked wearing his hat at a saucy angle with a cigarette dangling from the corner of his mouth. Once, when taking a booking photo, Higgins refused to open one eye, claiming the socket was hollow. He was also an avowed Socialist.

After the tills were cleaned out, Starr ordered Brewster and two bank customers, E. M. Michener, owner of a hardware store, and a farmer named William Murphy, into the washroom. Brewster had a trick up his sleeve. He stage-whispered to Michener not to worry because the washroom had a transom that would allow them to escape. Davis overheard Brewster and alerted Starr, who ordered them into the vault instead. Brewster had pulled a fast one: inside the vault was a burglar alarm.

Starr, Davis, and Higgins then smoothly exited the bank. Townsfolk observed the men leaving, but no one suspected they were bank robbers. The three men crossed paths with a young woman in the street as they headed for their horses. "They lifted their hats and stepped to one side for her convenience and passed on." Soon, they reached their horses, mounted up, and safely rode away with $8,452. When First National's bookkeeper, Walter Hartley, returned from an errand, the bank was empty. Then he heard a faint cry from inside the vault: "Let us out!" Despite his earlier bravado, Brewster had gotten cold feet and never sounded the alarm.

Six days later the Starr Gang robbed the Kiefer Central State Bank.[64] As the outlaws made their escape, they fired shots into the air, warning away anyone who might try to stop them. They needn't have bothered. Most of Kiefer's 1,200 residents worked at the Glen Pool District oil fields at that time of day, leaving it a ghost town. However, a small group of theatergoers watching a Western thought their movie suddenly had sound. A newspaper reporting on the heist noted, with overt racism, that Starr was Cherokee and "a dangerous man, especially when drinking."[65]

At this point Starr was robbing a bank every other week. The stepped-up timetable had a specific purpose: a reunion with a special someone.

Feathering a Tulsa Love Nest

Starr's bullet wounds for the bank heists of his youth had long been stitched, but there was a hole in his heart that only Retta Elwick could fill. With the ill-gotten gain from his crime spree, Starr splurged on a "pretty little bungalow" on East Second Street in Tulsa, boasting no less than five spacious bedrooms, a bath, electric lights, hot and cold running water, a telephone, wall-to-wall carpeting, and drapes.[66] Gone were the days of surviving on pocket change, living as a fugitive, or being locked up.

In October 2014 Starr sent a telegram to Retta in Holly, describing the love nest he'd feathered just for her. Retta immediately went to her bedroom and retrieved her trusty leather Gladstone—the perfect bag to carry her essentials but small enough not to raise suspicion. Inside she packed her nicest dresses, beaded handbag, and alluring lingerie. Guy Elwick asked her what the telegram said. Retta feigned being distraught, explaining that her sister in Kansas City was ill and she needed to be at her bedside. Snapping the suitcase shut, Retta gave a fleeting kiss to her children and headed toward the train station. Seemingly without regret, she was ready to begin a new life with Starr. Friends of Retta who knew of the affair were "at a loss to account for her infatuation with the outlaw." She was educated and refined, and Starr was an uneducated Cherokee "savage." How could she explain to people who only knew Starr from newspaper accounts about his intelligence and charisma?

Retta's plan to escape with Starr faced a daunting obstacle. The Colorado police had been on Starr's tail since he had broken parole, and they knew of his intimate relationship with Mrs. Elwick. Two detectives had been keeping a close eye on her, and they grew suspicious when they saw her at the station with her Gladstone. They listened in as she asked the cashier for a one-way ticket to Kansas City. Unbeknown to Retta, the detectives followed her onto the eastbound Santa Fe train. Starr, however, planned two steps ahead. He had anticipated Retta would be tailed and instructed her on what to do. As the train made its first stop at Coolidge, just across the Kansas border, Retta surreptitiously disembarked and transferred trains. When the initial train rolled into Kansas City and Retta wasn't onboard, the detectives realized the outlaw's sweetheart had given them the slip. Starr had outsmarted them.[67]

I'm on the Road Called Straight Now　　　　　　　　　　　21

Once Starr and Retta settled into Tulsa, they adopted the aliases of Mr. and Mrs. R. L. Williams—an inside joke since that was also the name of the newly elected governor of Oklahoma.[68] Starr took Retta on a lavish shopping spree. Arm in arm they visited Tulsa's finest boutiques. With a flourish a salesman showed them a fumed oak piano. After a smile and a nod from Retta, it was promptly added to the delivery list. They picked out an expensive Victrola with a range of records, including "Tipperary." Retta indulged in frivolous knickknacks to adorn the shelves of their new home. Starr and Retta then strolled through the Ford dealership, settling on a shiny new five-passenger Nash to park in their cement-floored garage. With her luxurious new possessions, Retta had her dream life—a far cry from her dull, hard-scrabble existence with Guy.[69]

To throw off the scent of determined bounty hunters, Starr employed a clever disinformation campaign. He cunningly leaked anonymous tips to newspapers far and wide that he and Retta were planning to flee the country. Starr's plan was so convincing that the *AHTA Weekly News* out of St. Paul, Kansas, reported that the couple had ridden overland to Texas and embarked on a ship bound for South America.[70] The *Arizona Republican* repeated the rumor, declaring that Starr had escaped to some foreign country. With the media being led by a string, Starr had detectives chasing their tails in a desperate bid to locate him.[71]

It wasn't until the spring of 1915 that Tulsa residents learned that Starr had lived under their noses for months. A splash headline in the *Tulsa World News* read, "Starr Walked Tulsa Streets While Officers Sought Him." Scandalized citizens wanted to know "how in the tarnation" Starr went unnoticed, living just blocks from the homes of Tulsa County Sheriff James Woolley, school board members, city and county employees, and even local newspaper editors. The public imagination went wild, picturing Starr taking leisurely walks around his family neighborhood, corrupting children on the playground of the Washington Public School, or mingling with God-fearing folks at the Grace Methodist Episcopal Church on Trenton Avenue.

Yet nobody noticed that the King of Bank Robbers lived among them. Tulsans would later wonder if their public officials were corrupt or merely incompetent. The *Tulsa World News* blasted Sheriff Woolley: "While police-men, detectives and deputy sheriffs of the west were on a sharp lookout for him; while his Bertillon picture and measurements were in the hands of every police department in the country, and rewards aggregating several thousand dollars were hanging over his head, Henry Starr was driving past the home of the Tulsa County sheriff almost every night."[72]

And where was Starr going on these evening excursions? He and Retta regularly attended motion pictures at Tulsa's Royal. The moviegoing expe-rience had changed since Starr first entered the Colorado State Penitentiary. In 1909 theaters were often abandoned stores converted to venues with a sheet tacked onto a wall for a screen, a projector on the floor, and spare kitchen chairs serving as seats. Showtimes weren't posted because films ran on continuous twenty- to twenty-five-minute loops, featuring documen-taries, dramas, comedies, and illustrated songs. Patrons could enter and exit at any time, morning to night. Storefront theaters provided cheap enter-tainment for the poor, immigrants, and truant schoolchildren who gathered along the sidewalks. On the streets theaters promoted their films like circus attractions, with painted signs and illustrations strung above the entrance with ropes.[73] Instead of tantalizing audiences with the opportunity to see the bearded lady in person, theaters drew customers in to watch human traffick-ing in action on the screen, which at the time was salaciously marketed as "white slavery." Inside, early theaters lacked proper ventilation. One patron described the experience as being stuck in a cattle car with "five hundred smells combined in one."[74] After affluent citizens began accepting motion pictures as legitimate entertainment, they established classier venues such as opera houses or private clubs.

Intense competition whittled down the number of storefront theaters that could survive economically, and projection booth fires, due to the high flammability of nitrate film, took the rest. When Starr and Retta attended the movies in 1915, circus-style exteriors gave way to bright, flashy electric lights and terra cotta facades. Bedsheet screens were replaced with plastered walls painted in flat light-blue enamel. Projectors were housed in fireproof booths made of brick or terra cotta and were placed above and behind the audience. The rear theater wall utilized a port for each projector and a lookout port for the projectionist. A third port served the stereopticon—a throwback to the magic lantern days—to project slides of illustrated songs, advertisements, and coming attractions.[75]

Starr and Retta settled into new padded seats to watch her favorite genre, Westerns. She was used to Starr whispering critiques in her ear. "If robbers really stopped trains that way, there'd be a lot more railroad accidents on record," Starr chortled. When he saw actors twirling guns and acting tough, it insulted his professional pride. "Makes me want to shoot holes in the screen," Starr grumbled.[76]

While at the Royal, Starr likely watched the pictures of two cowboy stars he used to know when they were outlaws: Alphonse "Al" Jennings and Emmett Dalton. Starr met Jennings while they were both locked up in the Ohio State Penitentiary. Emmett Dalton, the last surviving member of the Dalton Gang, he'd known his whole life. Emmett, Bob, and Grat Dalton had been US deputy marshals out of Fort Smith, where Starr spent time in prison. The entire Dalton Gang, except Emmett, were killed attempting the 1892 double daylight bank robbery in Coffeyville, Kansas.

Starr was amazed to witness two outlaws reinventing themselves as matinee idols. Starr must have wondered, "Why not me?"

Why not, indeed?

Al Jennings, the First Bandit Movie Star

Alphonse "Al" Jennings was born November 25, 1863, in Tazewell County, Virginia. He'd been a low-level, bungling outlaw in Oklahoma for only four months when he was captured and ordered to serve a life sentence in the Ohio State Penitentiary. Crime historian Jay Robert Nash dubbed Jennings "the Most Inept Outlaw of the Old West."[77] The first time he attempted to rob a moving train, he nearly got run over. The second time he galloped his horse alongside the roaring train, firing his pistol in the air, ordering the engineer to stop. "The engineer merely waved a friendly hello and kept going," wrote Nash. Learning from his mistakes, Jennings robbed a stationary train that had stopped to take on water. The booty was laughable—a meager fifteen dollars and a bunch of bananas.[78]

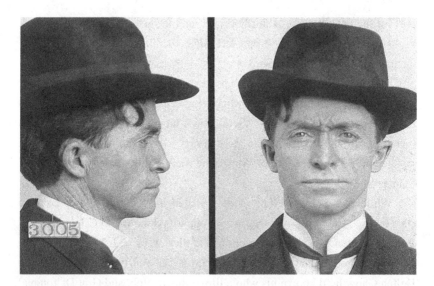

Figure 10 Booking photo of Alphonse "Al" Jennings taken at Leavenworth Penitentiary in 1902. Despite being called "The Most Inept Outlaw of the Old West," he sold his life story, *Beating Back*, to the *Saturday Evening Post*, which led to a motion picture of the same name and his own Hollywood production arm. Identifier: 571125, National Archives at Kansas City.

Will Irwin, who edited Jennings's autobiography, *Beating Back*, in 1914, described meeting the 48-year-old reformed outlaw for the first time: "He was a little man, hardly more than five feet tall; he had a shock of bright auburn hair and a face, what with tan and sun-wrinkles over a ruddy skin, looked like a baked apple."[79] Those qualities, plus a rubbery, expressive face, rivaled the diminutive silent film comedy greats like Buster Keaton and Charlie Chaplin.[80]

Of the three outlaws-turned-actors, Jennings's initial pivot from honest citizen to criminal was the most dramatic. In 1893, at age 30, Jennings and his brothers Ed and John opened a law practice in Woodward, Oklahoma. Their enterprise put them on a violent collision course with opposing attorney Temple Lea Houston, son of the Texas icon Sam Houston. Jennings's encounter with Houston would leave one of his brothers dead and another with a gunshot wound. Feeling betrayed by the legal system would turn Jennings from a Panglossian solicitor into an embittered outlaw.

I'm on the Road Called Straight Now

The trouble began in October 1895 when Ed Jennings and Houston squared off in court.[81] Ed was defending two boys falsely accused of burglary by Houston's client, Sheriff Jack Love. After a point of order, Houston slammed his fist on the table and declared, "Your honor, the gentleman is grossly ignorant of the law." Hot-tempered Ed countered, "Well, you're a liar." Flushed with rage, Houston reached for the Colt .45 on his hip, known as Old Betsy. But Jennings, sitting at the defense table with Ed, had his gun out first. "Lightning anger was striking in all directions," Jennings recalled. Before shots could be fired, men rushed at Jennings and Houston to disarm them.

The next day, Ed and John Jennings were playing cards at the Cabinet Saloon when Houston and Sheriff Love confronted them.

"Are you going to apologize?" Houston demanded.

"When you're sober, come back," Ed replied flippantly. "Apologies will be settled then."

Sheriff Love, standing behind Ed, shot him in the back of the head. Then Houston fired two shots from Old Betsy into his head from the front. John Jennings was shot in the arm in the exchange of gunfire as Houston and Sheriff Love fled.

Later, Temple and Love were charged with murder. Both men claimed they fired in self-defense, and they were acquitted. Jennings's faith in the law was shattered. Angry and embittered, he turned to crime. In 1897 he formed the Jennings Gang with another brother, Frank, and three other ruffians. Jennings's bumbling career lasted only four months before he was captured and given a shockingly disproportionate sentence of life in prison to be served at the Ohio State Penitentiary. After he served five years, Jennings's sentence was commuted by President William McKinley for good conduct.[82]

Once again a free man, Jennings returned to practicing law. However, his friendship with a lawman would soon pivot his career to motion pictures. In 1908 President Theodore Roosevelt was hiking through Oklahoma with his guide, US Marshal John Abernathy.[83] While on their journey, Roosevelt watched Abernathy capture a wolf with his bare hands. After returning to Washington, DC, Roosevelt regaled his society friends with his astonishing observation. They dismissed his outlandish tale as typical Teddy balderdash.

26   Reel One

Roosevelt was riled up by their humorous effrontery and was determined to prove his story true. He asked Abernathy to capture a wolf again but this time record it on celluloid film. Thus, US Marshal Abernathy became the first tin star filmmaker. He formed the Oklahoma Natural Mutoscene Company and hired the only man in the region with a camera, James "Bennie" Kent.

Kent was a watch repairman from Nottingham, England, who had relocated to Chandler, Oklahoma. He was ruddy faced, wore a derby hat, and smoked stogies, making him a doppelganger for Winston Churchill.[84] Kent was fascinated with photography and got his start shooting pictures for the Miller brothers' 101 Ranch out of Bliss (now Old Bliss), Oklahoma. When the brothers wanted to put their Wild West shows on celluloid, Kent bought a Moy 35mm movie camera.

Marshal Abernathy was friends with Jennings and cast him as one of the wolf trackers. The film became the quasi-documentary *The Wolf Hunt* (1908). Roosevelt held a screening at the White House with Jennings in attendance. Jennings was a raconteur equal to Roosevelt, and the president was so entertained that he later granted the outlaw a full pardon. Abernathy's film was a big success and later that year, Natural Mutoscene filmed the drama *The Bank Robbery* (1908). Abernathy recruited his pal, former US Deputy Marshal William "Bill" Tilghman, to direct with Kent again behind the camera. Jennings was cast in the lead role as a bank robber.

The Wolf Hunt and *The Bank Robbery* didn't immediately launch Jennings into a motion picture career. Instead, his ascent was gradual and quirky. In 1896, before being captured and sent to the Ohio State Penitentiary, Jennings and Frank fled to Honduras. While there they met William Sydney Porter, who became famous as the writer O. Henry. Porter was also a fugitive, hiding from bank embezzlement charges.[85] Remarkably, in 1898 Jennings and Porter found themselves reunited behind bars at the Ohio State Penitentiary and their friendship grew. In 1904, after both were free men, Jennings shared with Porter his rough attempt at writing a first-person train robbery story. Out of "innate kindness," Porter volunteered to "weed and slash the manuscript, hammer and pound Al's florid prose, and add 'lots of things that never happened.'"[86] The dubiously true tale "Holding up a Train" was soon published in *McClure's* magazine and later added to O. Henry's short story collection *Sixes and Sevens* (1911).[87] In 1913 Jennings met journalist Will Irwin in New York City and regaled him with

Figure 11 James "Bennie" Kent, a former watch repairman and still photographer, discovered a new calling with a cheap, portable motion picture camera. The Chandler, Oklahoma–based cameraman helped President Theodore Roosevelt establish the documentary genre, and he brought lawmen and outlaws to the screen, including Bill Tilghman, Cattle Annie and Little Breeches, Arkansas Tom Jones (Roy Daughtery), Al Jennings, Emmett Dalton, and Starr. https://www.findagrave.com/memorial/89071135/james-b-kent.

his lively—and highly embellished—life story. Captivated by Jennings, Irwin collaborated with the diminutive, red-headed ex-con on his biography, *Beating Back*. Irwin serialized the book in the *Saturday Evening Post*, making Jennings famous from coast to coast.[88]

On September 10, 1914, the Thanhouser Film Corporation out of New Rochelle announced *Beating Back* was being adapted into a motion picture: "Occupying six reels with Al Jennings himself, as the principal character, the picture marks an epoch in the search of the unusual themes for presentation on the screen." Despite his ne'er-do-well criminal career, the sun-wrinkled baked apple was about to be the first bandit movie star.[89]

Figure 12 Real-life outlaw Al Jennings jumps from the pages of *The Saturday Evening Post* onto a sprocketed film reel. A sales promotion for the film *Beating Back*, starring the former outlaw and candidate for governor of Oklahoma. *Moving Picture World*, Apr–June 1914, p. 556.

I'm on the Road Called Straight Now

Figure 13 Emmett Dalton booking photo, Kansas State Penitentiary, taken March 8, 1893. Emmett was the youngest brother of Bob and Grat Dalton and the only survivor of the Dalton Gang (including Dick Broadwell and Bill Power), who were killed by armed townsfolk during the failed daylight double bank robbery in Coffeyville, Kansas, October 5, 1892. Courtesy of Kansas Historical Society, Topeka; kansasmemory.org.

Emmett Dalton, the Second Bandit Movie Star

Emmett Dalton was the second outlaw to turn his criminal escapades into film stardom. In the crisp November air of 1907, Dalton walked out of the Kansas State Penitentiary a free man. He'd entered fourteen years earlier a tall, dashing young cowboy and was leaving as a flabby 36-year-old with a receding hairline.[90] Once spry, his body now ached from close confinement in a prison cell and the twenty-three buckshot wounds he sustained during the failed double bank robbery in Coffeyville, Kansas, in 1892. Despite multiple surgeries while in prison, his arm still pained him, and he feared it would one day need to be amputated.[91]

Upon his release, Dalton was inundated with opportunities from theatrical managers offering for him to appear on the stage or in a carnival Wild West show. He stated plainly that he had no interest in exhibiting himself as Emmett Dalton of the Dalton Gang. He said, "I am not an actor, never have

30   Reel One

been, and never can be."[92] Instead, he opted for a mundane and respectable career operating a grocery store and meat market in Tulsa with his cousin Scout Younger, a former Wild West show performer.[93]

A year later John Tackett entered Dalton's shop with a different type of opportunity. He had been a photographer in Coffeyville during the failed daylight double bank robbery. Tackett took the haunting death photos of the Dalton Gang, including Emmett's brothers Bob and Grat. The images were made into postcards and were reproduced for newspapers around the world. Tackett became rich and famous.[94]

Fifteen years later Tackett had a new idea for making money off the Dalton Gang. He had purchased a "motion picture machine" to add "cinema-photographer" to his repertoire. Tackett pitched an idea to the Coffeyville Commercial Club to make a film promoting the city. His vision was to contrast 1892 Coffeyville, known for the Dalton raid, with the modern city it had become in 1908.[95] The Commercial Club loved the idea. Tackett visited Dalton in person to see if he wanted to help write the robbery portion of the promotional film. The cinema-photographer hoped Dalton didn't hold any grudges for capitalizing on his family's misfortune. Rather than being offended, Dalton was eager to participate. He'd already been jotting down ideas for a book describing the methodology of the Dalton and Starr Gangs, and he told Tackett they could use his notes for the scenario.[96] Dalton believed a filmed recreation of the failed double robbery would serve as "a warning to impetuous youth" and that no one else could retell the story as accurately as a member of the gang.[97] Tackett and Dalton shook hands, and the reformed outlaw went to work putting the story to paper.

In 1892 the Dalton Gang was at the height of its infamy. Led by brothers Grat and Bob Dalton—ex–deputy US marshals turned outlaws—the gang included their 20-year-old kid brother, Emmett. "Brother Bob was determined to outdo the James boys," wrote Emmett. "He announced a plan which would make him and his gang the greatest desperados of this or any other country." Bob proposed robbing two banks simultaneously in broad daylight.[98]

On October 5 the three Daltons and cohorts Dick Broadwell and Bill Power rode into town early in the morning. Their goal was to rob the C. M. Condon and Co. and First National Banks as soon as they opened.[99] Bob had planned to hitch their horses on Eighth Street, directly south of both banks and an optimal location for a quick getaway following the heist. Unfortunately, the brothers hadn't done any recent reconnaissance and were surprised to find their preferred hitching posts had been removed. Grat, the eldest at 31, suggested they tie up their horses a block west, near the city jail. The decision proved fatal. A few hours later, Coffeyville citizens would pile their corpses in the cool confines of that same jail.

After tying their horses, the gang approached the banks on foot through a passage that would later become known as Death Alley. They emerged onto Walnut Street, three in front and two behind. The Condon bank was straight ahead, and First National was only a few hundred feet farther across Union Street on the east side. Aleck McKenna's dry goods store was on the south side of Death Alley. He was on his front sidewalk when the gang emerged from the alley. Since the Daltons were raised in Coffeyville, Bob wore a fake mustache and goatee and Grat a fake mustache and sideburns to avoid being recognized. McKenna recognized the brothers despite their disguises and watched as Grat, Broadwell, and Power peeled off for the Condon Bank while Bob and Emmett continued toward First National. Condon Bank had large front windows, and McKenna could see Grat raise his Winchester and point it at the cashier. The dry goods owner sounded the alarm.

Inside Condon Bank, Grat ordered the cashier, Charles Ball, to empty the vault.

"It has a time lock," Ball stammered. "It can't be opened until 9:30."

"What time is it now?" Grat demanded.

Ball fished out his pocket watch and said, "It's only 9:20."

The clock on the wall read 9:45, but Grat couldn't tell time. He told Power and Broadwell they'd wait the ten minutes.

Bob and Emmett were having better luck inside First National. The bookkeeper, Bert Ayers, was doing what Bob had demanded, quickly filling their sacks with money. Unbeknown to the brothers, the owner of Isham Hardware, next door, was handing out rifles and ammunition to a large group of men eager to defend the banks.

Meanwhile, Power, inside Condon Bank, was watching the cashier stuff currency from the till inside a sack. Behind him the front window spidered from a rifle blast. Power grabbed at his arm when he felt a bullet tear into his flesh. A Coffeyville man stood in the street just outside the bank's front door, cocking his rifle for a second shot.

Bob and Emmett exited the front door of First National, using Ayers as a hostage. The brothers were immediately driven back inside by a hail of bullets from the Isham's Hardware men. Bob and Emmett ran back through the bank and exited the rear door. When the brothers spilled out into the back alley, they were surprised to find a young man, Lucius Baldwin, waiting for them. Baldwin never fired his pistol. Bob shot him dead.

The brothers ran north to the end of the alley, then rounded west at Mahan and Custer's Grocery Store on the corner. Looping around to the corner of Eighth Street and Union, Bob and Emmett could see the front of First National and the Isham men waiting for them to come out. George Cubine, whose father owned Cubine's Boot and Shoe Shop, had his gun trained on the First National front door. He couldn't see Bob and Emmett crossing Union Street on his blind side. Bob shot him in the back, killing the young man instantly.

Another Cubine boot shop employee, Charles Brown, saw Cubine drop and ran to him. He snatched up the dead man's rifle and fired off one shot before Bob shot him dead as well. The First National bookkeeper, Ayers, had armed himself by this time and popped up behind Brown. Bob fired and nicked him in the head. In less than five minutes, Bob Dalton had killed three innocent men and left Ayers paralyzed for life.

Meanwhile, Grat could see the Isham men taking firing positions in the street facing Condon Bank. He, Broadwell, and Power ran for the west-side door and tumbled onto Walnut Street. The shortest route to their horses was across Walnut and through Death Alley. Grat, Broadwell, and Powell, cradling his bloody arm, sprinted toward the alley. A volley of gunfire zinged their direction, and they ducked their heads as if heading into a strong wind. Once inside the alley, Grat took cover behind a south-side staircase. Power stopped at a door in the alley and tried the handle. It was locked. The next instant his body was riddled with bullets. Broadwell emerged from the far end of the alley onto an open dirt road lined by split-rail fencing. He stumbled past a Shell Oil wagon with two horses that had been abandoned in the middle of the road when the shooting started. Ahead

I'm on the Road Called Straight Now

on his left, Broadwell could see the adobe brick jail and, just beyond that, the gang's horses tied up.

Marshal Charles Connelly, stable owner John Kloehr (pronounced Clair), and barber Carey Seaman met at the corner of Ninth Street and Walnut armed with rifles. They looked north just in time to see Grat, Broadwell, and Power disappear into Death Alley.

"Let's meet 'em on the other side," Connelly growled.

The men spun on the heels of their boots and raced west on Ninth Street, then cut north across an open field. Marshal Connelly saw that Broadwell had already exited the alley and was racing toward their horses. He split off west from Seaman and Kloehr to cut off Broadwell's path. Meanwhile, Grat was facing a barrage of gunfire as he hid behind the staircase. He watched the Isham men advancing and quickly abandoned his position. Grat covered his retreat with guns blazing, then turned and ran. He passed the body of Power lying dead on the ground, then took cover behind the abandoned Shell Oil wagon.

Farther west down the split-rail lined road, Marshal Connelly watched as Broadwell climbed in the saddle of his horse. He stepped into the road and shouldered his rifle. Marshal Connelly's bullet struck Broadwell solidly but didn't knock him out of his saddle. The outlaw spurred his horse and rode off, wounded. Marshal Connelly would never know that his shot was fatal and that Broadwell would be found dead a half mile outside of the city.

Grat heard Marshal Connelly's shot coming from his left. He turned his head and saw the lawman in the road firing at Broadwell as he galloped away. Grat shot Connelly in the back, killing him. By this time Kloehr and Seaman had arrived at the split-rail fencing near the exit of Death Alley. When Grat turned to shoot Marshal Connelly, Kloehr saw his opportunity and fired. His bullet hit Grat in the neck, snapping his vertebrae.

Bob and Emmett were on foot, headed south behind the Walnut Street storefronts. The plan was to arrive at the exit of Death Alley and turn west toward their horses. However, when they arrived at the intersection, the brothers were struck immediately by a hail of gunfire from the Isham men. Bob was hit and dropped to the ground. Emmett turned west and kept running. He passed the two dead horses that had been hitched to the Shell

Oil wagon. They'd been killed in the crossfire. Bob was gravely wounded but managed to crawl to the south side of the alley and sit up. Emmett reached the horses and swung up into his saddle. He tied his money sack to the pommel as gunfire dropped the horses on either side of him. The next barrage of bullets tore through his left hip and groin.

Kloehr repositioned to get an angle on Bob. They locked eyes. Bob fired first and wide. Kloehr fired second. Emmett, on horseback, turned in time to see Bob grab at his solar plexus and slump over. Emmett could easily have ridden safely away with the money, but Bob was his big brother and hero. He spurred his horse and galloped back to rescue Bob. Seconds after Emmett reined his horse next to Bob and reached down to pull him up, Seamon hit him with double buckshot in the arm and shoulder. Emmett fell from his horse and hit the ground, facing Bob. The money sack landed between the two brothers. Emmett looked over to his big brother, but Bob's eyes were already fogging into oblivion.

When the gunshots stopped ringing and the smoke cleared, the townsfolk emerged from their hiding places to assess the damage: four Coffeyville citizens and four Dalton Gang members were dead. Someone set out a wooden hay board, and the bodies of Grat, Bob, Broadwell, and Power were laid out on top of it for public display. Another person handcuffed the corpses on the off chance they made a miraculous recovery and tried to escape. The young photographer John Tackett arrived with his camera and took multiple photos of the outlaws laid out side by side in their stocking feet. The Isham Hardware heroes wanted photos of themselves with the outlaws, so the limp bodies of Bob and Grat were hoisted up and held in a standing position like marionettes. The jug-eared Bob and mustached Grat posed gracefully in the arms of Eternal Sleep.

Meanwhile, Emmett was carried up the staircase inside Death Alley to the office of Dr. Walter Wells, located above Slosson's Drug Store. Dr. Wells had just begun treating Emmett's injuries when he heard townsfolk gathered below, calling to hang the young outlaw. The physician stepped onto the landing and told everyone to go home. There would be no call for lynching because Emmett was unlikely to live. However, despite the odds, the youngest Dalton would survive.

I'm on the Road Called Straight Now

Figure 14 John Tackett, a still photographer, gained national acclaim for his ghoulish death photos of the Dalton Gang after their failed daylight double bank robbery in Coffeyville, Kansas, on October 5, 1892. The corpses (*left to right*) of Bill Power, Bob Dalton, Grat Dalton, and Dick Broadwell were laid out for public viewing. Despite the outlaws being dead, fearful townsfolk insisted their hands be bound or handcuffed. Souvenir hunters cut off pieces of Bob's left pant leg. Photo courtesy of the Oklahoma Historical Society, Frank Harrah Collection, 20193. *Inset*: Emmett Dalton, recovering from his gunshot wounds on the surgery table of Dr. Walter Wells. By 1909 Tackett had added motion pictures to his repertoire, collaborating with Emmett Dalton to produce several versions of the raid. Courtesy of the N. H. Rose Photo Collection, Western History Collections, University of Oklahoma Libraries.

Seventeen years later, in 1909, former Kansas Governor E. W. Hoch heard about the Coffeyville Commercial Club promotional film and was "greatly annoyed" that Dalton was involved. Hoch advised Dalton to abandon the project entirely, and the sooner the "whole unfortunate Coffeyville affair" was forgotten, the better. Ex-Governor Hoch feared that his decision to free Dalton would discredit his "liberal parole policy."[100]

Nevertheless, Dalton and Tackett went forward with the film, securing permission from Coffeyville Mayor Fred B. Skinner to use the city streets and alleys for filming. Rehearsals began in December 1908. Dalton was not an actor in the motion picture but was a technical advisor to the Morgan Stock Company actors.[101] Dalton also filled in as a stuntman. When re-creating crossing the Caney River into Coffeyville, Dalton's horse stepped into a deep hole. Both horse and rider disappeared under the water for several seconds. "Dalton was rescued in an exhausted condition, and the horse swam out."[102] The reformed outlaw lost both his pride and his rifle.

While the Dalton raid was meant to be "a mere incidental part" of the promotion, the audience went wild for the dramatic, action-packed sequences. Dalton and Tackett hit upon the idea of expanding the bank robbery scenes and scrapping the rest. For the reboot Dalton decided he was an actor after all. When *The Great Dalton Raid* debuted at Guthrie's Gem Theatre on September 26, 1909, the advertisement boasted that Dalton was "the figure wearing the white hat in all of these pictures."[103] In addition to the film, Dalton delivered a lecture on the futility of crime, and Tackett displayed his Dalton Gang death photos. *The Great Dalton Raid* was shown to patrons across Kansas and Oklahoma. At the Oklah Theatre in Bartlesville, the owner sold 3,500 tickets despite competition from the Barnum and Bailey Circus.[104]

In the summer of 1912, after three years of touring with *The Great Dalton Raid*, Dalton decided to shoot a twentieth-anniversary version of the Coffeyville robberies. For the remake Dalton, "who was never averse to increasing the candle power of his private spotlight," partnered with Scout Younger and Natural Mutoscene's James "Bennie" Kent.[105] The new film, *The Last Stand of Dalton Boys at Coffeyville, Kansas*, would be different in several ways. The new scenario would provide more backstory, show-ing the boys growing up in Vinita, and include the character of Emmett's heroic eldest brother, Frank, a US deputy marshal killed in the line of duty. Coffeyville didn't permit Kent to film in Coffeyville, so Dalton's crew had to improvise. They painted flats to resemble the Condon and First National Banks and mounted them on stage at the Oklah Theatre in Bartlesville.

By the end of January 1913, Dalton began touring with his new three-reeler. The *Bartlesville Daily Enterprise* described Kent's images as "unusu-ally fine and clear and are said to be in every way superior to previous Dalton pictures."[106] The poster described *The Last Stand of Dalton Boys* as "A motion picture that every man, woman, and child should see."[107]

Figure 15 A poster for the 1912 film *The Last Stand of the Dalton Boys at Coffeyville, Kansas*, directed by Jack Kenyon. Emmett Dalton portrayed himself as the only surviving member of the notorious Dalton Gang, who were killed attempting a daylight double bank robbery in Coffeyville, Kansas, on October 5, 1892. Dalton remade the film in 1918, titled *Beyond the Law*, this time portraying himself and his brothers Bob and Frank. Photo courtesy AAAVintagePosters.com.

The Bank Robber Bill

In contrast to Jennings and Dalton, who had hung up their spurs and pearl-handled revolvers decades earlier, Starr was still an operating and highly successful bank robber. From August 1914 to January 1915, bandits raided seventeen country banks in the Oklahoma, Arkansas, and Kansas tristate regions.[108] Most of the thrilling heists were blamed on Starr. Newspapers reported conflicting amounts stolen from each robbery, but taking the low estimate, Starr galloped away with $36,000, the equivalent of roughly $1 million today[109]—a figure the producers of *A Debtor to the Law* would exploit in its marketing campaign.[110]

Starr scoffed at the amount of money newspapers reported, insisting the bankers inflated the figures to bilk the private insurance companies. "They can't crook the books, but they can crook the cash when the bank is robbed," Starr said.[111] He gave an example of a bank being robbed of $180 in silver, but the bankers filed an insurance claim for $2,600. Starr felt aggrieved that prison was reserved for outlaws. He asked rhetorically, "Which is the worst, me or the bankers?"

Robberies were becoming so numerous and routine that after the Price State Bank in Prue, Oklahoma, had been robbed, the cashier, J. F. Comer, languidly dialed up the police to say, "I've just had my annual holdup, send officers."[112] The rash of heists made the secretary of the Oklahoma Bankers' Association (OBA), W. B. Harrison, apoplectic. He spoke daily with East Coast investors who read the reports in the newspapers and refused to invest in a state rampant with crime. "We could not spend $25,000 in advertising where it would do the state as much good as is the damage done by the report of a single bank robbery," Harrison said.[113] OBA members badgered Oklahoma's legislature to act against Starr, but lawmakers dragged their feet—that is, until County Deputy Sheriff Bob Moore was cold-bloodedly murdered.

On January 12, 1915, three teenagers, Bill Inhofe, James Spess, and Alonzo "Buz" Clark, entered the First National Bank in Terlton, Oklahoma, with guns drawn. After emptying the cash register, they forced the bank employees to march through town to act as shields. Deputy Sheriff Moore followed the gang as they made their way to their horses, but because of the

I'm on the Road Called Straight Now

39

hostages, he didn't have a clear shot. When the robbers released the hostages and mounted their horses, Moore found his opportunity. He fired one shot and missed. Spess fired back, sending a bullet through Moore's chest, killing him instantly.[114]

Once again, Starr was blamed for a bank robbery he had nothing to do with. "I was 100 miles away," Starr told the newspapers.[115] US Marshal B. A. Enloe, who was tasked with finding the bandits, admitted Starr hadn't robbed the bank himself but said the outlaw was the puppet master behind the robbery, operating from his bungalow in Tulsa.[116]

The senseless murder of Deputy Sheriff Moore, who left behind a wife and four children, so enraged the public that Oklahoma Governor R. L. Williams was forced to act. On February 6, 1915, he scratched his signature to the Bank Robber Bill, which offered a $1,000 reward for the capture of Starr for the December 29 armed robbery of the State Bank of Carney. But this was no ordinary reward; it included a chilling "dead or alive" clause straight out of the Old West.[117] With this proclamation, Governor Williams hoped to incentivize law enforcement officers who had become too friendly with outlaws or who wouldn't usually risk their lives.

Hugh S. Fullerton, a *Tacoma Times* special correspondent, dramatized Starr's reaction to being branded public enemy number one: "His lips curled in a half-smile of contempt. He had read that day in a scrap of newspaper that the legislature of Oklahoma had passed a law and authorized the governor to place a price upon his head. Nailed to a tree, he had read a notice that the state offered $1,000 for his body, dead or alive. Something akin to pride stirred his savage breast."[118]

Although Fullerton's description was melodramatic, it accurately pegged the spirit of Starr's response. The governor had thrown the gauntlet, and Starr was determined to double down. An opportunity presented itself when Starr went for a pleasant Sunday drive to Stroud, a small town fifty miles southwest of Tulsa. As Starr brought his Nash to a halt on the bustling corner of Fourth Avenue and Main Street, his eyes were drawn to the imposing new building that loomed over the intersection. The First National Bank building was a masterpiece of dark brick and cut-stone lintels, with a towering height that dwarfed all the other buildings in town. Its corner entrance was marked by a stone sign reading "BANK," but Starr saw something more than a commercial building. In his mind the gabled stone parapet resembled cat ears, and the arrangement of its dark windows gave the appearance of eyes and a gaping maw. Starr saw a black panther ready to pounce, and he was just the man to tame that beast.

Turning east, Starr spotted a second bank one block away. In contrast to First National Bank, the Stroud National Bank was warm, inviting, and almost comical. The one-story building had intricate tan brickwork over friendly curved windows. A pointed tower over its entrance, wrapped in scalloped shingles, resembled an upside-down ice cream cone. Starr chuckled, thinking how foolish it was to open a new bank so close to the old one with a clear line of sight.

But then, he had an idea: *Why rob one bank when it's just as easy to rob two?*[119]

Starr knew that pulling off the impossible, a daylight double bank robbery, would launch him into the pantheon of great bank robbers. The feat had eluded history's boldest outlaws, including Jesse James and the Dalton Gang. John Tackett's haunting death photos of Bob and Grat Dalton, Bill Power, and Dick Broadwell sent shivers down the spines of even the most fearless bandits.

But not Henry Starr.

Reel Two

The Stroud
Doubleheader

There never was a Wild West show or moving picture so exciting!
—J. M. Parks, Armour Packing Company salesman
and Stroud eyewitness

I n 1915 Lewis Estes arrived in Tulsa, Oklahoma, from Coburn, Missouri. He was a wide-eyed newlywed with a head full of dreams of a better life.[1] Estes had jug ears and large, wide-set eyes that added to the perception of his naivete. He wasn't bright, but the one thing he understood was that Tulsa meant opportunity.

Ten years earlier, on November 22, 1905, wildcatters had struck the Glen Pool—the richest oil deposit in the world at the time. When Estes arrived Tulsa had grown from a one-horse hamlet called Tulsey Town into the Oil Capital of the World.[2] Millionaires were made in Tulsa with names that became familiar at gas stations across the country: Henry Ford Sinclair, J. Paul Getty, and Frank, L. E., and Waite Phillips. There was plenty of work for unskilled young men. Even Starr, after President Roosevelt pardoned him, spent a short time as a driller on Getty's lot 50 well in the Osage.[3]

Now a new generation of men like Estes were drawn by the promise of wealth and opportunity. He found no trouble being hired as a teamster at the Bird Creek Oil Company. *Tulsa Tribune* writer Jessica D. Harper contemporaneously described her impression of oil boom towns: "What a revelation is the first view of the oil fields, the shadowy outline of the derricks against the sky, the whistle of a flowing well, the slowly moving pumps 'put-put-putting' all day and night and the thick smell of the oil over all!"[4]

Estes and his boss, Bud Maxfield, drove oil field wagons twelve hours a day in a hazy, gas-filled landscape, hauling pipe string, dirt, and lumber. The stench of crude filled Estes's nostrils and permeated his skin. The water he drank to slake his thirst tasted of oil. A fellow "boll weevil" told Estes the toxic gas fumes could cause blindness.[5] Estes's dream for a better life was clogged with crude, and he quickly yearned for a faster and easier way to make his fortune. He didn't need much convincing when Maxfield whispered in his oil-blackened ear that he knew of a business opportunity that could lift them both out of their miserable situation. Little did he know the job would involve the greatest heist in history with one of the most infamous bank robbers in the country, Henry Starr.[6]

In late March 1915, Maxfield invited Estes to his home in Turley, nine miles north of Tulsa, to begin their new assignment. Maxfield introduced him to two mysterious fellows who had just woken up, Charles Johnson and Claud Sawyer. Estes was unimpressed, seeing only a lazy rancher and a cocky pretty boy.

Maxfield told Estes they were going to ride into town to buy supplies. They purchased camping gear, a chuck wagon, and five horses. Estes's eyes popped when Maxfield pulled out a thick wad of bills to pay. Estes had never seen that much money in his life and wondered where Maxfield got it. When Estes and Maxfield returned with the wagon and horses, three new men had arrived at the home: Joe Davis, Elijah "Lige" Higgins, and Henry Starr. Estes recognized Starr's name, and suddenly the tumblers fell into place: he was going to be part of a bank robbery.

That evening Estes and the six other men huddled over Maxfield's dining room table. Starr pointed out features on a hand-drawn map of Stroud: the location of each bank, where they would stage their horses, the back alleys they would walk, and where they would ride off to escape. They would work in two teams: Starr, Johnson, and Higgins would hit the Stroud National Bank, the farthest point from their horses, while Davis, Estes, and Sawyer would take on First National, only a block away. Estes was glad to be assigned the bank nearest the horses, but he didn't like being paired with the two most obnoxious men in the gang.

Davis and Sawyer were boyhood friends born into wealth and privilege.[7] While both were tall and slim, Sawyer was more handsome and popular with women. They shared a taste for fancy clothes and wild nights at the Crowder, Oklahoma, honky-tonks.[8] Starr knew they would work well together. In retrospect, Starr should have placed Estes on his team.

At midnight on Monday, March 22, Starr and his gang rode out by the dim light of a quarter moon with their two wagons and seven horses for the sixty-mile journey from Turley to Stroud. Just as he'd done in the 1890s, Starr fitted a chuckwagon with camping gear and provisions.[9] He could have pulled off the heist using automobiles, but using horses and wagons was more than mere nostalgia. By 1915 cars were becoming commonplace, and even police departments, including those in Lincoln County, where Stroud was situated, had them. But in Starr's mind, using an automobile to pull a robbery still had too many disadvantages. In the 1930s John Dillinger would use the superior V8 engine on his Essex Terraplane to leave four-cylinder police cars eating his dust. Mass-produced V8s were still a decade away and not an option for Starr.[10] The roads in and out of Stroud weren't paved, so blowing a tire at high speeds was a legitimate possibility. And since there were so few roads at the time, law enforcement could easily set up roadblocks to cut off their escape. For Starr horseback was still the best method to elude pursuing posses since the gang could cut across open fields and then disappear in the thick blackjack forest where cars couldn't follow them for more than a few hundred feet.[11]

On Wednesday, March 24, 1915, Starr and the gang arrived in Stroud. Prior to 1907 Stroud was nestled on the border of the "dry" Indian Territory and was the go-to destination for outlaws and upstanding citizens alike seeking a good time and a stiff drink.[12] But after statehood Stroud changed. The cotton industry took hold, and by 1915 the once-rowdy cow town had become a bustling community with 1,600 residents, seven churches, four cotton gins, two newspapers, and a canning factory. More importantly for Starr, Stroud had two fat banks with vaults bursting with cash and coins.

Starr rode at the head of the caravan, leading them west on Main Street (then known as West Third Street). A mix of horse-drawn carriages, draymen on delivery wagons, and the occasional automobile bustled around them.[13] A teeming forest of newly erected telephone poles lined each side of the street, weaving a cat's cradle of telephone wires above their heads. Below them wagon wheels carved the frozen mud into French curves, swirls, and other assorted displays of non-Euclidean geometry.

Close behind Starr, Maxfield drove his team of horses to pull the oil field wagon. Stroud townsfolk would later learn that inside the wagon were seven Winchesters and boxes of ammunition that would bring terror to their lives. To Stroud residents Starr's caravan would have appeared like a horse trader's outfit and would not have caused anyone to be alarmed.

Just like he'd done in Bentonville thirty-three years earlier, Starr had the rest of the gang stagger their entrance on horseback alone and in pairs so as not to raise suspicion. Estes pulled up the rear in the chuck wagon. Oklahoma had the coldest March in a century, and the temperature was unlikely to reach forty degrees. The Starr Gang wore gloves, hats pulled low, and heavy coats buttoned tightly.

At the corner of Fourth and Main, the site of First National Bank, Starr turned left, heading south.[14] Maxfield followed him, the wheels of his wagon rumbling over the boards serving as a crosswalk. On their right, just past the bank, were the stockyards where pig farmers penned their hogs before loading them onto the train cars. Starr noted the pens were empty and ideally situated for staging their horses during the robberies.

The caravan crossed the railroad tracks and then stopped at a clearing. After everyone arrived the gang set up camp. George Rogers owned a farm adjacent to the clearing and took notice of the strangers. He spied on them from his farmhouse window and became alarmed when he saw them unloading the rifles. He rushed to his phone and dialed up the town marshal, A.W. Lycan:

"There are suspicious-looking men with guns on my property, Marshal," Rogers exclaimed. "I think they're going to rob the bank!"[15]

In the clearing Starr began digging a firepit with no idea that his meticulously crafted plan was unraveling before it even started.

Team Starr and Team Davis

On the other end of the line, Marshal Lycan weighed Rogers' words. Then:

"George, you're getting yourself worked up over nothing," Marshal Lycan said. "Of course, there are men with guns. It's hunting season."[16]

Rogers sputtered his objection, but Lycan rang off.

Starr's luck held out—for now.

The following day, Saturday, March 27, 1915, Starr and his gang broke camp at sunrise. Puffs of breath rose from the nostrils of the nickering horses as the men tacked up. At Starr's instruction Maxfield packed each saddle-bag with field glasses and fence nippers.[17] When everyone was ready, Starr led the heavily armed men toward town.[18] They crossed back over the railroad tracks and dismounted at the hog pens one block south of First National Bank. Every man had a firearm on his hip. From their saddle scabbards, they pulled Winchesters and secreted them inside their dusters.

Starr reminded them, "No shooting unless absolutely necessary."[19]

Nobody wore a mask, but Davis, with "stubby white whiskers on his chin," pulled automobile driving goggles over his eyes. Maxfield gathered their mounts and secured them inside the pen. He would stay with the horses and have them ready to go after the robberies. Davis understood the plan. His team would hang back until Starr, Johnson, and Higgins had time to reach Stroud National Bank on foot.

Team Starr

Starr, Higgins, and Johnson dogtrotted east along the back alley parallel to Main Street. At Third Avenue they turned a sharp left, quickly crossed Main Street, and stopped at Stroud National on the corner. According to local legend, when Starr arrived at the front door, he saw a placard dangling from the glass announcing a $1,000 reward for him, "captured or killed." Starr supposedly chuckled and pulled it down.

Team Davis

Davis led Sawyer and Estes from the hog pens toward First National Bank. J. M. Parks, a traveling salesman from the Armour Packing Company, remembered seeing them just before making a sales call at the Tartar Bros.

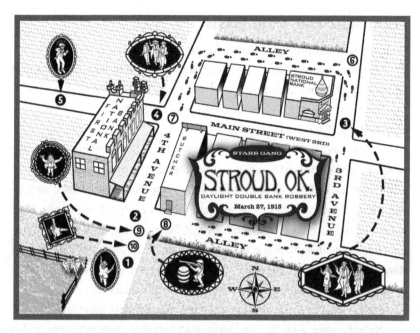

Figure 16 A schematic diagram of the daylight double bank robbery at Stroud, Oklahoma, on March 27, 1915. (1) At 10:00 Saturday morning, Starr's gang arrives in town on horseback. They dismount and corral their horses in a hog pen. Bud Maxfield stays behind to guard them. (2) Team Starr (Henry Starr, Lige Higgins, and Charles Johnson) and Team Davis (Joe Davis, Claud Sawyer, and Lewis Estes) split up. (3) Team Starr turns right and takes the back alley on foot, turns left on Third Avenue, and arrives in front of the Stroud National Bank. (4) Team Davis continues straight on Fourth Avenue and waits in front of First National Bank. At a signal from Starr, both teams enter the banks. (5) Grocer's boy Paul Curry hears that the First National Bank is being robbed. He enters businesses along Main Street, asking shopkeepers if he can borrow a gun. (6) After robbing the Stroud National Bank, Team Starr leads the hostages down the alley behind the bank and turns left on Fourth Avenue. (7) Team Starr and Team Davis meet up at the corner of the First National Bank. Using the hostages as cover, the group walks along Fourth Avenue back to their horses at the hog pen. Starr brings up the rear, exchanging gunfire with gathering townsfolk. (8) Grocer's boy Paul Curry has obtained a rifle and waits in the alley behind the butcher shop. (9) As Starr comes into his sights, Curry shoots Starr in the hip, dropping him to the street. (10) Lewis Estes sees Starr has been shot and runs back to help. Starr waves him off and tells him to save himself. As Estes flees Curry shoots him in the shoulder. Estes manages to reach his horse and rides off. The rest of the Henry Starr gang escapes with the money. Map by Artxie Media.

The Stroud Doubleheader

grocery store. They wore overcoats and overalls "much after the fashion of farmers" and Parks thought nothing more of it. When Davis arrived at the steps of First National Bank, he looked diagonally east toward Starr, standing in front of Stroud National a block away. Starr gave him the signal. The Stroud doubleheader was a go.

Team Starr

Starr assigned Johnson to stand guard at the corner entrance of Stroud National Bank. Then he and Higgins stormed inside like an Oklahoma tornado. Starr raised his Remington Model 8 rifle to his shoulder and barked for everyone to put their hands up. Higgins settled into a strategic position to cover the room. A customer, J. M Reed, watched in frozen amazement as Starr hopped the teller windows and landed in the counting room. Starr advanced menacingly on John Charles, the bookkeeper, and tossed him an empty flour sack.

"Empty that safe and put it in the sack," Starr barked.

Born into a banking family, Charles knew better than to resist. He took the sack and resignedly crossed to the open vault behind him.

Team Davis

Team Davis poured into the First National Bank like a pack of wolves—Davis from the grand front double doors and Sawyer and Estes from the sides. The command to "stick 'em up" came "like a thunderbolt from a clear sky," one witness breathlessly described later. Bank President O. E. Grecian and his staff shot their hands up. Clattering coins fell like rain. Estes covered the customers with his pistol, his hand shaking badly. Sawyer's Winchester was trained on the bank staff.

"Who is the cashier?" Davis barked.

Homer Breeding whimpered, "I am."

He caught a flour sack, and Davis ordered, "Fill it!"

Inside Tarter Bros.

Armour salesman Parks had just opened his display suitcase on the long front counter when a boy burst through the front door, yelling, "The First National is being robbed!"

48 Reel Two

Parks rushed to the front, jostling with the other customers to get a good view of the bank. First National had large windows facing Main Street, and Parks could see the "farmers" brandishing weapons. The bank staff had their hands up, and behind them, the bank's vault door stood wide open.

Team Starr

Stroud National had two vaults. The smaller one was a red brick barrel-roofed strongroom. The ship's-wheel door was already open. Charles quickly emptied the small combination safe inside. Starr ordered him at gunpoint to the other vault. The second vault was newer and larger. Its door was closed. Starr demanded Charles open it. Charles nervously stammered out that he didn't know the combination. Starr didn't believe him and placed the barrel of his Winchester on the bookkeeper's forehead.

"Open it right now," Starr growled, "or I'll put a slug through your head."

Charles closed his eyes and waited for the blast. Just then, the bank's vice president, Lee Patrick, spoke up.

"The safe is on a time lock," Patrick explained. "It can't be opened until the close of business." Starr turned and snapped his rifle at Patrick.

"You open it, then," Starr demanded.

"I can't open it. Don't you know what a time lock is?"

Starr's eyes narrowed, disliking Patrick's saucy attitude. He certainly knew what a time lock was. They had been around for twenty years. However, Starr hadn't seen one like this before. Below the ship's-wheel crank, he observed an inset bulletproof glass window with three tumblers resembling white clock faces. Behind the tumblers were gears and other strange gizmos made of machined brass. Nevertheless, Starr thought Patrick was bluffing.

"That's the oldest lie in the book," Starr seethed.

The *Stroud Democrat* later framed Starr's reaction with overt racism, writing, "The vicious Cherokee blood in the veins of the man surged again through his brain, and he leveled his gun for the second time at the head of Mr. Patrick."

"Now, I'm going to start counting down. Three, two . . ."

The Stroud Doubleheader

Before Starr reached the count of "one," Shirley Temple skipped into the bank through the side screen door. Well, not the actual movie star, but a dimple-chinned doppelganger named Lorene Hughes.

Team Davis

First National Bank felt like the monkey house at the zoo as Davis and his team yipped and terrorized the bank employees with sadistic glee.

"We want the money! Get us the gold!" Davis chanted while pounding his rifle on the counter. Sawyer, eyes glinting with malice, raked the barrel of his revolver menacingly across the bars of the teller cage. "Like a boy draws a stick over a picket fence," one terrified customer remembered. The carnival atmosphere made the bookkeeper nervous, and he dropped a cigar box filled with coins, sending them clattering and spinning across the floor.

"Pick 'em up!" Sawyer snapped at Grecian. The bank president quickly dropped to his hands and knees and began scooping up the coins like a common beggar.

Meanwhile, the cashier, Breeding, handed Davis a sack filled with gold and silver.

"Is that everything?" Davis demanded.

Breeding responded flippantly, "Do you want the pennies too?"

Team Starr

Little Lorene Hughes walked straight up to Starr and stared at him saucer eyed. She wore a black wool winter dress, white boots, and a black bonnet that framed her pudgy face like a sunflower. The petrified looks of the bank employees escaped her.

"My name is Lorene."

Starr had already lowered his rifle.

"Nice to meet you. I'm Henry," Starr responded gently. "But you must go, little one."

The moppet did not move. Instead, she defiantly balled her tiny fists inside her woolly white muff.

"Run home, little one!"

Little Lorene held her ground against the big, bad man.

50   Reel Two

The *Tulsa Daily World* captured the moment rife with sentimentality: "The Indian outlaw, with a great affection in his heart for 'kiddies' and animals, stopped, took from his sack of booty a small bag of new coins to keep her amused." Starr then lifted Lorene and placed her on a stool. He poured the pennies into her lap, saying, "Here honey, play with these and don't cry, and I will buy you some ice cream when we come back." Lorene settled obediently on her perch and busied herself with the pennies in her lap.

The *Stroud Democrat* told a variation of the "pennies" episode: Starr handed Lorene the sack of pennies and said, "Here, kiddie, take these and go and buy some ice cream." The little girl took the bag but climbed on a stool instead of leaving the bank.

In either version, Lorene refused to leave and sat politely in a chair.

"Oh, hell! She's up balling the game!" exclaimed Starr. "All right, kid, stick around for the big show."

At the Stockyard

Maxfield watched as a hog wagon clattered up to the gate led by a team of horses. Stroud pig farmer Thomas Hamer Godfrey pulled his wagon to a stop. His 10-year-old nephew Ernest Nichols sat on the buckboard beside him. Maxfield could hear the squealing hogs in the back of the wagon.

"What dern fool would put their horses in the hog pen?" Godfrey asked Maxfield.

"We'll only be a few minutes," Maxfield answered.

"What's goin' on around here?"

Maxfield boasted, "Henry Starr is robbing two banks this mornin'."

"Now, I ain't got time for pranks."

Maxfield revealed his Winchester.

"Ain't no prank, old-timer."

Godfrey's eyes bulged.

Team Starr

Starr's plan to slip in and out of Stroud National expeditiously had gone awry due to two unforeseen problems: the safe's time lock and little Lorene Hughes. Both hiccups made Starr late for his rendezvous with Team Davis.

Figure 17 Five-year-old Lorene Hughes wandered into the Stroud National Bank while it was being robbed. Starr gave her a lapful of new, shiny pennies to play with and a promise to buy her ice cream if she was good. Photo: *Lincoln County News*, May 2, 1982.

He could feel the sand shifting beneath his feet as if he were standing in an hourglass. Starr decided to cut his losses. He ordered Patrick, Charles, and Reed out the side door, tumbling them onto Third Avenue rather than the busier Main Street. Starr barked at them to lower their hands "and do just what I tell you to do, or I'll kill you by God." Starr stuffed the flour sack with $1,000 in his overcoat pocket and ordered Charles to carry the bag filled with silver. The civilians would serve as shields as Starr, Higgins, and Johnson proceeded down the back alley, back toward First National.

"Let's go!" Starr demanded.

Patrick balked, "You can't order me around!"

"I can," said Starr calmly. "And I'll take this, too." He plucked a diamond stickpin from Patrick's cravat.

"Please, don't take that," Patrick pleaded. "My mother gave me that diamond just before she died."

Starr chuckled, "Yes, I've heard that mother story before, but it don't go with me." Starr slipped the diamond into the inside breast pocket of his overcoat.

Team Davis

Davis checked his pocket watch. Starr was late, and it made him edgy. Moments earlier he'd heard the cry in the street, "They're robbing the bank!" They'd been discovered, and if Starr didn't show up soon, he would head back to the horses—with or without him. Davis ordered the civilians to line up. They began to cry out and beg fearfully, some believing they were about to be executed. Davis yelled for them to shut up. He flashed his revolver and asked, "How would some of you fellows like to smell this?" Davis looked each of them in the eyes, "Who's the bad man in here?"

The answer was obvious.

Curry Grocery Store

Two buildings west of First National Bank, teenager Paul Curry was counting eggs in his father's grocery store. When he heard a shout that the bank was being robbed, he ran out onto Main Street. Curry had his life savings of fifty dollars in the bank, and he'd be damned if he'd allow it to be stolen.

The Stroud Doubleheader   53

Curry needed to find a gun, and his best bet was the butcher's shop. Unfortunately, he would have to pass the large front windows of First National Bank to get there. Curry took the risk and sprinted toward the east side of Main Street.

Team Starr

Starr led the hostages at a quick step. When they reached Fourth Avenue, they startled Dr. Charles McLarty, a dentist who inadvertently walked straight toward them.

"Hold on there!" Starr shouted, raising his rifle. The dentist threw his hands up and froze in terror. Satisfied the dentist wouldn't cause any trouble, Starr led the gang south toward First National.

Patrick chittered in Starr's ear, "I'd like mighty well to get that diamond back."

"I want it myself. Got a girl I want to give it to."

"How about I trade you my watch?"

Starr chuckled.

Team Davis

Davis could hear the bank clock ticking as he watched from the First National front windows. Stroud citizens began collecting on the sidewalks across the intersection with weapons in their hands.

"What's keeping Starr?" Davis wondered. Maybe he'd been caught and killed.

If Starr didn't show, Davis felt no obligation to protect innocent civilians. If the townsfolk wanted a bloody shootout, Davis was happy to deliver.

Henry's Waterloo

> The notorious band of bank bandits led by Henry Starr met its Waterloo at 10:30 o'clock in this town.
>
> *Guthrie Daily Leader*
> March 27, 1915[20]

54   Reel Two

Just as Davis was preparing his team to shoot their way out, Starr, Higgins, and Johnson arrived at the intersection. Davis prodded his hostages into the street at gunpoint. Together, as one chaotic mob, Team Starr and Team Davis moved toward the hog pens.

The armed townsfolk collected at a right angle to First National Bank, peeking out from behind wagons, barrels, and awning posts. They had no clear shot. Deputy Sheriff Isaac Dodrill seethed as he watched the Starr Gang moseying away like a herd of cattle. Impulsively, he fired two rounds above their heads. The shots echoed through the town. The bubble of pent-up tension had been pierced and suddenly, the hounds of hell were unleashed. A volley of gunfire erupted from both sides.[21] The air was quickly blackened by gunpowder and filled with the screams of terrified bystanders.

Outside of town a farmer and his boy looked up from their work planting potatoes. The sound of gunfire crackled in the air.[22]

"Something's wrong," the father said. "You stay here and keep planting." The father turned and ran toward town.

The boy was torn. He didn't want to disobey his father, and yet he didn't want to miss the excitement. So he dropped his whole peck in one large pile—technically planting them. Then he raced along a shortcut and arrived at Main Street ahead of his father.

Starr took the rear position as his gang and their hostages moved toward the hog pens. From Starr's blindside Charles Guild burst from the R. J. Miller hardware store with a double-barrel shotgun. Starr spun and pointed his rifle at Guild. Starr could have sent a bullet in the man's forehead or heart, but he only wanted to force the man to reconsider his life choices. Starr fired a bullet through the flap of Guild's coat with precision. Guild instantly realized he was no match for a skilled rifleman and ducked for cover.[23]

Meanwhile, Deputy Sheriff Dodrill climbed atop a feed sack and fired three rounds at Starr. Each bullet sailed high but tragically ended the lives of three windows of First National Bank. Marshal Lycan thought he saw an opportunity to shoot Starr after the outlaw had turned toward Guild. The lawman stepped from the crowd, but Starr spun with catlike quickness. Marshal Lycan was caught dead to rights. He froze, anticipating his death flaring from the end of Starr's rifle. Once again, Starr had the advantage and could have killed the

The Stroud Doubleheader

lawman. Instead, Starr fired a round between Marshal Lycan's feet. No longer immobilized with fear, the marshal turned tail and ran.

In the Butcher's Shop

Paul Curry, the teenage grocer's son, had just entered the meat market across from First National Bank when he heard the popping of gunfire in the street. The butcher was peeking out the front window with a .44-caliber hog gun gripped tightly in his hands.

"You gonna put that thing to use?" asked Curry.

"Heck, no. I ain't going out there."

"Then give it to me."

Curry snatched the gun from the butcher's hands and hopped to the back of the shop. The rear door opened onto the southside alley—the same one Team Starr had taken thirty minutes earlier to get to Stroud National Bank. Curry found cover behind a barrel with a clear view of the bandit/ hostage procession. A hog rifle was not Curry's weapon of choice. He was a crack shot with a Winchester. His older sister teased him about spending so much time practicing as if he was preparing for something big. Here was his moment.

Along Fourth Avenue

Starr continued trailing the procession with Patrick at his side, protecting their rear. As he walked backward, he looked right and spotted Curry behind a barrel. He dismissed the young man as a threat. "I didn't think the blamed kid would shoot," Starr recounted later. "I was watching the others." Starr didn't have much time to ponder Curry's intentions. A farmer named Walter Martin stepped out from the crowd with his rifle trained on Starr.

"Get back!" Starr yelled.

Martin kept coming.

"I'm warning you, get back!"

Once again Starr fired with precision, his bullet striking the fabric of Martin's heavy winter coat at the shoulder. Having enough of close combat, the farmer turned and ran.

56   Reel Two

"You shot at that man!" exclaimed Patrick.

"But he'll live to tell a good story."

Starr heard a blast from his right. Seconds later, a .22 LR bullet smashed into his hip. Starr spun and crumpled into the hitching post wire along First National Bank. Estes, a few feet ahead, heard the blast and turned back.

"Don't worry about me," Starr said, waving Estes on. "Keep going!"

Curry stood up from behind his barrel and fired at the retreating Estes. The bullet bit into the flesh above Estes's clavicle but didn't drop him.

Curry then raced over to Starr. The outlaw's rifle lay on the ground and out of reach, so he drew the pistol on his belt.

"Throw that gun, or I'll kill you," Curry ordered.

Starr dropped his weapon.

At the Stockyard

Maxfield was mounted up and had the horses ready. Davis, Johnson, and Sawyer reached the pens first, mounted up quickly, and galloped off. Higgins's bay panicked, fighting the reins, and whirled about. Starr's decision to buy new horses for the robbery meant they weren't comfortable around gunfire. Higgins's money sack dropped to the ground. One of the hostages picked it up and kindly handed it back to him.

Estes, bleeding profusely from his neck like the Spindletop gusher, stumbled toward the hog pens. He pointed his gun at First National Bank President Grecian and hardware store owner R. J. Miller and ordered them to help him onto his horse. Once Estes was in his saddle, he rode off after the others.

While Curry kept his gun trained on Starr, his little brother Dewey rode up with the family's grocery delivery cart. He'd been gathering asparagus four blocks south of town when the shooting started. Curry and another brother, Clark, jumped aboard the cart, and Dewey snapped the reins. The three Curry brothers boldly chased after the departing outlaws.

Townsfolk pulled Starr from the hitching post wire, and the outlaw dropped to the street, writhing in agony. A spot of blood was expanding from his hip, soaking his serge wool suit pants. Starr looked toward the hog pens. His once flawless plan had been shattered like the bones in his hip. However,

Figure 18 In a scene from Starr's biographical film, *A Debtor to the Law* (1920), a Starr Gang member based on Lewis Estes (William Karl Hackett) is shot during his escape following the Stroud, Oklahoma, daylight double bank robberies. The 26-year-old Hackett was a Broadway actor before being hired by director P. S. McGeeney for the reshoots. Courtesy of the Glenn D. Shirley Western Americana Collection, Dickinson Research Center, National Cowboy and Western Heritage Museum, Oklahoma City (RC2006.068.32.6.12).

his boys were gone, which meant he had pulled off the first successful daylight double bank robbery, besting Jesse James and the Dalton Gang.

Starr gritted his teeth—a strange smile mixed with pain.

In Hot (and Cold) Pursuit

With the pounding of hoofbeats beneath them and dust kicking behind, Davis, Sawyer, Johnson, and Maxfield raced for the blackjacks at a breakneck pace.[24] They executed Starr's escape plan flawlessly. When they came to a fence, the lead rider jumped off and used the nippers to cut through the wire. The others scouted the horizon with their field glasses. Within seconds they were on their way again.

Higgins was far behind and galloping hard when the money sack tied to his saddle split open. Glittering coins sprinkled across the ground behind him like a trail of silver breadcrumbs. Higgins immediately pulled the reins and swung back around. When he reached the coins, he jumped from his saddle and hot-footed it, gathering them up. While Higgins was filling his pockets, his horse spooked and bolted away. He tried chasing after the skittish bay, but it was gone. Higgins cursed the horse and his bad luck.

Just when Higgins's situation appeared most dire, he saw a horse and rider approaching from a distance. Higgins pulled his revolver, anticipating a posse. Instead, the rider turned out to be Estes. Blood was gushing from his neck, and he looked ragged and weak. *It figures the greenhorn got himself shot.* Higgins took the reins and ordered Estes to slide back. He then grabbed the pommel and swung into the saddle in front of him.

"Hang on tight," Higgins said. "If you fall off, I ain't stopping for you."

Higgins snapped the reins, and the two desperados galloped off.

Davis, Sawyer, Maxfield, and Johnson had paused at the tree line, using their field glasses to look for any signs of the others. When they spotted Higgins and Estes, they rode down to meet them. Estes's face was pale from the loss of blood, and the ride had sapped his strength.

"He's as good as dead," Davis said.

"Let's set 'im against a tree," Johnson suggested.

Maxfield and Johnson helped Estes to the ground and then placed him at the foot of a blackjack.

"Sorry 'bout this young fella," Maxfield said.

"Mount up!" Davis called.

Estes watched helplessly as the gang galloped away.[25]

Twenty minutes later Estes heard the roaring of an automobile and then saw it bobbing across the rocky landscape.[26] He waved at them with what strength he had left as a sign of surrender. After the two posse men pulled to a stop next to Estes, they climbed out and began searching his pockets. They found seventy-five dollars in silver coins.

"I need a doctor," Estes moaned.

One of the men ran back to the car. Estes hoped he had a first aid kit.

Instead the posse man returned with a bucket, and the two men began filling it with other coins scattered about. Only after they had recovered every coin did they lift Estes into the car and drive back toward Stroud. Estes, barely conscious, hoped he could get back before bleeding out. Unfortunately, whenever the possemen spotted loose coins, they stopped the car to fill the bucket. For Estes the delay was excruciating.

Lincoln County Attorney Streeter Speakman arrived in Stroud within the hour and immediately called in the state militia headquartered in Chandler.[27] With bugles blaring Company B of the 1st Oklahoma Infantry boarded the train headed for Stroud led by Captain H. B. Gilstrap. When the eleven militiamen arrived at the Stroud depot, they were hustled into a phalanx of waiting automobiles and driven toward the Osage Hills. Armed posses formed in Bristow, Sapulpa, Okemah, Mounds, Drumright, and Beggs. Phone lines buzzed with promising reports from the field indicating the posses were hot on the bandits' trail. But hours into the chase, the posses didn't know if they had the Starr gang on the run or were chasing their tails. As Starr predicted, automobiles were useless in the heavily timbered woods. The drivers had to drop the soldiers off to scour the forest on foot.[28]

Lawmen were angry that area farmers refused to lend them horses.

"Why do you need my horses?" the farmer asked.

"We lost the trail of some bank robbers out of Stroud," one marshal responded.

"Well, I ain't lost no bandits," said the farmer thoughtfully. "Tell them bankers to use their own horses."[29]

Farmers were understandably miffed at the banks. In 1915 newspapers reported that three hundred Oklahoma banks were charging farmers interest rates considered usurious. Weeks before the Stroud robberies, the Oklahoma Bankers Association successfully lobbied state lawmakers to defeat the Glasco Usury Bill that would have protected farmers from being gouged.[30] From then on, given a choice, the farmers preferred the bandit holding a gun to the one carrying their loan.

After twelve hours on the chase, Captain Gilstrap called County Attorney Speakman and sheepishly admitted defeat. The militia had found neither hide nor hair of the robbers.

Talk of Lynching

Starr lay on the frosty ground in front of First National Bank, bleeding out. The townsfolk, no longer timid, gathered around him and jeered. Some demanded to know his name, while others called for him to be hanged. J. M. Parks, the Armour Packing Company salesman, stepped forward and rifled through Starr's pockets. In one pocket he found a photo of Retta, and from another he retrieved a packet of bills amounting to $1,000. Starr asked Parks to wire his mother in Tulsa and tell her to come quickly. "It's all off with me," Starr croaked, believing he was dying.[31]

Dr. J. J. Evans parted the circle of onlookers and examined the downed outlaw.

"I need to get him to a clean room," the doctor said, addressing the crowd.

"You can use my office above the bank," an attorney said. "I can set up a cot."

Starr was shifted to a horse blanket. Then four men grabbed the corners and lifted him up. Just then, a shout rang out. "The bandits are coming back!"[32] Like a scene from a Keystone Kops comedy,[33] the men immediately let go of the blanket and dropped Starr hard to the ground. One can imagine the slapstick hijinks as the men tried to hide by diving headfirst into a rain barrel, pulling a bear skin rug over themselves, or pretending to be a cigar store Indian. After the rescue attempt turned out to be a false alarm, the men wiped their collective brows and continued carrying Starr up one flight of stairs to the attorney's corner office.

A few hours later, Dr. Evans was monitoring Starr's condition in the makeshift doctor's office when two possemen arrived, carrying Estes.[34] The newlywed outlaw looked half dead.

"I'd rather have been killed myself than have them catch you," Starr told him.

He then turned to the doctor. "That Estes is sure some fine kid. Fix 'im up, Doc, and I'll pay for it." Starr later signed over his horse, which was valued at over six hundred dollars.

"I wouldn't bother patchin' up these fellers," one of the possemen told the doctor. "The town is fixin' to lynch them."

The Stroud Doubleheader 61

Dr. Evans walked to the window. From the second story, he had a bird's-eye view of the intersection below, where a "howling mob" was gathering. The possemen said a rumor was swirling that someone had killed a man in the First National Bank for not raising his hands fast enough.

"Doc, have you got any poison?" Starr croaked. "I don't give a damn about dying, but I don't want to be strung up."

"Cooler heads will prevail," the doctor assured him. "I will let them know no one has been injured except you and Estes."

Stroud National Bank Vice President Lee Patrick found himself among the hue and cry of the mob below First National Bank.[35] He didn't know that when he was caught in the crossfire earlier, his daughter saw what was happening and quickly peddled home on her bicycle. Arriving at the Patrick home, she yelled, "They're robbing the bank and killing Papa!" Patrick's wife, Cosette, rushed to the scene, but by the time she'd arrived, Starr had already been moved to the second-floor law office. She found her husband standing outside with the angry townsfolk, eyes glazed and still shaken from the traumatizing experience. Instead of comforting him, she pointed out his missing diamond stick pin.

"Where did it go?" she demanded.

"A bandit took it," Patrick answered quietly. "The one they carried upstairs."

"Well, you better get yourself right up there and get it back!"

Patrick was afraid to see Starr face-to-face again, but when push came to shove, he was more terrified of Cosette.

Upstairs, Starr was stretched out on a cot, lying comfortably with sheets, a blanket, and a pillow. The sedatives had kicked in, easing his pain. Starr heard a knock at the door, and the guard in the hallway opened it to reveal Patrick standing in the doorway.

"I guess you want your diamond back," Starr said.

Patrick entered sheepishly as if a death sentence were over his head.

"That would make my life a whole lot easier."

"It's still inside my coat pocket. Just reach in there and take it."

Patrick gratefully plunged his hand into the coat pocket. His fingers fished around—then his face dropped.

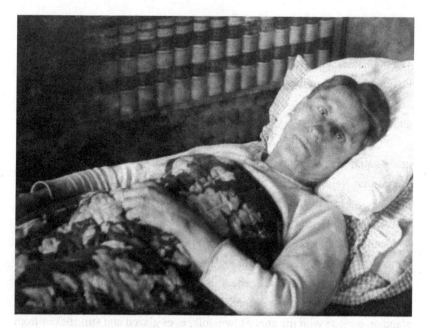

Figure 19 Starr recovers from his gunshot wound at the hands of Stroud grocer's boy Paul Curry. A makeshift hospital is set up in a law office on the second floor of First National Bank, which the Starr Gang had just robbed. The photo was made into a postcard and sold as a souvenir. Courtesy of the A. B. MacDonald Papers, Box 7, Library of Congress.

"The bottom is out of the pocket!" Patrick exclaimed.

"Yeah. Meant to have that hole sewed up."

Frightening scenarios raced through Patrick's mind. The diamond could have fallen out anywhere, perhaps in the street, and someone took it, or it was being trampled by the mob, never to be found.

"Keep poking around. Things fall into the lining."

Patrick frantically dug deeper, his fingers searching. Then a look of relief washed over him. The banker pulled out the glittering stick pin.[36]

Starr had a question for Patrick, and the relieved banker felt chatty.

"What kind of gun did that boy have?" Starr asked.

"I don't know, but I heard he got it from the butcher."

Starr shook his head with wounded pride. "A hog gun and a kid, too. I wouldn't have minded it so much if a man had shot me."

The Stroud Doubleheader

As Dr. Evans predicted, the mood in Stroud shifted dramatically. Record crowds came to Stroud in the days following the robbery. Visitors spent money at the shops and dined at the restaurants, greatly improving the mood of the town merchants.[37] Tourists wanted to see the bullet holes that were still lodged in the walls, posts, and barrels. Over fifty shots had been exchanged, but no civilians were wounded. Charles Guild and Walter Martin told and retold their near-death experiences, agreeing that Starr could have easily shot them dead if he'd wanted to. A local merchant admired Starr for waiving off Estes and nixing a potentially bloody rescue attempt. "Starr's signal prevented a lot of new made graves at Stroud," he assented.[38]

Stroud residents agreed Curry had nerves of steel, but reports differed on his true age. Newspapers called Curry a boy, a lad, or a kid. The *Stillwater Gazette* editor said waggishly, "That boy who shot Starr at Stroud with a hog gun, ranges in age from 16 to 20, according to the imagination of the correspondent. It is a safe guess that he is not too old to be ruined by the notoriety."[39] In the days following the holdup, Curry had become the cock of the walk among local girls, strutting around with one on each arm. They would clutch tighter when he bragged that his life could still be in danger if Starr's gang returned for revenge. Privately, Curry was worried. Only one person knew whether his life was truly in danger—Henry Starr.

One night, he came to Starr's bedside.

"You think your gang might come back and kill me?"

Starr smiled.

"Son, won't nobody harm you," Starr assured him. "You go home now, and don't get swelled up over what you did."[40]

Curry also had money on his mind. The day of the robberies, he'd put in for his reward, sending a succinct telegram to Governor R .L. Williams:

I shot Starr through the leg and captured him. I also shot one other robber, and he was captured. Will hold for your disposal and claim reward.

Respectfully,
Paul Curry[41]

Curry believed the reward would change the trajectory of his life. He spent evenings gazing at the stars and calculating his windfall: the state of

Oklahoma owed him $1,000 for the capture of Starr, plus another $1,000 for Estes, and Colorado was offering another $1,400 because Starr had broken his parole. Curry remained coy about how he planned on using his newfound wealth. His sister said Curry had always dreamed of attending the Agriculture and Mechanical School of Oklahoma. However, his family could never afford it.[42] Paul's father, L. W. Curry, didn't support his son's college ambitions and wanted him to carry on the family store. So at least publicly, Curry stated, "If I get the money, I am going into the grocery business with my father."[43] For Curry the easy part was daydreaming about the money. Getting the states and the bankers to pay the $3,400 reward would be fraught with excuses and double-talk.

William Tilghman, the Second Tin Star Filmmaker

Although talk of lynching had quieted, Starr didn't put much faith in the fickle nature of mobs. He dictated a telegram to former Deputy US Marshal William Tilghman, who lived fourteen miles away in Chandler: "You are the only officer who ever spoke kindly to me and gave me good advice. I don't want to be lynched." Shortly after receiving the telegraph, Tilghman boarded the Frisco bound for Stroud.[44]

When the guard opened the door to law office above First National Bank, Starr looked over from his cot and saw Tilghman filling the frame. It wasn't until Tilghman pulled up a chair next to him that Starr could see that since lawman's glory days, his hair and mustache had turned from blond to gray. However, despite being 62, his eyes were bright and his mind keen. In a grandfatherly tone, Tilghman informed Starr that he'd tamped down any talk of stringing him up. Starr was relieved and not a bit surprised that the Stroud townsfolk listened to Tilghman; he was a legend. As a young man, Tilghman was Bat Masterson's deputy during Dodge City's wild and woolly days and served alongside Wyatt Earp. He'd also been an Oklahoma state senator and the Oklahoma City chief of police.[45]

Tilghman asked perfunctory questions about the identities of his accomplices, but Starr refused to name names, instead spinning an absurd story about recruiting some strangers he and Estes met on the road outside Stroud.[46]

The Stroud Doubleheader 65

Tilghman didn't seem to care about the lies, and his eyes danced when he got to the real reason for his visit:

"I'm shooting a motion picture about the most famous lawmen and outlaws in the Oklahoma and Indian Territories," Tilghman said, barely hiding his excitement. "And I want you to be in it."

"I'll have to check with my appointment secretary, Bill," Starr said. "But I think I'm unavailable for the next five to ten." Starr showed Tilghman his wrist handcuffed to the cot.

"Just allow my cameraman to film you going to jail, and I'll pay you."

When he got Starr's telegram, Tilghman had been in Chandler shooting *The Passing of the Oklahoma Outlaws*. "'Hold the camera!' I told Bennie Kent," Tilghman recalled.[47] The cameraman and former deputy marshal were collaborating seven years after filming *The Bank Robbery* (1908) for US Marshal John Abernathy's Natural Mutoscene Company. Abernathy, the first tin star filmmaker, begat the second—Tilghman. Initially Abernathy wanted Kent to direct *The Bank Robbery*, but Kent liked to plant his tripod and crank the camera, not direct actors. Abernathy and Kent turned to Tilghman.

"Why, I don't know anything about moving pictures!" Tilghman protested.

"You know how to get things done," replied Kent. "We'll put you in full charge and do what you say."

The Passing of the Oklahoma Outlaws was conceived out of spite. After working together on *The Bank Robbery,* Tilghman and Jennings wanted to turn the book *Beating Back* into a motion picture.[48] The pair traveled to the Thanhouser Film Corporation in New Rochelle, New Jersey, and pitched the idea to studio head Charlie Hite. Jennings would star as himself, and Tilghman would direct. Both Oklahomans were excited to enter the big-time motion picture industry. Hite had recently produced *The Million Dollar Mystery*, the most profitable motion picture serial at the time.[49] Hite agreed to make a film based on Jennings's life story, but Tilghman later discovered the two men had cut him out of the deal.[50]

After *Beating Back* was released, Tilghman was angered to discover the film presented US marshals as corrupt. Tilghman wanted revenge. He contacted his former boss, US Marshal Evett Dumas "E. D." Nix, and

Figure 20 The Old Wild West meets the New Wild West of motion picture production. William Tilghman (*inset*), a Dodge City lawman and buffalo hunter, becomes Bill Tilghman (*far right*), a motion picture producer, director, photoplaywright, and actor in *The Passing of the Oklahoma Outlaws*. Seen here, Tilghman holds a revolver from his gun collection as part of his *Passing* roadshow. Tilghman rescued Starr from an angry lynch mob after the Stroud, Oklahoma, robbery and was the first person to place Starr in front of a moving picture camera. Courtesy of the Oklahoma Historical Society.

they formed the Nix-Tilghman Anti-Outlaw Movie Company (later renamed the Eagle Film Company) to produce their own film refuting Jennings while highlighting their heroics.[51] They hired a Hollywood scenarist to write *The Passing of the Oklahoma Outlaws*, aided by Tilghman, who shared his "storehouse of Western knowledge." The film was shot in real locations with many of the actual participants on both sides of the law. Tilghman and Nix played themselves, and the lone survivor of the Doolin Gang, Roy Daugherty (a.k.a. Arkansas Tom Jones) re-created his role in the infamous Battle of Ingalls. Wannabe "girl outlaws" Cattle Annie and Little Breeches had minor roles in the film, pretending to be captured by Tilghman. Al Jennings, however, would not be playing himself. Eagle Films vowed to present his career "stripped of any fiction." Tilghman exacted his revenge by hiring an actor to portray Jennings as a foolish and failed outlaw.

The Stroud Doubleheader
67

Upon hearing about the daylight double bank robberies, Tilghman's first thought was, "Henry Starr did what the Younger boys and the James brothers were never able to do."[52] His second thought was, *I must get the King of Bank Robbers into my film.*

Now, at Starr's bedside, Tilghman made his proposal: he would provide safe passage for Starr and Estes to the Lincoln County Jail in exchange for letting Kent capture the event on film.[53]

"Any money you make off me should go to my boy."

"Deal."

Outlaws of Other Days

As the Frisco chugged into the Chandler depot, Bennie Kent stood on the platform with his box camera ready.[54] Three hundred people gathered excitedly around the station, spilling into the streets and bobbing for the best view. Tilghman was the first to step down from the express car, followed by Deputy Sheriff George Wilson. The crowd buzzed excitedly when Starr and Estes were borne out on stretchers carried by a platoon of militiamen. Kent followed the action as the outlaws were loaded onto a waiting hay wagon. There was quite the hubbub as the swarming crowd followed the wagon to the Lincoln County Jail. Kent jumped in his car and raced ahead to get the angle of their arrival.

The militiamen offloaded the stretchers and carried Starr and Estes from the wagon at street level to the basement of the Lincoln County courthouse. The relentless jostling of the train car and the bone-rattling wagon ride left the outlaws in excruciating pain. Starr and Estes were laid side by side in a cell with one window covered in steel mesh and iron bars and with double steel doors with bars and sheet metal.[55] Dr. J. W. Adams had been awaiting their arrival and swiftly set to work. He administered anodynes to alleviate their suffering and stripped away their ragged and bloody bandages to examine their injuries. Starr's femur was shattered, and sepsis had set in, ballooning his leg to three times its normal size. Dr. Adams told Starr he believed he could save his leg by removing the bone shards and bullet fragments and draining the festering fluids.

68   Reel Two

After Starr and Estes received treatment and their pain had subsided, newspaper reporters were allowed in. Hungry for a scoop, they shouted questions.[56]

"How did your gang elude the posses?"

"We never worried about posses," Starr answered. "They don't have the heart to confront men like mine."

"You're calling them chicken livered?"

Starr smiled like the Cheshire cat: "You've heard that story about the tramp who was hunting for work and praying he couldn't find it? That's the way it is with posses."

Hours later another train arrived at the Chandler station from Tulsa. Retta Elwick and Starr's mother, Mary Gordon, stepped onto the platform and were greeted by Tilghman and a man in a derby hat cranking a movie camera. Gordon set her fierce black eyes disdainfully toward the crowd gawking at her. Next to her stood Retta, draped in a somber black ensemble, exuding an aura of both beauty and defiance.[57]

"Ladies, I'm Bill Tilghman, and this is my cameraman, Bennie Kent."

Kent waved his cigar from behind the camera.

"Now, Henry and I have an agreement to let Mr. Kent use his motion picture camera to record said events."

The women shared a look.

"The money will go to Starr's boy," Tilghman added.

Gordon and Elwick sighed.

"Fine, if you'll face the camera then."

Kent put the stogie back in his mouth and returned to cranking. He chronicled their carriage ride from the station to the Lincoln County Jail.

When Starr's cell door was unlocked and Gordon was allowed to enter, her heart broke seeing her boy's battered body on a cot. Over the next few days, she transformed the jail cell into a sanctuary of care and nourishment. Daily she delivered bowls of homemade soup. In a tableau reminiscent of Michelangelo's *La Pieta,* Gordon propped Starr's head on her lap and spoon-fed her son a healing elixir. "Henry is my own dear boy, no matter what happens," she told reporters.[58] Newspapers buzzed with gossip about Starr's adulterous relationship with Retta. A wag from the *Bartlesville Independent* wrote, "Henry Starr not only was apt in robbing banks but seemed to have the facility of robbing a man of his wife."[59]

Word of Starr's incarceration spread, drawing a motley crew of characters to Chandler from far and wide. The *Kansas City Star* wrote, "Outlaws of other days, and friends of outlaws, and men who were famous as outlaw chasers dropped into Chandler from all around to say 'Howdy' to Henry Starr, for Starr is considered the 'king of 'em all.'"[60]

Lincoln County Sheriff George Arnold welcomed the colorful parade of visitors, and soon the air in Starr's jail cell hung heavy with the aroma of smoke, chewing tobacco, and lively conversation. The loudest visitor was larger-than-life Colonel Zach Mulhall, a renowned Wild West showman. When Mulhall—loud, bold, and richly mustached—entered a room, it was like "diving headlong into a tank of ice water. It makes you gasp."[61]

"Ay-ooo-dy-ooo-deday-lo-oo," Mulhall sang, explaining it was a song he used to put herds to sleep with.

Mulhall wore an expensive cowboy hat with wide eaves and carried a pistol on his hip. The gun, he explained, came in handy when making his six-shooter cocktail. Instead of straw, he used the barrel to stir his intoxicating libation.

Mulhall regaled the group with the story of how he had helped Starr hide from the law one time by hiring him as an actor in his Wild West show. One of Mulhall's set pieces featured a stagecoach being chased by bandits around the arena. During one performance Starr was inside the stagecoach when it flipped over. "Starr was as mad as a hornet," Mulhall said, his laughter echoing in the jail cell. Starr smiled ruefully at the memory of breaking his wrist.[62]

Beside Mulhall sat the notorious former Doolin-Dalton Gang member Arkansas Tom Jones. He was in Chandler recreating his role in the Battle of Ingalls for *The Passing of the Oklahoma Outlaws* when he'd heard about Starr's double bank robbery.[63]

"How many did you kill in that fight at Ingalls, Tom?" Mulhall asked.

"They laid three on me."

In fact, Arkansas Tom had only killed one deputy marshal during the 1893 Battle of Ingalls but was charged with murdering three lawmen and served seventeen years behind bars. After being released in 1910, he vowed

Figure 21 Visitors to Starr's Chandler jail cell included the loquacious, avuncular Wild West showman Zach Mulhall (*left*), who gave Starr, as a young fugitive, a role in his live show (photo by Vincent Dillon, October 24, 1927; Fred J. Acton Collection, Oklahoma Historical Society), and Roy Daugherty (a.k.a. Arkansas Tom Jones; *right*), a former member of the outlaw Doolin-Dalton gang who was in Chandler re-creating his part in the Battle of Ingalls gunfight for William Tilghman's motion picture *The Passing of the Oklahoma Outlaws* (photo: https://www.findagrave.com/memorial/42340221/roy-daugherty/photo).

to go straight and opened a restaurant in Drumright, Oklahoma. Five years later former marshals E. D. Nix and Bill Tilghman entered his establishment, wanting a word with him. He was afraid they had a warrant for his arrest, but they surprised him with an offer to play himself in their moving picture.

At 45 Arkansas Tom's hairline had crept back to the crown of his head, but his prodigious English mustache remained the same, extending well beyond the pipe he clenched in his teeth. His name wasn't Tom, and he didn't hail from Arkansas. He was born Roy Daugherty in Missouri. Two of his brothers became preachers, but Arkansas Tom preferred outlawry. In 1893 he drifted into Oklahoma Territory and soon joined the Bill Doolin–Bill Dalton bank and train robbery gang.

On August 31, 1893, the Doolin-Dalton Gang descended upon the small town of Ingalls, thirty miles north of Chandler.[64] In addition to Jones, Bill

The Stroud Doubleheader

Doolin, and Bill Dalton (older brother of Emmett), the gang included Bob Yocum, George "Bitter Creek" Newcomb, Dan "Dynamite Dick" Clifton, Tulsa Jack, Slaughter Kid, and Red Buck. Business owners welcomed the colorfully named gang because they spent lavishly on liquor and gambling without causing trouble.

When Guthrie's Deputy Marshal John Hixon heard the Doolin-Dalton Gang was in Ingalls, he devised a simple but audacious plan reminiscent of the Trojan horse in Greek mythology. While the gang was sleeping at the OK Hotel—the only two-story building in town—Hixon planned to roll in with two covered wagons filled with deputies. At the stroke of midnight, the lawmen would leap out and surround the hotel, capturing the outlaws as they slept. Unfortunately, the plan went awry when the second wagonload of deputies was late.

Hixon and his deputies waited all night for the reinforcements to arrive. When the sun began to rise, he and his men watched helplessly as the gang members exited the hotel, stretched, yawned, and casually ambled toward Ransom's Saloon. Every gang member left the hotel except Arkansas Tom, who was sick and stayed behind in his room on the second floor. Hixon had to improvise. He deployed his men to cover the exits out of town until the second wagon arrived. "Bitter Creek" Newcombe was sitting on the porch of Ransom's Saloon when he spotted Deputy Marshal Dick Speed slinking down an alleyway. Without hesitation Newcombe fired at him. Deputy Speed shot back. Hixon's surprise siege had now wholly unraveled.

From the second floor of the OK Hotel, Arkansas Tom heard the gunshots and sprang out of bed. He grabbed his rifle and rushed to the window. Below, he witnessed deputies descending upon Ransom's Saloon. From his perch Arkansas Tom drew a bead on Deputy Marshal Thomas Hueston and shot him dead. With Arkansas Tom providing cover fire, the gang made their way to their horses. Bill Doolin killed Deputy Marshal Speed, and Bill Dalton shot and killed Deputy Marshal Lafayette Shadley. Dalton and Arkansas Tom kept the lawmen at bay until the gang reached their horses and rode to safety.

Hixon's remaining men surrounded the OK Hotel. He called to Arkansas Tom, "Give up peacefully or we'll throw dynamite through the windows." Arkansas Tom tossed his rifle out the window and surrendered.

72   Reel Two

Twenty-two years later Nix and Tilghman built a set to look like Arkansas Tom's second-story room at the OK Hotel. They also gave him a costume similar to the one he had worn during the Battle of Ingalls.[65] Arkansas Tom told Mulhall and the other visitors that he liked the moving picture business and was considering working in Hollywood.

Perhaps a seed was planted in Starr's mind.

Courting Justice

Almost from the first moment they had to share a jail cell, Starr began grating on Lewis Estes's nerves. First was the endless parade of visitors, including melodramatic Retta and Mary Gordon, who spoon-fed her son like he was a little boy. Then Estes watched enviously as Starr had a brass bed delivered with an expensive "easy springs" mattress. The only amenities Estes enjoyed came on Tuesday during house cleaning day when his mattress was dragged outside and the flea-infested straw disgorged and burned. And don't get Estes started about the food. While he ate bland jailhouse grub, Starr ordered delivery from local restaurants.[66]

Despite the indignities, Estes had to admit Starr had been kind to him. The outlaw told the marshals to take it easy on him, saying, "He's just a hard-working boy that I led off, and this is his first robbery."[67] Starr was also paying all his doctor bills. However, when Estes was in a foul mood, he grumbled that he wouldn't need a doctor had he never met Bud Maxfield and Starr.

Tilghman visited Estes and badgered him to give up the names of the other gang members, but he always refused. Then, one day, the simmering resentment Estes felt boiled over, and he "showed the white feather." Tilghman relayed Estes's information, and soon Claud Sawyer and Charles Johnson were arrested.[68] It hadn't taken long for Lige Higgins to get into another scrape. He was currently in custody in Pueblo, Colorado, in connection with the murder of a Santa Fe railroad detective.[69] Bill Tilghman captured Joe Davis, but prevailing warrants kept him from immediately facing charges in Chandler.[70]

In August 1915 the trial of the Starr Gang commenced before District Court Judge Charles B. Wilson.[71] The proceedings were the biggest event of the summer, eclipsing July Fourth celebrations the month prior.

Figure 22 The ill-fated rookie bank robber Lewis Estes joined the Starr Gang and was shot in the shoulder by grocer's boy Paul Curry. While in the Chandler, Oklahoma, jail, and the cellmate of Starr, he became embittered and "peached" on the rest of the gang to get a lighter sentence. His plan failed. Photo: *Tulsa Daily World*, July 21, 1915.

Women brought their knitting, and men traded snarky comments from the back row. Estes made a deal with Lincoln County District Attorney Streeter Speakman to testify under oath against the gang in exchange for leniency. Estes felt no qualms about "peaching" on his cohorts and was ready on day one. First up was Claud Sawyer, who sat at the defendant's table wearing a stylish blue serge suit, a white shirt, and an expensive sombrero. A wag in the audience whispered, "If that handsome fella was being tried in front of a jury of ladies, he would be acquitted." In addition to Estes's testimony, four First National Bank employees identified Sawyer and, inexplicably, the twenty-dollar bill found in his possession. The jury found the stylish outlaw guilty, and Judge Wilson sentenced Sawyer to serve five years of hard labor at the Oklahoma State Penitentiary in McAlester—Sawyer's hometown.

Next, Estes testified against 40-year-old Charles Johnson.[72] On the witness stand, Johnson's defense lawyer, J. R. Charlton, ripped apart Estes's testimony, explaining to the jury that Johnson didn't need to rob a bank because he had a good-paying job with a large-scale cattle-buying operation. The jury acquitted Johnson.

Since Bud Maxfield never entered either bank, no witnesses identified him as part of the gang. However, the oil field wagon found at Stroud was identified as his. The jury found Maxfield guilty, and Judge Wilson sentenced Maxfield to five years in prison.[73]

On Friday, August 20, Estes came due for sentencing.[74] He was smug, anticipating a light sentence from the judge for ratting out his friends. A courtroom observer commented, "We'll see if Estes gets off easy. He sure delivered the goods." Judge Wilson had other ideas. He stunned Estes and the courtroom by sentencing him to five years of hard labor—the same as Sawyer and Maxfield, who clammed up. Speakman rose from his chair to protest, but Judge Wilson shut him down.

"I am under no obligation to honor any of your promises, prosecutor," Judge Wilson said flatly.[75]

On the day of Starr's sentencing, dark clouds dropped sheets of rain.[76] Chandler had received unprecedented precipitation that month—over six inches in the first ten days. But bad weather couldn't keep the

Figure 23 Outside the Chandler, Oklahoma, courthouse (1915), Starr poses for a publicity photo for William Tilghman's *The Passing of the Oklahoma Outlaws*. Starr was still on crutches due to his gunshot wound in the hip. Note he's wearing a sock on his left foot because it was too swollen to fit in a boot, and he is using his left hand to balance himself against the Chandler Courthouse wall. Courtesy of the Oklahoma Historical Society.

standing-room-only crowds away. Since Starr wasn't contesting the charges, he didn't require a defense attorney. However, he was allowed to present character witnesses. Lee Patrick, the man who looked straight into the barrel of Starr's rifle and had his diamond stickpin stolen, took the stand and shared how he'd come to know Starr as a kind and intelligent man. He asked the judge to give Starr a lenient sentence.

Then, it was Starr's turn. He made a dramatic humbling entrance, hobbling on crutches up the stairs from the jail downstairs, aided by his common-law wife, Retta.

"Henry George Starr," the bailiff called.

The gallery buzzed with anticipation as Starr stood unsteadily before the judge.

"Your Honor," Starr began. "I would like to apologize to the kind people of Stroud for my actions."

Judge Wilson looked about, gauging the reaction in the room.

"As you can see, I will be a cripple for the rest of my life," Starr continued. "And I ask that you consider my infirmity as you determine my sentence."

All eyes in the courtroom turned to the judge as he sat up and cleared his throat.

Scenes and Incidents Authentic

"Mr. Starr," Judge Wilson began. "I'm sure the good people of Stroud appreciate your contrition; however, I believe a criminal should suffer for his acts."

Starr swallowed hard.

Forty-year-old Judge Wilson had a long, narrow face and spoke with a firm, horizontal slash for a mouth.[76] He was nearly the same age as Starr, but their life journeys were very different. Wilson came to Lincoln County from Missouri, obtaining property during the '89 land rush. He enjoyed all the benefits of influence, wealth, and privilege. Judge Wilson followed his father into law and rose quickly.

Judge Wilson continued, "I sentence you to twenty-five years of hard labor at the Oklahoma State Penitentiary."[77]

The Stroud Doubleheader

77

An audible gasp erupted in the courtroom. The sentence was shockingly punitive; Starr's sentence was five times longer than the rest of the gang members. Retta's eyes blazed with anger at the injustice against her man.

As Starr was escorted from the courtroom by armed guards, a reporter shouted a question to him: "Do you regret not squealing in exchange for a lighter sentence?"

"The world may regard me as a bad man," Starr responded. "But I have not reached the point where I will betray a friend."[78]

Later, as a measure of gratitude, Starr gave Patrick his Remington Model 8—the one he'd threatened to shoot him with.[79]

After sentencing Starr languished two more weeks at the Lincoln County Jail recuperating. Teddy visited his father for three days, and then he and Mary Gordon left. Retta took over as both cook and nurse. She made Starr his favorite meal of fried squirrel and arranged for Dr. E. S. Lain, a specialist out of Oklahoma City, to x-ray his hip. Starr's femur had been shattered, and two large cracks emanated down his leg from the bullet fragments that hadn't been removed. The doctor determined Starr's bones were knitting well. "This is my 24th day. Have got 18–20 more flat on my back," Starr wrote to journalist A. B. MacDonald. "It's pretty tough, but part of the game."[80] The prognosis was that it would be a few more weeks before Starr could safely put any weight on the injured leg. He "laughed heartily" after reading a spurious newspaper report that he'd escaped from the Chandler Jail—on foot.[81]

Tilghman sent photographer Tony Mitchell to the Lincoln County Jail to take promotional photos of Starr.[82] The convicted double bank robber hobbled outside on crutches wearing a dark plaid suit, white shirt, and a wool square-end tie. Setting the crutches outside the camera frame, he stood as upright as possible without putting weight on his left leg. Starr's left foot was covered with a black sock since it was too swollen to wear a shoe. He bent his left arm behind his back and steadied himself against the courthouse wall. Mitchell took several shots as Starr stared stoically into the camera. He had lost a lot of weight and color from being locked up.[83]

The publicity photo was one of Tilghman's final checklist items. Kent's terrific documentary footage of Starr, his mother Mary Gordon, Retta, and

Ollie gave him the idea to release a stand-alone featurette focused solely on Starr. To add excitement to the footage, Tilghman hired Paul Curry to reenact shooting Starr.[84] To appear in the film, Curry took time from track practice, where he was a pole vaulter at Stroud High School. His track uniform bore the school's initials, S.H.S, which his chums joked stood for "Shot Henry Starr."[85]

During filming Curry complained to Tilghman that he still hadn't received his reward money. The two Stroud banks had given him "a handsome gold medal," and he took photos with the bank presidents, but he expected to receive $3,400.[86] Governor Williams was balking over technicalities, explaining that the $1,000 reward wasn't for capturing Starr per se but for whoever was tried and convicted of robbing the Carney Bank in December 1914. There would be no reward for capturing Estes because they'd never posted one. The State Bankers Association offered a $200 reward for the capture and conviction of bank robbers, but they informed Curry they would only pay out $100 because he stopped Starr and Estes while they were escaping, not inside the banks committing the crime. Once again, the banks demonstrated why regular folks hated them. After hearing how Governor Williams was cheating Curry, Starr confessed to the Carney robbery so the boy would get his money.[87] On October 19, 1915, Governor Williams cut a check for $500, and that was expected to be the limit Curry would receive. So much for risking one's life to stop bank robbers.

On April 21, 1916, Tulsa's Wonderland advertised the exclusive feature "*The Capture of Henry Starr*, the Most Desperate Outlaw of Modern Times. Scenes and Incidents Authentic, Taken at Stroud Immediately After His Last Exploit. Not Motion Pictures."[88] The true-crime film debuted only one month after the real daylight double bank robbery. After seeing Tilghman's short film, producers from a Tulsa film company visited Starr in jail and offered 20 percent of ticket sales for the rights to his story. Starr turned them down.[89] Four years later he would have a different answer.

In May Tilghman and the Eagle Film Company released its six-reel $50,000 motion picture *The Passing of the Oklahoma Outlaws*, including the new Starr footage.[90] At a preview screening in Oklahoma City, the audience was "loud in their praise." On Tuesday, May 25, the film screened

Figure 24 Stroud grocer's boy Paul Curry poses with Starr's .35-caliber Model 8 Winchester after he felled the bandit with a shot to the hip. Trophies at his feet (*left to right*): a bandit's hat, Starr's revolver, and a bullet. Curry reenacted his heroic moment in three films: *The Capture of Henry Starr* (1915), *The Passing of the Oklahoma Outlaws* (1915), and *A Debtor to the Law* (1920). Courtesy of the Museum of Pioneer History, Lincoln County Historical Society, Chandler, Oklahoma. Originally a gift from Mr. and Mrs. Dewey Curry.

at Chandler's Odeon on a continuous loop from 1:00 p.m. until midnight. The *Chandler New-Publicist* predicted the film would create a "furor" and that Tilghman and Nix would profit handsomely.

For the Stroud screening, the advertisement copy read, "These pictures will show the reproduction of the robbing of two Stroud Banks by Henry Starr and his band of outlaws a few weeks ago. See Paul Curry fire shots that resulted in the capturing of Starr and Estes. See how the people of Stroud perform under such circumstances."[91]

Jessica D. Harper, a writer for the *Tulsa Tribune*, described seeing *The Passing of the Oklahoma Outlaws* at an oil boomtown theater outside the city. When she arrived there was already a long line of people waiting for the doors to open: "And what a heterogeneous crowd! Sunbonnets, sombreros, spurs, bare feet; blanketed Indians, old men with white whiskers stained with tobacco, boys and girls in faded overalls and calico dresses, nearly all with protruding teeth and shocks of yellow hair, women with tiny babies in their arms but looking haggard and work-worn so they would be thought to be 60 years old. Sallow skins and freckles predominated."[92]

The ticket taker informed Harper he was the son of the man who received $5,000 for "getting" Bill Doolin, and another patron bragged that Paul Curry was her uncle. During the show, an old man in the audience "drinking in the story" spoke aloud to himself: "Yes, that's jest exactly how it was."

Finally, on August 16, Sheriff Arnold and three deputies escorted Starr and Estes to the train station for their trip to the Oklahoma State Penitentiary. They missed their connection in Oklahoma City and had to spend the night in the local "Bastille." Word got out that Starr was being held there, and little boys buzzed around the Oklahoma City Jail, hoping to glimpse the famous bandit. An officer shooed them away, telling them they would be disappointed. Starr didn't have "a big bushy set of whiskers, or chaps or two big guns."[93]

The next day, Chief W. B. Nichols took custody of Starr and Estes and escorted them on the next train to McAlester. Starr was familiar with the intake process: photos, measurements, and questions:

> Age: 42
> Height: 5'10"

Weight: 150 lbs.
Eyes: brown
Hair: brown
Complexion: light brown
Alcohol: No
Smoke: No
Chew: No
Religion: None
Number of years in school: 3
Read: Yes
Write: Yes
Cause of your downfall: Robbery
Relatives: two sisters and a mother
Married: Yes, Loretta Starr[94]

In his booking photo, Starr holds a haunted gaze as if he is looking into the abyss. He appears resigned to a bleak future.

A reporter for the *Stillwater Gazette* crowed that the King of the Bank Robbers would never follow in the footsteps of Emmett Dalton and Al Jennings: "Henry Starr was a stellar performer in the role all right, but the chances are he never will play it now in a picture show."[95]

He couldn't have been more wrong.

Intermission

Starr's in Stripes Forever

> Let's all go to the lobby,
> Let's all go to the lobby,
> Let's all go to the lobby,
> To get ourselves a treat.
> —Technicolor Refreshment Trailer No. 1 (1957),
> produced by the Filmack Trailer Company

In 1912 the French film *Les Amors de la Reine Élisabeth* debuted at New York's Lyceum Theatre.[1] The motion picture featured an unheard-of four reels that required the projectionist to switch them three times. Thus, the movie house intermission was born. Like those audiences, Starr was forced to endure an intermission before the action could start again.

On December 2, 1915, Starr celebrated his 42nd birthday in prison stripes. If he served his full twenty-five-year sentence at McAlester, he'd be nearly 70 before seeing the outside world again. Retta Elwick, who publicly referred to herself as Mrs. Henry Starr despite never formally marrying, planned on finding work in McAlester. "If I can make a little extra money, it will go to buy Henry tobacco, knick-knacks, and other luxuries to be found in penitentiaries," she said.[2]

83

The prospect of being locked away for decades ate at Starr. He yearned to contribute to society instead of being known as an outlaw. During his incarceration two opportunities arose for Starr to change the public's perception of him. In March 1916, after President Woodrow Wilson sent General John "Blackjack" Pershing to Mexico to capture Francisco "Pancho" Villa, Starr dashed off a letter:

> Colonel Roy Hoffman
> Commander of the First Regiment Infantry of the Oklahoma National Guard
>
> Dear Colonel,
> With my experience I ought to make good in the style of fighting to be done in Mexico.
>
> Yours very truly,
> HENRY STARR[3]

Hoffman supported the idea. "Starr's absolute fearlessness and his ability as a fighter would be a valuable asset to the regiment," he declared. If the guard were called up, Hoffman would ask for special permission to have Starr join his ranks. Newspaper editors disagreed with Hoffman. The *Tulsa World* wrote that Article 849 of the US Army regulations prevented anyone convicted of a felony or serving in a penitentiary from joining the service. So Starr would be disqualified, "as likable as he may be, as true as he may be to his friendships." Besides, the newspaper added, "The fellow who is noted for shooting from the hip seldom proves to be a good soldier, for he is not amenable to discipline."[4]

The Great War was Starr's second opportunity to change the public's perception of him. On May 18, 1917, President Wilson signed the Selective Service Act to expand the national army. By June 1918 800,000 US troops were fighting in Europe, with 3 million more expected to be called up in the next six weeks.[5] Starr watched enviously as people from his past joined the war effort. Paul Curry reported to Camp Travis to try out as a sharpshooter to "help capture the Kaiser."[6] Homer Breeding, Stroud's First National Bank cashier, also signed up. "Having been through one experience with bank robbers and come out of it alive . . . [he] decided to try his hand at killing Germans," the *Daily Oklahoman* reported.[7]

Meanwhile, Starr's field of operations was the prison mess hall. "I can do my country more good handling a machine gun against the Germans than I can running this kitchen," Starr groused to a reporter. He vowed to kill one German a day if the government issued him a .44 Winchester.[8] The *Bartlesville Examiner* was onboard but wanted Starr to fight the Germans Old West style: "Henry would be worth more with both hands filled with six-guns playing a lone hand in offense or defense."[9]

Starr wrote to Governor J. B. A. Robertson explaining his desire to serve his country:

> From the time I was 15, I always had an ambition to do something Big and Honorable. Something that would stand out in history. For instance, the knight that rode ahead of the column at the Battle of Hastings and asked the privilege to be the first to die, and Marshal Ney as he led the old guard at Waterloo and the English captain that headed the charge at Balaklava and Napoleon 1st at the bridge of Lodi. Those fellows, governor, reached the apex of human emotion and lived more in 10 seconds than the ordinary man lives in a century.
>
> Very respectfully,
> Henry Starr
> General Delivery Tulsa[10]

Once again, Starr offered his services to Roy Hoffman, now the brigadier general of the Oklahoma National Guard.[11] Even though Hoffman supported the idea, the governor didn't, and Starr had to sit out the war despite his patriotism and marksmanship.

On January 6, 1919, Starr read in the newspapers that Theodore Roosevelt died at his home at Sagamore Hill on Oyster Bay, Long Island.[12] Motion picture historian Kevin Brownlow considered *The Wolf Hunt* a watershed moment in cinema's progress. "Roosevelt was as much the father of factual film as the Lumière brothers, for he created a market for the documentary."[13] Inadvertently, Roosevelt was also instrumental in the unlikely transformation of outlaws and lawmen into filmmakers.

Starr's mother, Mary Gordon, deeply felt Roosevelt's death. She loved telling the story about meeting him in the White House while seeking a pardon for Starr.[14] In December 1903 Gordon took the train to Washington,

Figure 25 Mary Gordon, Starr's mother, was born April 21, 1849, in Fort Gibson, Indian Territory. She married George Starr on March 26, 1868, and they had four children: Elizabeth, Adna, Sterling (died at birth), and Henry. She was of French, Scottish, Irish, and Cherokee descent. Photo: *Daily Oklahoman*, February 25, 1921.

Starr's in Stripes Forever   87

DC, to visit Pennsylvania Senator Matthew Quay. The congressman had distant Native American ancestry and, therefore, lent a sympathetic ear to the old mother's plight. The following day, Senator Quay called at the White House with his special guest, Mary Gordon. Roosevelt welcomed her with his wide grin and folksy manner. He asked what was troubling her, and she told him about Henry. The president listened thoughtfully.

"Was your son the prisoner who disarmed Cherokee Bill at Fort Smith?"

"Yes," Gordon replied. "And he had saved many lives that day."

"Well, I think more of a brave man in a dungeon than I do a coward outside," Roosevelt told her. "We'll have to help your boy."

Gordon teared up.

"Have you spoken to my Attorney General, Philander Knox?"

"No, Colonel. I heard he was a big-headed Yankee."

Roosevelt stifled a laugh, charmed by Gordon's plainspokenness and astute character evaluation. "We can't ignore him completely," he said with a wink.

Roosevelt pulled out a sheet of his official stationery and dashed off a personal instruction to Knox. The next day Starr received a wire from the president: "Will you be good if I set you free?"

The outlaw vowed to go straight, and he was pardoned. Gordon told the Oklahoma newspapers about her meeting at the White House, crying tears of gratitude. "I have a boy that is bad, and here I come before the president of the USA, and he treats me like an ambassador or something, and I just don't deserve it."

Gordon and Starr never forgot Roosevelt's kindness. Upon hearing of the former president's death, Starr became a leading donor for a memorial in Tulsa.[15]

By March 1919 Starr was the only one of the Stroud robbers sentenced by Judge Wilson still locked up in the Oklahoma State Penitentiary. Tilghman wrote to Oklahoma Governor Robertson suggesting, in fairness, that Starr should not serve longer than the other guilty parties. Lincoln County prosecutor Streeter Speakman also wrote a letter in support of Starr's release: "He is a man of unusual intelligence. He is not a low, depraved type of humanity and is capable of making a good citizen."[16]

Governor Robertson agreed the time was right for Starr to be set free.

On the day of his release, a large brown paper package tied with string was delivered to Starr's cell. Inside, he found a brand new western-cut suit. The card was signed, "Best of luck on your new start, Henry. The Miller Brothers."[17] Starr was touched. He'd known the Miller boys from the 101 Ranch since his 20s when he worked the horses for their Wild West show. In 1915 Starr had been admitted to the penitentiary wearing an expensive blue serge suit, but it had stitches over the bullet hole in the leg. A new suit would give him a fresh start. Starr folded up the old suit nicely and gave it to Ance Rogers, a convicted murderer—a kind gesture Rogers never forgot.[18]

Ollie and Teddy accompanied Starr as he limped out of the prison. He paused to speak with awaiting reporters: "Every outlaw sooner or later comes to the point that he realizes the game is against him and he must quit. . . . I've promised my son, my mother, and my friends. I want to get on a farm and stay there." Teddy, now a Muskogee high school student, told the press he liked his dad's idea of becoming a farmer. Ollie added, "Henry has buried the past, and is going to work. He has some friends who are going to help get something he can do."[19]

Retta Elwick, Starr's dedicated lover, wasn't there. Starr never spoke of how their relationship ended.

While in Chickasha, Oklahoma, promoting *The Passing of the Oklahoma Outlaws*, Bill Tilghman offered his perspective: "There comes a time in every criminal's life when he realizes there's a superior being that controls his life, and he desires to go straight. I believe that time has come for Henry Starr."[20]

Reel Three

Henry Movie Starr

> That is the true myth of America. She starts old, old, wrinkled and writhing
> in old skin. And there is a gradual sloughing off of the old skin, toward a
> new youth. That is the myth of America.
> —D. H. Lawrence, *Studies in Classic American Literature* (1923)

Ollie, the former Mrs. Starr, compared Starr's newfound freedom to a child being let out of the house to play on a spring day. "While he is 45 years old, he is like a boy starting life anew," she said.[1] Starr wrote to a relative in Bartlesville, "Put the pot on the fire and have a good feed ready when you see a man with a limp and a hungry look, for that will be me."[2]

Starr's friends offered to back him in a business in Tulsa or Bartlesville. He contemplated opening a glove-making factory or a bakery, leveraging the skills he'd gained while an inmate, or perhaps "life in the open" as a farmer.[3] However, the most tempting offer came from a motion picture company that promised him the "proper backing" if he wanted to become a movie star.

90   Reel Three

A columnist for the *Oklahoma City Times* wrote a waggish poem suggesting Starr shun movie stardom:

"A Hint to Henry"*

As a daring desperado, we'll concede that Henry Starr
Could be quoted on the market a figure over par,
And he may succeed at farming, should he choose to till the soil,
Or amass a frenzied fortune as a magnate selling oil.
Having gained extensive freedom, after years of durance vile,
There are endless occupations which can help him make a pile.
But with hope that springs eternal we beseech that man to shun,
A career among the movies as a bad man with a gun.
So we sound the hope that Henry will not be a movie Starr.
With a line of bogus battles our artistic sense to jar.
But will hie him to the prairie or a place among the sticks.
And produce more beans and onions like the other helpful hicks.

*The first, second, and sixth stanzas[4]

Tilghman was "inclined to discourage" Starr from entering motion pictures, but the reformed outlaw took his cue from Al Jennings and Emmett Dalton.[5] The ex-outlaws-turned-matinee idols had become tremendously successful since Starr and Retta watched their early films at Tulsa's Royal in 1915.

Al Jennings

In 1916 Jennings found Oklahoma's prejudice against reformed train robbers becoming movie stars stifling. So he packed up his motion picture dreams and moved to California. He was soon rubbing shoulders with top Hollywood stars like Douglas Fairbanks and Harry Carey.[6]

Over the next two years, Jennings churned out numerous quickie two-reelers. In 1918 Jennings produced a second autobiographical picture, *The Lady of the Dugout*. In the film Al and his real brother Frank help a young mother save her farm from creditors. *Moving Picture World* touted the film as "refreshing in its naturalness and freedom of the false and melodramatic atmosphere that mar many productions that pretend to depict frontier life."[7] *The Lady of the Dugout* screened in California, New York, and every state in between. Later that year the film was shown at the Philharmonic Hall in London.[8]

By September 1919 the Capitol Films Company in Hollywood gave him his own motion picture arm with dedicated stages and a budget for a crew. Capitol marketed Jennings as "The Bandit King of the Screen."[9] He would produce, direct, or star in twenty-four two-reelers, including *Fugitives Who Came Back*, which re-created his life as a "soldier of fortune" in Honduras with O. Henry. In Hollywood Jennings was practically printing money on the "leaves from his outlaw past."[10]

Emmett Dalton

In 1916 Dalton expanded his oeuvre beyond Coffeyville by producing the fact-based film the *Hatfield-McCoy Feud*.[11] He took his life in his own hands by trekking into the backwoods of West Virginia. Dalton spoke to the patriarchs on both sides about telling their monumental story on film. He appealed to their vanity, describing his project as "a historic picture to show how brave men met brave men and noble women bore their part like Spartan mothers of old." Both sides agreed to let Dalton make his movie. His big casting coup was getting "Devil" Anse Hatfield to portray himself. The production had challenges unlike any other motion picture. Each day of production, Dalton had to personally inspect the rifles for both sides to ensure they weren't cheating and firing real bullets. After completing the film, he invited both families to the screening. Dalton had the lofty idea that when the men saw their petty behavior projected on the big screen in front of an audience, they would feel ashamed. Instead, they watched themselves on screen "tickled as children."[12]

In 1918 Emmett celebrated his 47th birthday with a new job as head of the Southern Feature Film Corporation (SFFC) out of Gastonia, North Carolina. In the public investor statement, the company vowed, "We are going to make the Southern Feature Film Corporation stand for all that is clean, pure, and high-class in motion pictures."[13] The SFFC prospectus noted the film business was the fifth-largest industry in the United States, and they were presenting a rare opportunity to more than "thrible" their investment.[14]

In November 1918 SFFC released its first production, the six-reel motion picture *Beyond the Law* (*BTL*). Once again Dalton dipped into his bag of tried-and-true Dalton Gang stories.[15] In *BTL* Dalton played not only himself but also his brothers Frank and Bob.[16] The movie, directed by Theodore Marston and written by William Addison Lathrop, was filmed on the actual prairies with cactus, shrubbery, and local color "which breathes of the West."[17] However, while locations lent authenticity, the scenario misrepresented Bob and Grat as honest US deputy marshals "who were driven to desperate deaths through oppression."[18] Clearly, Dalton hoped to reframe public opinion by creating the false narrative that his brothers, Bob and Grat, were cheated out of money the government owed them for their work as lawmen. In fact, the Dalton brothers were crooked marshals, and they killed four innocent Coffeyville men in a matter of minutes. Nevertheless, *BTL* ends on an upbeat and factual note with Emmett's parole and new life as a law-abiding citizen.

Moving Picture World reviewer Margaret I. MacDonald wrote that *BTL* was not intended "to meet the highest standards of artistic picture craft" but had the same appeal "a small boy feels for his storybook heroes."[19] State and foreign distributors agreed and clamored for the rights to the picture—at least according to the (very likely paid) promotional story.[20]

While Dalton may have been a limited storyteller and lacked artistic vision, he proved to be a savvy businessman in the early days of film. Dalton had wisely serialized the *BTL* story in a prominent London magazine prior to its US release. The Apollo Trading Company quickly snapped up the foreign rights for *BTL* because the film already had a built-in audience. For the US rollout, Dalton provided a detailed plan on how to capitalize on his notoriety and charisma. "This picture must be worked as a big special," Dalton explained. "I am going to open the picture myself in leading cities of each of the big territories, showing exhibitors how to get the maximum publicity."[21]

Dalton's roadshow began on March 3, 1919, in his adopted backyard of North Carolina at the Broadway in Charlotte. During the screening Dalton delivered a short moral lecture "wearing his sombrero and strikingly individual clothes."[22] He returned to New York at the end of March after selling the states' rights for *BTL* in Georgia, Florida, Alabama, Virginia, and North and South Carolina. Once again, Dalton was a savvy marketer, using the strong box office receipts from one state to get a more profitable deal in the next. Money rolled in, and Dalton wrote more Westerns with himself in the "stellar role" and with "that very important element of successful pictures—a virile plot."[23]

While Starr was in the Oklahoma State Penitentiary, Jennings and Dalton had become a polished motion picture hyphenate: producer, actor, director, and writer. Starr was indeed the King of Bank Robbers, but in the realm of moving pictures, he was a mere knight-errant.

Upon his release Starr, the reformed gunslinger, faced a new Wild West.

A Pioneer Motion Picture Man

Witnessing the success of Jennings and Dalton, P. J. Clark, president of the Pan-American Motion Picture Corporation, was eager to meet with Starr. Thirty-six-year-old Clark was amid a career pivot himself, from being an intrepid freelance photographer capturing Tulsa's seamy underbelly for the local newspapers to becoming a motion picture mogul.[24] In 1917 his photos were key evidence against local police officers who had ambushed and gunned down an unarmed taxi driver they suspected was a bootlegger. When called, Clark took the stand and displayed his crime scene photographs: a bullet-riddled windshield, a blood-soaked bench seat, shell casings, and the slumping corpse of a young man. When the prosecutor pointed out there was no gun pictured in the photographs, the crowd in the gallery jeered at the police officers sitting at the defense table.

Although newspapers dubbed Clark a "pioneer motion picture man," he had only purchased his camera a few months before forming Pan-American with two partners.[25] Clark knew that several motion picture companies were courting Starr, so netting the infamous former outlaw would be a coup beyond his wildest dreams.

When the tall, gaunt outlaw took a seat in his Muskogee office, Clark was excited to explain how Starr would be a bigger hit than Jennings, Dalton, and even William S. Hart. First, Jennings, as they both knew, was not a legitimate outlaw. "Starr's way was the way of the Daltons, the Cooks, Cherokee Bill and dozens of others," wrote the *Tulsa Daily World*.[26] "Al Jennings was spectacular, but he was more in the newspapers than at the business end of a six-shooter." Sam Konkel, owner and editor of the *Springfield Democrat-Herald*, knew Jennings and called his *Beating Back* biography "fishy."[27] Starr told Clark that he and Jennings met at the Ohio State Penitentiary back in 1899. "I knew Al like a book," Starr joked, referring to the biography. "The movie stuff is just make-believe and not from the heart," Starr agreed. "But I like Al. He's a fine fellow, personally."[28] Clark proposed that if Jennings could turn four months of bungled robberies into a big payday, imagine what they could do telling the life story of the King of Bank Robbers.

Next, there was Emmet Dalton. The Coffeyville, Kansas, double-header was undeniably spectacular, and Dalton's multiple filmed versions had been a gold mine. However, Dalton was a minor player, the kid brother in the failed heist, whereas Starr had orchestrated the seemingly impossible feat at Stroud. Additionally, Starr had much more material to mine. While Dalton's outlawry ended at age 20, Starr's continued into his 40s.

Finally, there was William S. Hart. In 1918 Hart was the top Western motion picture star and 2.5 million *Motion Picture Magazine* readers voted him the number-five most popular screen actor in a poll.[29] William Surrey Hart was popular because he broke new ground as a silent film performer. He brought all of his experience as a Shakespearean actor to the camera when he created the "good, bad guy" Western screen persona.[30] Hart's characters start out living an immoral life, such as an outlaw or gambler, but through the story they are revealed to have "a heart of gold, and [are] eventually set on the path of good, clean, honest living by the end of the movie."

As Hart gained more influence in Hollywood, he demanded more realism in his Western pictures, reflecting his lived experience. However, his expertise in that area was paper thin. Hart biographer Ronald L. Davis wrote, "The actor exaggerated his knowledge of the West, and his life on the frontier was more as a circumspect tourist than a longtime resident."[31] Hart was born sixty miles outside of Manhattan in Newburgh, New York, on December 6, 1864. His perspective on the West grew from boyhood travels with his father, Nicholas, where he played with Sioux children in Orinoco, Minnesota, and learned their language. His time on the prairie was short, and soon he was back in Newburgh developing into a moody teenager.

At 18 Hart left for Europe to study acting in London and Paris. He returned to New York City two years later to begin his American stage career. Over the next quarter of a century, Hart pieced together a career in Shakespearean tragedies and nineteenth-century melodramas. In 1914, at age 50, he headed to Hollywood to make short films with pioneer filmmaker Thomas Ince. Hart quickly moved up the Hollywood food chain to become its top Western star.

Starr far eclipsed Hart in the authenticity rubric. "[Hart] remembered playing outlaw and pretending that the fence around his family's yard was a robber's cave," Davis wrote.[32] In contrast, Starr spent his childhood at the real Robber's Cave outside Wilburton, Oklahoma, where his cousin Sam, Belle Starr, and the James-Younger Gang used it as a hideout. And, of course, Starr wasn't merely "playing outlaw."

While Clark made a convincing argument that Starr could be bigger than Jennings, Dalton, and Hart, he had an ace up his sleeve. Starr had previously shared with reporters, "If I consent to enter the movies, I will insist on taking part in no picture that my boy could not see and be helped by."[33] Taking that cue, Clark proposed making a Western "entirely different from anything like kind," where there would be "no glory attached to outlawry."[34] Starr welcomed the idea that his biographical motion picture would make the life of the outlaw unappealing to young men and boys.

In April 1919 P. J. Clark and Starr struck a deal. Merely a month after being released from the Oklahoma State Penitentiary, the King of Bank Robbers was on the path to moving picture stardom.

A New Type of Gang

In April 1919 the Pan-American Motion Picture Corporation publicly announced its deal with Henry Starr. "The producers of this picture believe the name will be a drawing card that will bring audiences by the thousands to see the story of his life and absorb the moral of it," said P. J. Clark.[35] Starr added that he was on "a mission to show the youth of the present day that it doesn't pay to do otherwise than to go straight." A reporter from the *Bartlesville Daily Enterprise* asked pointedly if a "bandit picture" wouldn't do the opposite, giving boys bad ideas. "I've got a 14-year-old boy over in

Muskogee," Starr clapped back. "Do you think I want to put on a motion picture stunt that will inspire him to follow in my footsteps? Not much."[36]

Pan-American placed an advertisement in the *Tulsa World Daily* seeking investors:

IF
You're Seeking a Gilt-Edge Investment
HERE IS YOUR OPPORTUNITY!

The Pan-American Motion Picture Corporation, a Tulsa enterprise, has contracted for the production of a feature picture based on the life of HENRY STARR, which, in the opinion of men thoroughly acquainted with the movie picture industry, will prove one of the biggest successes ever attempted in the history of the Motion Picture business. . . .

The work of making the "Feature" is rapidly progressing, but until the stock is sold necessary to complete the picture has been subscribed, actual production will not begin . . .

We offer a limited amount of stock at the par value "$10 per share."[37]

The *Beaver Herald* offered waggish gratitude for the honest solicitation: "Henry Starr, recently paroled, is advertising the sale of stock in his proposed picture company. Evidently, he does not intend to take the hazards of former days to get the money."[38]

Pan-American's effort to raise financing wouldn't be as simple as placing an ad in the newspaper. Oklahoma's Blue-Sky Commission—whose mission is to protect consumers from fraud—denied Pan-American's application to sell securities because half of the money raised would go toward marketing and salaries, including Starr, a convicted felon.[39] Clark's lawyer redrew the paperwork, removing Starr's stock option (valued at $12,500) from the application. Upon refiling the commission approved Pan-American's bid to sell $20,000 worth of stock. As a compromise, Starr would receive $2,000 cash and 25 percent of the net—not gross—proceeds.[40] Although Starr couldn't have predicted at the time, the new arrangement may have contributed to his subsequent financial undoing.

The *Oklahoma City Times* editor, with a fondness for alliteration, weighed in on the production moving forward: "The state has decided that Hank's movie company can proceed with the sale of $20,000 worth of stock, thereby financing the plan for preserving the bold bandit's dashing deeds in deathless celluloid, or thereabouts, to make an Oklahoma holiday. The boob birthrate being what it is, a flossy future may be forecast for this latest flier in the filmy firmament."[41]

Clark originally planned to direct Starr's "photoplay" with the working title *Unto Him Who Transgresses*. However, when financing rolled in, Clark had the funds to hire George E. Reehm, an experienced director out of New York City.[42] Reehm apprenticed under D. W. Griffith for two years, including working on *Birth of a Nation*. Following that he spent eight years working at Lubin and three with Vitagraph. Clark told Reehm that most of the exterior scenes would be shot in the exact locations but promised him that Pan-American would build a studio for the interior scenes.

Clark's good fortune continued when an experienced screenwriter—known then as a scenarist or photoplaywright—landed on their doorstep. Her name was Vivian Woodcock Kay, but a besotted reporter from the *Tulsa Morning News* dubbed her "Vivacious" Vivian.[43] As a college actress at the University of Illinois Urbana-Champaign (U of I), friends said she was typecast as the strong-willed and sharp-tongued Phoebe in William Shakespeare's *As You Like It*.[44] In 1916 the moving picture fad sweeping the nation arrived at U of I, and Woodcock Kay wrote a four-reel picture titled *Pro Patria*.[45] She produced the film and cast it with fellow actors from the drama club Mask and Bauble. Filmed over the summer when the campus was quiet, Woodcock Kay's plot was ripped straight from the newspapers, where the Mexican revolutionary Pancho Villa topped the headlines. In the story Woodcock Kay portrayed the freshman sorority girl Betty Gamble, who has a crush on the rich, handsome Mexican exchange student Eduardo Salazar. Unbeknown to Gamble, Salazar is secretly a Mexican revolutionary with plans to blow up the university with a wireless explosive. After Salazar's nefarious plot is foiled, Gamble finds a more sensible love interest in the American student Happy Harding.

In August 1916 *Pro Patria* was screened for Essanay studio head George K. Spoor, whose company had recently produced *The Tramp* with Charlie Chaplin.[46] A director at Essanay liked the picture and hired two of the actors to be in his next five-reel picture.[47] The Lubin Film Company also saw

Figure 26 Pioneering motion picture producer, photoplaywright, and actress Vivian Woodcock Kay became the scenario writer for *A Debtor to the Law*. Billed as Mrs. Vivian Kay, she cast herself as Betty in the self-produced film *Pro Patria*. University of Illinois Urbana-Champaign, *Illio Yearbook*, 1918, courtesy of the Illini Media Company, illioyearbook.com.

Pro Patria and hired Woodcock Kay to write the five-reel scenario *Rosemary, for Remembrance*.[48]

When Woodcock Kay began writing for Lubin, the company was on the downslide. The founder, Sigmund Lubin, a Jewish optician originally from Poland, built the most advanced studio of its time, Lubinville. Located in downtown Philadelphia, Lubinville featured rooftop stages, film-processing laboratories, and editing suites.[49] In 1910 Lubin innovated further, building the Betzwood studio lot in North Philadelphia. Betzwood had a Western village set, a glass-enclosed "daylight" studio, a "dark" studio with state-of-the-art Cooper Hewitt and Klieg lights, a film-processing plant, and a cafeteria that provided free lunches to the cast and crew.

Unfortunately, Lubin hit hard times. World War I devastated the foreign film market, the pandemic shuttered theaters domestically, and a disastrous fire at the studio destroyed most of his film slate. After creditors seized Lubinville and Betzwood, Woodcock Kay's moving pictures dream appeared dead.[50] When her husband Fred, a geologist with the Twin State Oil company, was transferred to Tulsa in 1918,[51] she resigned herself to being a housewife and kept her mind active by entering newspaper puzzle contests.[52]

Fortunately for Woodcock Kay, a year later, in 1919, the Oklahoma film industry was booming. She sent her resume to Clark at Pan-American and was hired immediately. On her first day, she met Reehm and recognized him from her days at Lubin. "Weren't you an actor in my *Rosemary* story?" she asked. He was, and they spent the rest of the afternoon talking shop about what she called the "fillum" business.[53]

Soon, Woodcock sat poised behind her typewriter, tapping out the story of Starr's picaresque journey, eight reels worth of material to depict "the folly of a life such as he lived." For the Stroud scene, when Louis Estes turns to help Starr, who is lying wounded in the street, the dialogue card read: "We can't beat the law, Louis; we might as well give up."[54]

While Starr's new film gang worked on preproduction, he traveled to McAlester to recruit Claud Sawyer, recently released from the Oklahoma State Penitentiary, to play himself in the Stroud recreation.[55] "Henry had proved himself a stickler for detail," Al Jennings wrote, reflecting on his outlaw-turned-motion-picture-star counterpart. "He insisted upon real punchers, ranchers, bankers—and real outlaws. None of the clipped and roughed up Hollywood actors for him!"[56] No acting talent was required. When Starr and Clark were at the Lee-Huckins Hotel in Oklahoma City, they spotted a man who still dressed like he'd stepped out of the terri-torial days. He was hired on the spot.[57] Turned out he'd lived the life of a plainsman years ago and could perform the rough riding needed in the film. Starr also planned to have Teddy portray him as a teenager in the Fort Gibson scenes.[58]

The Specter of Bentonville

In June 1919 Starr and the Pan-American production team left for the Osage Hills to rehearse. Not a frame of footage had been shot yet, and already Oklahoma newspapers were denouncing Starr. The editor of Ardmore's *Daily Ardmoreite* wrote, "Ex-Outlaw Henry Starr, for instance, should be exercising his forgetter instead of being up in Osage country doing stunts before a camera for a movie thriller in which his past misdeeds are to be displayed before audiences made up largely of children and youths of both sexes."[59]

"It's wrong," Muskogee Police Commissioner Warren Butz told the *Muskogee Times-Democrat*. "The boys see the picture and think that if they can get away with the money and hide, and even if they are sent up for a little while and are pardoned, it is worth it."[60] Butz added that men on his force had been offered roles in Starr's motion picture, but they refused because they knew it would have a bad influence on children.

P. J. Clark responded quickly. "A number of persons in the state of Oklahoma are taking it for granted that we are about to flare forth with another of these 'wild and wooly' western outlaw tales, which always breed a flock of young bandits," Clark said. "I ask those persons to refrain from passing judgment until they understand the moral of this picture-play. One cannot rightly condemn what one knows nothing about."[61]

Nevertheless, the unwanted publicity reawakened the dormant Arkansas state prosecutor's office. When Starr returned home from rehearsals, he received a call from his longtime friend Tulsa Sheriff James Woolley.[62]

"Henry, I just received a warrant for your arrest."

"For what?"

"Bentonville."

"Woolley, that was twenty-six years ago!"

"I know it, Henry," Woolley said. "All the same, I expect you to turn yourself in."

Starr felt sick. He couldn't believe Arkansas was hounding him again. Last time he'd returned to bank robbery, in 1907, Ollie left him and he became estranged from his boy. Twelve years later, Starr faced the same question: *Should I own up to my past or flee?*

At 9:30 Monday morning, June 17, Starr arrived at the Tulsa courthouse and turned himself over to Woolley. The sheriff placed him in a cell, then phoned Arkansas and said, "Come and get him."[63] Fortunately for Starr the process would not be that simple. The office of Oklahoma Governor J. B. A. Robertson informed Woolley that Arkansas's state prosecutor was required to present an official request to him before Starr could be taken out of the state. Woolley unlocked the cell and released Starr on his own recognizance.[64]

However, Starr wasn't out of the woods. He still had to await the governor's decision.

A cloud of anticipation hung over the Pan-American offices that afternoon, having nothing to do with the two days of gloomy weather.[65] Behind his desk Clark worked on the budget to keep busy. Woodcock Kay sat perched on her desk, legs crossed, a smoke sculpture rising from her lit cigarette. Starr paced the floor.

Meanwhile, a *Tulsa Times* reporter hung out in the office, peppering them with questions.

"Does Arkansas really want Mr. Starr after so long?"

"Darling," Woodcock Kay said, "if Arkansas were serious about arresting Henry, they would have waited until the production showed up in Bentonville."

"Didn't you know they'd come after him?"

Clark looked up.

"Write this down, direct quote," Clark said. "Before making the contract with Starr for the film, all of these details were worked out. We went into the matter thoroughly and had the best legal talent in Oklahoma look up the status of just such a situation. The lawyers advised us that we were safe to go ahead with our plans, and we feel confident that within a week, this block in our plans will be out of the way."[66]

"What if Arkansas keeps you out of the state?"

"Hah, Arkansas thinks they can spoil my story?" Woodcock Kay asked rhetorically. "I'll show them. I'll write a new reel and won't even mention them in the picture."

"No scenes of the Bentonville bank robbery then?"

"We may have to cut Bentonville, but it will serve them right," she laughed saucily.

Unfortunately, there is no surviving evidence to show whether the Bentonville bank robbery scenes were ever filmed—inside or outside of Arkansas. The heist was the second most dramatic bank robbery in Starr's life and certainly would have been cinematic. Bentonville put Starr on the map and cemented his reputation as a fearless gentleman bandit.[67] Although he was only 19 at the time, it was a testament to Starr's confidence and maturity that he was able to convince hardened criminals to follow him into a deadly endeavor.

In 1893 Bentonville was a wealthy agricultural region surrounded by farms and fruit growers.[68] The social and business center was the park square, with the courthouse on one end and local merchants bordering the other three sides. On Saturday evenings, everyone—from farmers to Southern colonels—gathered around the bandstand in the center of the park to hear local musicians play. Bentonville residents were naïve because they hadn't experienced the level of crime and violence seen in the Oklahoma and Indian Territories. In fact, county peace officers "found it hardly worthwhile to go armed all the time." Even as a teenager Starr was a master planner, and when he performed reconnaissance in Bentonville, he learned that residents kept their rifles stored unless they were hunting squirrels, quail, or rabbits. He also heard that a big crop of strawberries had been brought to market, so the vault inside the People's Bank of Bentonville was swollen with cash.

Starr later wrote, "I spent a week in that town, planning the robbery, studying the habits of the men in the bank, seeing when they opened it and laid the money out, acquainting myself with every street and alley, store and vacant lot. . . . I got acquainted with the town Marshal and studied his habits. . . . I'll venture to say that after a week in that town, I knew it better than any man in it."[69]

On June 5, 1893, Starr sent a teamster named Happy Jack into town with a buggy laden with large-caliber Model 1886 Winchester rifles. The other six members of the gang rode into town on horseback in ones and twos, a mile apart. Starr enjoyed making a stylish entrance. Each man in his gang was "superbly mounted" on well-bred horses with cowboy saddles. They wore gleaming spurs and two fine Colts in wide leather belts. "I conceived the idea of recruiting a band of men so desperate that everyone would stand in fear of us," Starr wrote.[70] Happy Jack, whom Starr described as 27 years old, squarely built, and "full of sand," parked the buggy in an alley behind the *Bentonville Sun* newspaper offices.

The gang gathered at the buggy and retrieved their rifles. Starr then led their march, "single file Indian style," toward the bank one block away. Maggie Wood, a 19-year-old compositor for the *Bentonville Sun*, watched the outlaws as they crossed the street-facing windows. Their boots thunked on the wooden sidewalk, and their spurs jangled. Wood was the quintessential Victorian ideal of young womanhood, "the kind one associates with ribbons and laces, curls, modishly slim waists, and modesty." She wore her long tresses parted in the middle and tied up in a neat Psyche knot. Wood had a keen mind and quickly pieced together what was about to transpire and declared to the rest of the newspaper staff, "My God, they're going to rob the bank!" However, *Sun* newspaper offices didn't have telephones to call the town marshal. Wood and her colleagues had to watch helplessly as the inevitable events unfolded.

The People's Bank of Bentonville was located at the southwest corner of the park square. It had a snubbed-off corner entrance with five steep steps. White Doric columns flanked each side. Starr tapped John "Kid" Wilson to enter the bank with him. While they were both teenagers, Wilson and Starr were exact opposites. Starr was tall, dark, and collected. Wilson was short, blond, and hot-headed.[71] Link Cumplin, ten years older, would stand guard outside the entrance—the deadliest position of all. Along the march the four other gang members peeled off and took rear guard positions. When Starr and Wilson arrived at the bank entrance, they skipped up the steps, guns drawn, and burst inside. Cumplin stopped at the top of the steps and turned. In a "stentorian" voice he announced, "The bank is being robbed! Everyone, stay off the streets!"

Cumplin put a fine point on his message with a blast from his Winchester.

"It was as surprising as a clap of thunder," wrote W. L. Marley, then a young peace officer. "The people of Bentonville were suddenly face-to-face with an emergency for which they had made no preparation." Nevertheless,

Figure 27 Maggie Wood (*left, center*), fifty-four years after the bank robbery, stands between the iron pillars of the former People's Bank of Bentonville, Arkansas, pointing out to visitors the bullet holes still visible from Starr's raid on June 5, 1893. At 19 (*upper right*) Maggie Wood is the ideal young Victorian woman who rescued a hostage and $1,000 in silver from the Starr Gang. Photos courtesy of the *Arkansas Democrat Sunday Magazine*, July 27, 1947. *Inset:* The *Bentonville Sun* offices where Maggie Wood worked when she rescued a hostage and a sack of silver. Courtesy of Randy McCrory, VintageBentonville.com.

at the sound of Cumplin's rifle, men ran to their nearby homes and grabbed their weapons. Some curious citizens moved closer to the bank to get a better look. Cumplin warned them to take cover for their own safety.

Arkansas historian Clara B. Kennan noted, "And it proved a blessing to Bentonville that he [Starr] hated killing and instructed his men to confine their shooting to over-aweing the people and keeping them in off the streets until the robbery was completed."[72]

Cumplin did as Starr instructed and fired over the heads of the gathering townsfolk. Although Cumplin had the high ground, more and more armed men arrived, and soon he found himself dodging bullets like a mechanical bear in a shooting gallery.

Cumplin cracked open the front door and called inside, "Hurry up! It's getting hot out here!"[73] When he turned back, Cumplin took a bullet in his eye. Another in his arm. One more in the leg.

Moments later Starr and Kid exited the bank, encircled by bank employees and customers carrying bags of silver and gold. Cumplin joined them.

"You all right?" Starr asked him.

"Sure, I'm hunky," Cumplin responded bravely.

Starr heard the blood squishing in Cumplin's boots as they trotted for their horses. He'd once thought Cumplin might be "chicken-livered," but now he realized the man was the toughest outlaw he'd ever known.

On their return to their horses, Starr and the gang had to, once again, pass in front of the *Bentonville Sun* front windows. Starr brought up the rear. Ahead of him he prodded the bank's cashier, George Jackson, who bore a flour sack of coins on his shoulder. Wood, the compositor, waited for her moment. When Jackson "got even" to the *Sun's* front door, she threw back the bolt, grabbed Jackson, pulled him inside, and locked the door. Starr looked back through the window and smiled wryly. Wood, ever ladylike, denied grabbing Jackson and said he merely fell inside the open door. Yet, while the men in the *Sun* stood around dazed, Wood, weighing 120 pounds, carried the 65-pound sack of silver up a flight of stairs and locked it away in a safe. Starr didn't have time to retrieve the sack of silver, and he and the gang continued toward their horses and mounted up. Later, after Starr counted their "boodle," the total came to $11,500. Nevertheless, the Bank of Bentonville was able to open the following day with the $1,000 in silver Wood had rescued. She said the bank never thanked her.

Arkansas had a long memory. Nearly three decades later, the specter of Bentonville cast a pall on the Pan-American production team. If Governor Robertson granted the extradition, more than just the Bentonville scene would be cut; the motion picture faced a complete shutdown, and Starr would be led away in handcuffs.

Lining Up in Opposition

The long hours had ticked by in the Pan-American production offices when a reporter from the *Oklahoma Democrat* burst in. He raced up to Starr and handed him a special edition. Starr's eyes scanned the front page, then he looked up: "Get this, from Governor Robertson," Starr said, reading. "Starr's enemies are behind this thing. Unless the facts are different from what they were when Governor Haskell refused to honor a similar requisition, I shall not honor one. Starr's parole shall not be affected either."[74]

A cheer erupted in the office.

"I'll be right back," Starr said as he "hot-footed" out the door. Clark shot Woodcock Kay a curious look, and she shrugged. Fifteen minutes later Starr returned with a tray of ice cream sodas.

"It's my treat," Starr announced, handing out the tulip-shaped glasses.

The *Tulsa Times* reporter later wrote, "He wore a typical Starr grin that had refused to come out during the entire afternoon."[75]

While Governor Robertson's decision was sweet news, Starr and Pan-American's troubles weren't over. Realizing Starr's biographical film was moving forward lit a fire under his political opponents. Oklahoma's Senator Thomas Gore and House Representatives John Harreld and William Hastings introduced identical censorship bills in the US Congress to prevent Starr from distributing his moving picture. Congressman Harreld was coy about targeting Starr specifically, hinting that the legislation was intended to stop an outlaw who "was arrested in the act of robbing a bank. His arrest was accomplished by a sixteen-year-old boy." Harreld continued, "After his release, this man formed a motion picture company and made a film of the incident and has been going over the country exhibiting these pictures. Oklahoma has already secured all the advertising of that kind it wants."[76] The congressman may have confused *Unto Him Who Transgresses*, which was still in production, with Tilghman's film *The Passing of the Oklahoma Outlaws*, which was in theaters and had been since 1915.

Nevertheless, these three federal lawmakers hoped to classify the distribution of bandit films as a violation of interstate commerce. The Gore-Harreld Bill would prohibit the US Postal Service from transporting "films purporting to show or simulate the acts and conduct of ex-convicts, desperado, bandit, train robber, bank robber, or outlaw in the commission of crime or acts of violence."[77] Harreld aspired to drive all "Wild West, gunplay, and bank robbery" movies out of existence.[78] The Oklahoma City Commissioners took their cue from the Gore-Harreld Bill and unanimously passed a resolution instructing the municipal counselor to draft an ordinance to bar Al Jennings and Henry Starr productions specifically.[79]

Gore, Harreld, and Hastings were digging into an old bag of censorship tricks when they wrote their legislation. In 1873, the same year Starr was born, Congress passed the Comstock Act, a federal statute for the "Suppression of Trade in, and Circulation of, Obscene Literature and Articles of Immoral Use." Henceforth, it was a crime to send any material considered obscene—including personal letters—that included references to contraceptives, abortifacients, or sex toys through the US Postal system.[80]

The act was named for a puritanical former shop clerk named Anthony Comstock, who arrived in Washington, DC, with a valise full of money provided by industrialist John Pierpont (J. P.) Morgan to influence legislators. The postmaster general appointed Comstock as US postal inspector to oversee search and seizure. Not satisfied with controlling sexual conduct and repro-duction, Comstock also wanted to monitor what children read. In his book *Traps for the Young* (1883), Comstock wrote that Satan was more interested in the child than the parents who allowed their children to read dime novels: "Step up, parents, and buy a cheap way of getting rid of your boys! Supply these books and papers, and your boy will soon be behind prison bars and be off your hands!"[81]

Among the most popular dime novels at that time that *Traps for the Young* was written were blood and thunder outlaw stories. In 1881 publisher Frank Tousey produced the first Frank and Jesse James book as an edition of The Five Cent Wide Awake Library, titled *The Train Robbers: Or, A Story of the James Boys*.[82] Street & Smith published The Log Cabin Library series, which also featured Frank and Jesse James. Starr had his own novels as part of the library, including *Hank Starr at Pryor Creek*—the only outlaw besides the James brothers to headline his own series.

For Comstock, stories about bandits like Starr had to be stopped. In 1898 7-year-old Willie Addison was arrested for stabbing his 5-year-old friend to death after reportedly reading "trashy novels of the Wild West stamp" and wanting to emulate the hero.[83] Stories like these compelled Comstock to use the power of his office to harass, intimidate, and even jail publishers who didn't acquiesce to his censorship demands. He arrested Tousey and

108   Reel Three

threatened him with the loss of his second-class mailing privileges if he didn't stop writing salacious stories that corrupted children's minds. Tousey promised to destroy the plates of the offensive titles.[84]

Comstock found an ally in his fight against moral turpitude in the Women's Christian Temperance Union (WCTU), which had already formed a Department of Impure Literature. WCTU President Frances Willard shared Comstock's belief that dime novels turned killers and thieves into heroes and her organization advocated strict censorship. By 1903, working in concert, Comstock and the WCTU shut down Tousey and Street & Smith's dime novel publications completely.[85]

In 1908 Comstock shifted his focus to moving pictures. He convinced New York City Mayor George B. McClellan Jr. to have his police officers shut down 550 movie houses and nickelodeons on Christmas Day.[86] The US Constitution provided no censorship protection for film producers and exhibitors. In the *Mutual Film Corporation vs. Industrial Commission of Ohio* (1915), the US Supreme Court ruled that motion pictures were not protected free speech under the First Amendment. The court went one step further, declaring it legal for the police to enforce censorship laws.[87]

The court's decision emboldened Oklahoma's ministerial leaders and women's organizations. They sharpened their knives when Al Jennings released *Beating Back*, saying his autobiographical outlaw film glamorized crime. However, despite the WCTU's best efforts to demonize Jennings, *Beating Back* was a big hit with audiences. "Had a state censorship been established two years ago, the public would have been saved from the malevolent influence of the Al Jennings pictures on the youth of the state as manifested in the small thieving and the increasing bank robberies," the WCTU spokesperson declared ruefully.[88]

W. B. Harrison, secretary of the Oklahoma Bankers' Association, shared the opinion of the WCTU, stating, "Doubtless we are reaping as we have sown. Pictures of bank robbers and train robbers have been exhibited freely in Oklahoma and the perpetrators of such crimes are held up to our people as heroes."[89] On "The Lord's Day," December 12, 1915, Cora D. Hammett, president of the Central WCTU, set in motion a plan to pressure state lawmakers to take action on censorship.[90] She coordinated with ministers throughout

Oklahoma City to present a resolution to their respective congregations demanding the city commissioners establish a "strong board of censors" for motion pictures and vaudeville. Nearly every congregation signed the resolution, and Hammett delivered them to the Oklahoma statehouse.

During the regular session of Oklahoma's Fifth Legislature, Representatives L. N. Barbee and Sam Hargis drafted a bill, referred to commonly as the Beating Back Bill. Section One made it unlawful for a theater manager to show "material deemed obscene, licentious, or immoral, [and] any violation of the law such as murder, and especially bank or train robbery." In addition, section one granted the county attorney, mayor, and chief of police of any Oklahoma city the right to establish a board of censorship to determine which films were acceptable for public viewing. Theater owners, out of compliance, faced having their "moving picture machinery and appliances" confiscated and sold by the sheriff. The courts had the right to send an exhibitor to prison for one to five years. Section two made it illegal for motion picture companies to produce or manufacture any film featuring outlawry and real-life outlaws convicted of crimes "or other depredations" within the state of Oklahoma.[91]

The Beating Back Bill spawned vigorous debate. Representative Lewis Hunter called the legislation a naked attempt to put Jennings out of business and punish a political rival. The Democratic speaker ruled him out of order. However, none of the Beating Back Bill supporters seem to understand the bill would also prohibit fellow Democrat William Tilghman from showing *The Passing of the Oklahoma Outlaws*. Representative Kelley Brown scoffed at the bill, saying putting the police in charge of censorship "just gives the local officers one more excuse to fool away their time in picture shows." Representative J. T. Dickerson declared the bill unconstitutional since it "conferred judicial censorship authority." Representative E. E. Glasco thought the bill would hurt his constituents, saying it "punished the small-town picture showman."[92]

Ultimately, the Beating Back Bill lost steam because Representatives Barbee and Hargis couldn't gather the votes. In 1914 the *Tulsa Daily World* reported eight million people a year attended motion pictures across the country, with a revenue of $319 million.[93] Motion pictures were a nitrate gusher, to put it in Oklahoma oil parlance, and pragmatic business owners and their elected representatives didn't want militant moralists killing the golden goose that motion pictures provided the state. Legislators quietly "re-committed" the Beating Back Bill, sending it to amendment purgatory.[94]

While censorship advocates like the WCTU were seemingly hit with a knockout punch, in fact, they were merely down but not out.

Revenge of the WCTU

Two months before Starr's release from the Oklahoma State Penitentiary, Congress passed groundbreaking legislation: the Eighteenth Amendment of 1919, known commonly as Prohibition. The manufacture, sale, and transportation of alcoholic beverages were henceforth illegal.[95] With passage, the number one mission of the WCTU had been realized.

Some people wondered, *What will we do with all that extra time on our hands?*

Goldwyn Pictures producer Rex Beach had an inkling, quipping, "Thousands of these people who licked the Rum Demon at so much per lick are now out of work and will hop on the movies like a duck on a June bug."[96]

Beach was prophetic.

For nearly two decades, the WCTU kept censorship simmering on the back burner. In 1919, with Starr set to become a matinee idol, they were ready to turn up the heat. Their comrades in the Oklahoma State Bar Association (OSBA) joined their cause by passing resolutions to prevent theaters from showing films where "criminals of nationwide reputations were allowed to assume the role of hero bank robbers, highwaymen, etc." The OSBA sent their symbolic resolutions to the governor and state legislators, demanding they be codified into law.[97]

Bowing to the collective pressure of the OSBA, the WCTU, and ministerial leaders, Oklahoma legislators floated the idea of appointing a commissioner of vice to weed out "unsavory" content in motion pictures. The state's proposal was the hot topic at the 1919 Oklahoma Exhibitor's Association convention at the Lee-Huckins Hotel in downtown Oklahoma City. The three hundred theater owners were in an uproar when they learned that under the legislature's plan, the commissioner of vice would oversee a censorship committee whose only qualifications were being male and willing to pay a one-dollar administrative fee. Theater owners grumbled that these unqualified and unelected public citizens would file innumerable complaints arising from personal morals and vendettas. Some exhibitors threatened to shut down their theaters rather than operate at the whim of a few priggish locals. Cooler heads at the convention didn't believe the bill would ever become law.[98] After a few weeks of debate, the commissioner of vice plan withered on the legislative vine.

Undaunted, in February 1919 Oklahoma State Senator Luther Harrison introduced Bill No. 283, establishing an Oklahoma Board of Review.[99] Under this law the governor would appoint a three-person board with the right to shut down the exhibition of any film they deemed objectionable. Motion picture producers would be forced to submit their films, posters, and advertisements to the board for review prior to being deemed appropriate for public viewing. The board would be funded by the motion picture producers, who would be compelled to pay $2 per film. Theater owners who showed an unsanctioned film faced a fine between $25 and $100 for a first offense and a $500 fine plus up to thirty days in jail for multiple offenses. Ultimately, this legislation also failed to find support in the divided statehouse.

The censorship resolutions passed by the OSBA weren't a complete failure. They inspired the Gore-Harreld Bill that threatened to kill P. J. Clark and Pan-American's planned Henry Starr film. Congressman John W. Harreld cited the OSBA's work along with Starr signing a motion picture contract for the need to expedite his bill to the US Congress.[100] Senator Thomas P. Gore wrote identical legislation that prohibited transporting films that "show or simulate the acts and conduct of ex-convicts" across state lines. The *Hominy News* reported that under federal legislation, "Henry Starr pictures can be outlawed."[101] If the combined legislation known as the Gore-Harreld Bill passed, motion picture censorship would be taken out of the hands of the states and put under federal oversight under the auspices of the US Postal Service.[102] The Oklahoma Press Association (OPA), which in contemporary times would be expected to champion the right to free speech, enthusiastically supported the Gore-Harreld censorship. The OPA publicly opposed outlaw pictures featuring "Al Jennings, Henry Starr, and other famous bandits." The *Dustin News* fervidly predicted that it was only a matter of time before the legislature would "abolish this evil in the state of Oklahoma."[103]

The editor of the *Hominy News* thought film censorship was "too suggestive of German practice and the old idea of monarchy." However, in one area he waggishly supported censorship: "There should be a special censor for the idiots who read the screen descriptions aloud and said censor should be equipped with a fool-proof baseball bat about ten feet long."[104]

Jokes aside, police officers and juvenile custodians were motivated by the churches, women's organizations, and the newspapers to stop Starr and Pan-American. They testified before the Oklahoma City Board of Commissioners that the recent "wave of juvenile crime" was directly traceable to bandit movies.[105] In response, the commissioners instructed the municipal counselor to draft an ordinance barring motion pictures featuring outlaws.

Pan-American president P. J. Clark realized that if big cities like Oklahoma City banned his $30,000 motion picture, he would never recoup his investor's money. Sensing that some newspaper editors had grown weary of the morals martinets, Clark reached out to the *Daily Oklahoman*. A year earlier the newspaper had printed "Letters from the People" declaring that outlaws becoming motion stars was a bad idea, evidenced by "crimes by boys attempting the feats seen in the pictures of Emmett Dalton and Al Jennings."[106] By February 1920 the paper was willing to listen to Pan-American's side of the censorship debate. Clark explained that in *The Man and the Law* (the new working title), Starr was not the film's hero. "The real hero is to be the law and that throughout the film, the law will be triumphant over the outlaw."[107] *Daily Oklahoman* columnist Edith C. Johnson came out publicly against "extreme reformists who are striving to place the American people in a moral straitjacket." Further, Johnson warned that censorship boards with Puritanical ideas "may force the exhibition of a dull, uninteresting type of picture which the public will not pay to see."[108]

Despite hints that the public might not support censorship, Ralph Talbot, president of the Theatre Owners and Managers Association (TOMA), decided to be proactive.[109] During their annual meeting at the Lee-Huckins Hotel in Oklahoma City, Talbot convinced his fellow theater owners to make a Faustian bargain with the legislators. TOMA theaters pledged to voluntarily ban any motion pictures "made by persons discharged from penitentiaries or prisons and depicting therewith their careers in crime." The *Enid Daily News* welcomed the self-censorship: "Never more will 'wild-eyed Willi' after serving an indefinite term in the pen for 'sticking up' a train or robbing a bank, blossom out into a full-fledged movie star and show the younger generation how he did it. At least not in Oklahoma."[110]

Talbot sent a telegram to Representative Harreld requesting that he and Senator Gore withdraw their legislation in exchange for TOMA's promised self-censorship. Before the Gore-Harreld Bill could gain traction, it was withdrawn.

The death of the Gore-Harreld Bill was a double-edged sword for Starr and Pan-American. On the one hand, there wouldn't be a federal ban on interstate commerce for their film. On the other hand, when their film was completed, they would be shut out of the largest and most profitable theaters across Oklahoma.

Lights, Camera, Stroud!

On Monday, October 27, 1919, the Pan-American Motion Picture Corporation rolled into Stroud to begin two days of filming for *Unto Him Who Transgresses* (the title had been changed back). Adults and children gathered in the streets with smiles and waves as if greeting a circus parade, many hoping to be selected as extras in the film. Pan-American President P. J. Clark promised the townsfolk they would debut their Starr biography at the local Rialto, allowing them to be the first to watch themselves on the silver screen. The board of directors of First National and Stroud Banks refused to cooperate with the filming.[111] "This is good business for Henry Starr," a board member harrumphed, "but very bad business for the state."[112]

The *Tulsa Daily World* sent a reporter to the Stroud movie set for a thrilling front-page story: "Rifles cracked and bullets rang through the air as in the days of old when Henry Starr, king of Oklahoma outlaws robbed two banks at Stroud yesterday, duplicating the stunt he performed on March 27, 1915, which won him his title. Instead of frightened citizens scurrying here and there at the sound of the first shots, everyone in town was out on the streets calmly reviewing the spectacle . . . but of course, they were out of range of the motion picture camera, which clicked through the entire performance."[113]

Starr sat in a makeup chair for an exclusive interview with the *Tulsa Daily World*. Townsfolk said he was noticeably thinner than five years earlier, and many didn't initially recognize him.[1114] Starr was decked out in full costume: an expensive dark topcoat, a silk suit, and a dark Alpine fedora.

"Mr. Starr, I notice you don't wear fur-trimmed chaps, carry silver-plated revolvers, or ride on diamond-studded saddles like an average Western thriller."

"No sir, I'm trying to make a higher type of film by showing the truth in every detail," Starr responded. "I have a real story the public would benefit from seeing, unlike impersonators like William S. Hart."

"Why not retire quietly?"

Starr shifted in his chair, making the wood creak. Starr looked the reporter in the eye with a knowing smile. "I am in this game for two reasons. First, to make money, and second, to teach a lesson that when it comes to beating the law, there is nothing to it."

"Will you keep making motion pictures?"

Starr leaned back as the make-up artist dusted yellow Max Factor powder onto his face with a puff.

"I can't say just yet."

Part of Starr's commitment to authenticity included Pan-American hiring actual participants in the event. Paul Curry had recently returned from fighting in the Great War.[115] On the day of filming, Curry changed into a grocer's boy costume and re-created his movements for the camera, including hiding behind a barrel and shooting Starr as he walked in the street. Little Lorene Hughes, the 6-year-old Shirley Temple doppelganger whom Starr distracted with a handful of shiny copper pennies, had aged out of the

Figure 28 Starr (*center*) on location outside the Stroud National Bank in Stroud, Oklahoma, re-creating his daylight double bank robbery for the film *A Debtor to the Law*. The young actor (Anna Lee Amerman) portrays Lorene Hughes, the little girl who interrupted the robbery in real life. Courtesy of the Glenn D. Shirley Western Americana Collection, Dickinson Research Center, National Cowboy and Western Heritage Museum (RC2006.068.32.6.13).

role. Pan-American replaced her with a younger actress, Anna Lee Amerman. Because Stroud National Bank wouldn't let them shoot inside, George Reehm staged their scene on the sidewalk outside. When the director called, "Action!" Starr took a knee next to Anna Lee and wrapped his arm gently around her shoulders. The little pixie, wearing a stylish hat and a long velvet coat, listened as Starr explained that she must go home. Starr casually holds a rifle in his right hand, while in the background two other actors playing gang members scan the streets for trouble.

After Reehm called "Cut!" Starr looked over and spotted the real Lorene in the crowd. He approached her, and they exchanged grins.

"Remember I promised to buy you some ice cream if you were good?"

116   Reel Three

She nodded. [116]

"Well, I never forget a promise," Starr said, handing her a dollar. "Here, kid, go and get your ice cream."

Lorene took the dollar, and she and her two friends excitedly ran toward the Bon Ton confectionery shop. Later, when Starr finished shooting another scene, Lorene tugged at his coat. "Here's what's left over," Lorene said, holding out some coins.

"Keep it," Starr laughed. "I didn't expect any change."[117]

The *Tulsa Daily World* printed a portion of Woodcock Kay's photoplay *Unto Him Who Transgresses*:

> *On the morning of March 27, 1915, a strange caravan, fated to gain a place in the sun, could be seen entering the little town of Stroud, which bustled about its early morning activities all unmindful of the 'spot' it would hold in Oklahoma history.*

"We'll go easy and quick about it, boys."

> *It was the master bandit, Henry Starr, who spoke to his six men as they quickly dismounted and made preparations for carrying out their chief's orders, for as usual, Starr had planned everything days before down to the minutest detail.*

"Remember, no shootin' unless absolutely necessary."

> *Starr gave this command curtly.*[118]

A few days later, Clark, Starr, Woodcock, Kay, and Reehm gathered in the Pan-American offices to watch the footage that had come back from the developer. They had shot hundreds of feet of film and discovered "the lighting was all wrong" for the interior scenes. Reehm blamed the cameraman, saying he lacked "considerable expertise."[119] The giddiness surrounding the first days of filming had disappeared.

Starr and Clark shared a look. The motion picture was ruined.

Patrick S. McGeeney, the Third Tin Star Filmmaker

Despite Clark's promise to Reehm, Pan-American hadn't built interior sets with the proper lighting. Now the production's future was in jeopardy. Fortunately, Reehm had a possible solution. He recalled meeting Patrick Sylvester (P. S.) McGeeney a few years earlier, who owned Shamrock Photoplay Corporation in San Antonio. They had interior stages, a backlot, and even a repertory company. There was one potential complication Reehm admitted. McGeeney was a former US deputy marshal who might not want to work with a convicted felon.[120]

Clark thought it was worth a shot. Reehm called McGeeney and explained the trouble they had filming interiors on their production.

"What's your film about?' McGeeney asked.

Reehm swallowed hard.

"We're telling the life story of Henry Starr."

There was silence on the other end.

"Hello. McGeeney?"

"You know, Henry Starr stuck a gun in my belly once," McGeeney responded evenly. "He's why I became a lawman."

The confrontation took place on May 19, 1893, when McGeeney was a 19-year-old brakeman on the 403 Santa Fe passenger train.[121] Always keen and observant, McGeeney noticed that US Marshal Heck Thomas and two deputies had boarded the train armed with rifles. Suddenly, he realized the rumors that Henry Starr was going to rob the train were more than just idle talk. The next station was Old Ponca, which served the Ponca and Osage Reservations.[122] Texas cattlemen would offload their cows at Old Ponca and let them graze. Often, a portion of the herd would be sickly and die. For a mile each side of the station the land was dotted with rotting cattle carcasses whose hides had been stripped.

That evening was sweltering. Inside Old Ponca station, twenty Texas cattlemen were killing time playing seven-up and rolling dice. Despite the heat the windows were closed. They'd rather sweat than gag on the stench of decaying cow flesh. Suddenly the men heard gunshots and someone barking orders. Then, three bandits entered the station.

"I'm Henry Starr!" the tallest outlaw said. "And if any of you buzzards move, I'll smear this platform with your blood."

One of the cattlemen later commented, "Their game was to keep us intimidated, and they certainly played it." Every one of the Texans was armed, but none of them dared confront the bandits.

Just then Starr heard the 403's whistle in the distance. He turned his rifle on the pumpman and ordered, "Flag that train down!"

As the train approached the station, the conductor, Al Glazier, saw the pumpman frantically waving his lantern. He knew something was off. Old Ponca was not a scheduled stop. Glazier was also aware that the Henry Starr Gang might try to rob the train. Out of caution he hit the brakes, and the train came to a halt three hundred yards from the station.

McGeeney climbed down from one of the passenger cars with his lantern. He walked up to the engine as it steamed and huffed.

"I'm going to check out what's going on," McGeeney called up to Glazier.

"Don't be a fool; the railroad doesn't pay you enough to risk your life."

McGeeney shrugged with the invincibility of a teenager and walked toward the station, his lantern throwing a circle of light on the crushed stone path. As he approached the depot, he could see a bullet hole in the ticket window. Nevertheless, he climbed the steps of the platform. Starr emerged from the darkness with Bill Doolin and George "Bitter Creek" Newcomb on either side. They had their rifles trained on him. McGeeney had heard lots of terrible stories about Starr, but seeing him in person, he realized they were the same age.

"Why'd the train stop?" Starr demanded.

"The engineer thought there was trouble."

"There's going to be if you don't get that train up here," said Starr, pointing his gun at McGeeney. "Signal him forward."

McGeeney was frightened by Doolin, but somehow Starr seemed like a person he could reason with. He explained that they needed to get the 403 past the station as quickly as possible because an express train was coming up behind them and wouldn't have time to brake. A deadly collision was inevitable.

"I know you don't want to kill anybody," McGeeney said.

"No, no, by God, we don't," Starr agreed.

Glazier, observing from a distance, made a plan of his own. He backed the train up a mile to the top of the hill, then opened her up to seventy miles per hour. Starr and his gang fired at the train as it sped past the station "in a blur of fire and smoke and steel." McGeeney couldn't show it, but he was giddy inside. He'd "danced to the music" long enough to distract Starr. Seconds later officers from the Ponca Agency arrived. Gunshots were exchanged, and Starr and his gang were forced to ride off. A week later the government rewarded McGeeney for his bravery by appointing him a US deputy marshal—the youngest in the Oklahoma Territory.[123]

McGeeney's path from lawman to studio mogul was filled with unlikely twists. In 1906, after thirteen years in law enforcement, McGeeney moved to Mexico City to become a construction superintendent for the Mexican Central Railway. While in San Luis Potosi, Mexico, McGeeney met Gaston Méliès, the elder brother of the great French film pioneer Georges Méliès.[124] As the head of Star Films in Paris, Georges revolutionized motion pictures using in-camera special effects, including multiple exposures, time-lapse, and substitution splices. He also pushed the boundaries of the imagination with elaborate sets and costumes. One of his hundreds of films was *Le voyage dans la lune* (1902), which brought a Jules Verne–inspired lunar mission to life with stunning visuals.[125] In the United States, Star Films was forced to become a member of Thomas Edison's Motion Picture Patents Company (MPPC) or face lawsuits for using the patented Edison Kinetograph movie camera. The French genius fell into line along with other companies, including Essanay, Kalem, Pathé Frères, Selig, and Vitagraph.[126] Membership in the MPPC meant each filmmaker had to produce one thousand feet of finished motion picture footage weekly. As part of fulfilling that obligation, Gaston Méliès traveled to Mexico to capture the armed rebellion against President Porfirio Diaz in 1910 on celluloid. After Gaston met McGeeney, he invited the American to join his crew.

Later that year Gaston moved the Méliès Manufacturing Company from Fort Lee, New Jersey, to San Antonio, Texas, establishing the Star Film Ranch. Gaston established the infrastructure of a studio, including interior stages, a backlot, and film-processing labs. Two years later Gaston moved the company to Santa Paula, California. McGeeney didn't initially join Méliès when the Frenchman relocated to San Antonio. He stayed in Mexico to work as a train conductor. However, by 1912 the revolution made working for the national railroad too dangerous. When Méliès moved his operations to California, McGeeney relocated to San Antonio and took over the property, renaming it the Shamrock Photoplay Corporation.[127]

McGeeney hired experienced Hollywood talent to work in front of and behind the camera and added lighting to the production stages. He solicited production companies from both coasts to come to San Antonio and take advantage of the Texas scenery, the pleasant weather, and the longer daylight hours. In 1918 Samuel Goldwyn of Goldwyn Pictures Corporation selected Shamrock as the location for his feature *Heart of the Sunset*.[128]

Two years later, in early 1920, McGeeney sat in his screening room watching the Stroud dailies with P. J. Clark and George Reehm. He agreed with the Pan-American team that the Stroud exterior scenes were fine, but the interior shots were unsalvageable. McGeeney was open to helping Pan-American, but as a former lawman, it disturbed him greatly that Starr had murdered fellow US Deputy Marshal Floyd Wilson in cold blood. McGeeney wanted to know Starr's side of the deadly confrontation that took place back on December 11, 1892. For his part, Starr had always been forthcoming about what transpired, even to his detriment. He testified at his murder trial that Wilson was wounded and lying on the ground unarmed when he stepped up and fired two bullets into his chest.[129] Reportedly, the barrel of Starr's gun was close enough to leave powder burns.

McGeeney remembered reading newspaper reports describing Wilson as a "brave and fearless officer."[130] On the other hand, depending on the political proclivity of the newspaper, Starr was described as a "savage," a gentleman bandit, and sometimes even a modern-day Robin Hood.[131]

McGeeney had to reconcile Starr's true nature and insisted on meeting him face-to-face before moving forward.

A Debtor to Robin Hood

Eric Hobsbawm, in his seminal book, *Bandits*, coined the term "social bandits" to define outlaws who rise to notoriety when governments (civil or royal) or banks oppress peasants and laborers. These outlaws, whom Hobsbawm

Figure 29 Starr in costume for *A Debtor to the Law* (1920) publicity photo. Contemporaries considered him a gentlemen bandit, but his fit within the Robin Hood academic rubric is up for debate. Courtesy of the Bartlesville Area History Museum, Bartlesville, Oklahoma.

dubbed interchangeably noble robbers and Robin Hoods, are members of the peasant society and are seen by the community "as heroes, champions, avengers, fighters for justice."[132]

Paul Kooistra, in his book *Criminals as Heroes: Structure, Power & Identity*, noted that "social" banditry in the United States materializes during economic volatility.[133] For example, the post–Civil War 1870s wrought Frank and Jesse James and Cole, Jim, and Bob Younger. In the 1890s the Oklahoma land rush spawned the Dalton Gang, the Rufus Buck Gang, Cherokee Bill, and Starr. The Great Depression launched John Dillinger, Bonnie and Clyde, and Charles "Pretty Boy" Floyd. During these societal upheavals, Kooistra argues, "people turn to symbolic representations of justice outside the law," what he calls American Robin Hoods.[134]

It's important to understand that Robin Hood was not a real person, and his legendary exploits are a work of fiction. Kent Ladd Steckmesser, in his book *Western Outlaws: The "Good Badman" in Fact, Film, and Folklore*, traces the Robin Hood mythos to 1500 CE, with the printing of four ballads, "The Lytell Geste of Robyn Hode."[135] A "geste" was a tale of adventure, and the ballads established the classic Robin Hood tropes that are recognized five hundred years later. He is a commoner who steals from the rich—noblemen and religious leaders who've grown fat and happy while the common people suffer—and gives to the poor. Robin Hood is a skilled archer and swordsman who utilizes these skills to fend off the forces of his rival, the Sheriff of Nottingham. While the wild imagination of the press and public anoints bandits with Robin Hood–style qualities, Hobsbawm argues, "If there were no relation between bandit reality and bandit myth, any robber chieftain could become a Robin Hood."[136]

In *Bandits* Hobsbawm developed a nine-point rubric that an outlaw must meet to be defined as a Robin Hood or noble robber:

The Noble Robber :

1. Is thrust into a criminal career by injustice
2. Rights wrongs
3. Takes from the rich and gives to the poor
4. Never kills unless in self-defense or justifiable revenge

Henry Movie Starr

5. Returns to his community as an honorable citizen
6. Is admired, helped and supported by his people
7. Dies through an act of treason
8. Is invisible and invulnerable
9. Not an enemy of the king or emperor, only local oppressors, such as clergy and officials[137]

Steckmesser modernized, modified, and shortened the list of defining qualities:

The Good Badman must:

1. Serve a Higher Law
2. Be generous
3. Have a redeeming personality ·
4. Be perceived as the victim of circumstances
5. Display the intellect and cunning of a trickster
6. Die in action[138]

Through Hobsbawm and Steckmesser taxonomies, one can measure how Starr's behavior stacks up as a Robin Hood or noble robber.

Generosity

The keystone in the arch for a Robin Hood–style outlaw in both rubrics is stealing from the rich to give to the poor. However, Steckmesser tempered unrealistic expectations of any real-life bandit. Referring to "The Lytell Geste of Robyn Hode," he wrote, "No one in 1500 was under the illusion that Robin Hood had been running a one-man Community Chest. Nor does the geste have him handing out loot to the poverty-stricken."[139]

Nevertheless, Starr's reputation for generosity began at twenty following the Pryor Creek, IT, train robbery in 1893. No less an impartial witness than A. A. Mosher, president of the Kansas City & Independence AirLine, gave a lengthy firsthand account of the theft to the *St. Louis Weekly Gazette*, May 11, 1893.[140] When the train pulled into the station, Henry and his gang surprised the engineer and conductor and covered them with rifles. Then, the bandits went through each car, taking the passengers' watches, cash, and jewelry. According to Mosher, Starr had instructed his gang to feel the hands of the passengers first, "and some of those who had hardened hands, indicating severe toil, were not robbed." The sub-headline in the article read, "Nor Did They Rob Any One Whose Hands Were Hard and Horny." In this case Starr robbed the rich and spared the poor, which isn't the same as divvying up the spoils.

Four months after the Pryor Creek robbery, Starr received his own ballad of sorts along the lines of "Lytell Geste." On August 17, 1893, Street & Smith published the dime novel *Hank Starr at Pryor Creek, or, Old Jack Drew Heard From*.[141] Written by Jim Kearney (pseudonym for Oliver "Oll" Coomes) for the new Log Cabin Library series, the novel weaves blood and thunder action with humor while also imbuing Starr with "social bandit" qualities that would endear him to many in the public.

In the story, when Starr rides up to a home on the prairie, the farmer is initially spooked. "Don't get excited, Mr. Hayseed," Starr says calmly. "You've nothin' fear. We don't rob poor, working people. It's only the rich we call on. We're Communists—Populists and believe in the rich dividin' up with the poor."[142]

After enjoying a hearty meal, Starr hands Mr. Hayseed a twenty-dollar bill, paying not only for his fare but also for the bounty hunters chasing him who had eaten for free earlier: "Here's for our dinner and that of the officers and a little over. There may be some others along wanting food, and so I'll pay in advance."

"'Thankee, sir; if you be a robber, I'd like more like you hit this mansion. That's more money than I've seed since Heck was a pup,' the farmer said, looking at the bill with smiles all over his bronzed, hairy face."

The dime novel may not have veered far from the truth. Wild West performer Milt Hinkle said that after the train robbery at the Old Ponca Depot in 1893, Starr took refuge at Hose Kaiser's ranch in the Osage country.[143] The next day, before he left, Starr gave Kaiser $100 to show his gratitude. Nevertheless, the irascible Kaiser shot at Starr as he rode away. Starr turned his mount and shot Kaiser in the knee. A month later Starr returned to see how Kaiser was recuperating. To make things right, Starr offered Kaiser $15,000 to pay off his home loan. Kaiser stubbornly refused.

Figure 30 *Hank Starr at Pryor Creek; or, Old Jack Drew Heard From*, Log Cabin Library no. 231, August 17, 1893, written by Jim Kearney (pseudonym for Oll Coomes, 1845–1921). At 19 Starr joined Jesse James as the only outlaw to have their own half-dime series (thirteen novels). The sombrero-wearing, mustache-bearing character on the cover bears no resemblance to Starr. The hairs-breadth tale inside positively portrays Starr as an outlaw with honor and a sense of humor. Courtesy of the Dime Novel and Popular Literature Collection, Digital Library at Villanova University, Villanova, Pennsylvania.

"I know that damn bank in Arkansas City wants to take your place," Starr said.

Kaiser insisted he didn't want to take the money.

"You are an old man, and it's too late to make any money," Starr said. "Do as I say."

Kaiser reluctantly took the money and paid off the loan.

In subsequent newspaper accounts, Starr displayed other incidents of benevolence, but they were more of the spur-of-the-moment variety rather than a philosophy. In a 1915 *Guthrie Daily Leader* article, an anonymous man from the Cherokee country claimed that during the 1893 Caney Bank robbery, Starr came upon a stack of farm mortgages and notes twelve inches thick. Starr said, "These things are of no value to me, but I'd hate it if the farmers had them to pay."[144] With that Starr took the documents. Later, when he arrived at California Creek in Northern Oklahoma, he tied a stone around the mortgages and dropped them into the water. The article explained that he didn't burn the mortgages because the smoke might bring a posse to their hideout. The fact that the storyteller wasn't there during the robbery to witness the incident and his desire to remain unnamed puts the story's veracity in doubt. However, for many in the public, Starr's gentleman bandit mythos took hold.

A month earlier another generosity story appeared in the *Bartlesville Morning Examiner*. Reportedly, a merchant named Herman Stump was in the Carney State Bank making a deposit on December 29th, 1914. Stump, described as a "5x5 man" because he was "five feet tall and five feet wide" and weighed three hundred pounds, had just placed his money on the counter of the deposit window when Starr arrived. The outlaw grabbed Stump's money and tossed it into his grain sack along with the rest of the bank's loot. Then, Starr and his partner prodded everyone into the street to act as shields as they made their way to their horses. While marching Stump whined that it was unfair of Starr to take the money because the bank hadn't yet issued him a certificate of deposit. Starr said, "I'll show you that my heart is right. You reach in that fellow's pocket and pull your sack of money out."[145] A few minutes later, Stump was set free with his money returned. Like the Caney generosity story, this story lacks the details that make it feel true.

Stump's surname is either a pseudonym, a nickname, or an unfortunate coincidence, given his height and weight. Shortly after the robbery, Caney cashier J. W. Austin gave an interview to the *Daily Oklahoman* and never mentioned the Stump incident.[146]

Veracity was beside the point. In print, Starr displayed the attributes of Robin Hood.

A Redeeming Personality

In *Hank Starr at Pryor Creek*, Starr values the founding American principle of democracy. He calls a vote to ensure each man has the free will to decide for himself to rob the Bentonville bank. Starr's other admirable qualities included loyalty: "It shall never be said that Hank Starr deserted a friend even though all the marshals, sheriffs, and police of this Kingdom Come were skulking in the shadows."[147]

Steckmesser wrote that the "good" badman should be "light-hearted and show some humor now and then." In *Thrilling Events* Starr unspooled tales of life on the lam, often poking fun at himself. During one incident he helped a "minister of the gospel" by clearing out his property of prairie dogs with a gun. The following morning, in a sign of dubious gratitude, the reverend skinned and pan fried the varmints and served them to Starr for breakfast. The outlaw wrote "these ancient pups frying was neither fragrant nor edifying." Nevertheless, out of politeness, Starr ate one queasy bite. In another tale the same reverend brings a reluctant Starr to a raucous tent revival where the "shouting continued until 12 o'clock." When the devout crowd turned to Starr to testify his love for the Lord, he pretended to look away. However, the "older, bolder, and more enthusiastic dames" grabbed him anyway and forced him to the stage. Despite eschewing organized religion, Starr could think on his feet and cleverly repurposed the previous speaker's testimony. The crowd bought it, and he artfully won the moment.[148]

A corollary to having a redeeming personality is displaying a fondness for children. Steckmesser wrote that no outlaw "will ever be called a Robin Hood if he barks at youngsters."[149] There are several eyewitnesses to Starr displaying this endearing quality. In April 1893 Alexander Huling recalled meeting Starr when the outlaw attempted to ford the Little Caney River, five miles north of Dewey. Starr gave a 12-year-old boy "the thrill of his life" by allowing him to hold his gun to keep it out of the mud. Huling recalled Starr turned to the youngster and said kindly, "Here son is a piece of money for holding my gun."[150] Another example of Starr's kindness to children occurred during the Stroud bank robbery when Little Lorene Hughes showed up unexpectedly in the middle of the heist. He put her in a safe spot, gave her a handful of pennies to keep her occupied, and promised to buy her ice cream if she was good. Years later, while filming *A Debtor to the Law*, Starr would make good on that promise, giving Miss Hughes the money to buy an ice cream.

Victim of Circumstances

Steckmesser asserts that the public must believe the outlaw would have been a fine, upstanding citizen had there not been an unjust course of events that bent them on reprisal.[151] Starr vigorously felt he was the victim of a corrupt US marshal system that incentivized deputies to arrest Blacks, Native Americans, and poor whites on false charges to earn per diem. In *Thrilling Events* Starr wrote, "These same deputies were willing to arrest innocent and harmless boys and drag them off to jail, and with the fees thus, gained drink at Fort Smith and pose as heroes before the demimonde."[152]

In addition to personal victimization, the economic upheaval during the 1880s led to the criminality of Starr, the Dalton Gang, Al Jennings, Cherokee Bill, and many others. On April 22, 1889, President Benjamin Harrison opened nearly two million acres of Indian land to settlers during the Land Rush.[153] By 1905 most of the Indian Territory was in white hands. Over his lifetime Starr had observed the shifting economic and personal relationship between whites and Native Americans in the Indian Territory. Starr recalled in *Thrilling Events* that when he was a boy, the white settlers treated their Cherokee landlords respectfully and courteously. He remembered the settlers pouring in year after year "in covered wagons with many dogs and tow-headed kids peeping out from behind every wagon-bow, and who, at the very best, made only a starving crop." The directors of Indian schools let the white children attend for free, but after Oklahoma statehood on November 16, 1907, the Cherokee became an outcast on their own lands. According to Starr, hundreds of full-blood Indians quit school because they were "taunted and insulted about their nationality." White men could not be arraigned in court for any offense against the life or property of an Indian citizen. "The white man holds power, and the same hypocritical renter has now grown arrogant and insulting," Starr wrote. "Whenever the Indian is spoken to at all, it is with a sneer."[154]

The US Marshal system and settler encroachment fit with Hobsbawm's definition of the Robin Hood / noble robber being forced into outlawry by injustice.

Service to a Higher Law

By robbing banks the "social bandits" were taking revenge on the "fat cat" bankers and industrialists who pushed them around, and in a manner the average person didn't dare. A "good" badman could not risk being viewed as the "bad" badman, which Steckmesser defines as one who "doesn't give a damn if officials are corrupt, if bankers are cheating poor widows, or if greedy landowners are bullying the tenant farmers. He just wants his share of the pickings and devil-take-the-hindmost."[155] For Hobsbawm, noble robbers never lost the support of people, and neither did Starr. For example, Claremore's Lew Blackburn hid the outlaw despite him having a $10,000 reward on his head. "Nothing can make 'em talk if they are your friend," he said.[156]

"Moderation in the use of violence is an equally important part of the Robin Hood image," Hobsbawm wrote.[157] In *Hank Starr at Pryor Creek*, Starr's respect for human life is established in the narrative: "It was not his desire to kill men for the pure love of killing, unless in absolute defense of his own life." Just as Robin Hood could split an arrow that already occupied a bullseye, Starr was shown to be equally adept with a pistol: "As if by accident, the outlaw's pistol went off, and the pencil over Cashier Andrews' ear was picked from its perch and sent flying across the room. Andrews felt the wind of the bullet, but not a hair of his head was touched."[158] Readers understood that the fictional Starr had the skills to be deadly but chose to be a "good" badman.

In real life, how the "social bandits" conducted themselves determined how long they remained in the public's good graces. From the outset of his criminal career, Starr planned robberies with the mindset that he didn't want any innocent bystanders or bank personnel killed. Most notably, Starr demonstrated this when facing armed mobs during the Bentonville and Stroud robberies. McGeeney knew that in contrast to his contemporaries—like Bob Dalton, Cherokee Bill, Bill Doolin, and the Rufus Buck Gang—Starr didn't kill with sociopathic indifference.

Nevertheless, Starr did kill Floyd Wilson, who left behind a wife and two children. The murder was the one bloody stain on Starr's bank-robbing career, and despite many people believing the Cherokee outlaw was a gentleman bandit, McGeeney needed to meet the reformed outlaw in person to make sense of it.

A Meeting in Muskogee

P. J. Clark arranged a sit-down between McGeeney and Starr in Muskogee. McGeeney hadn't seen Starr in twenty-seven years, describing him as well-dressed, a man of fine appearance, and "more handsome an Indian" than he had remembered.[159] McGeeney laid his cards on the table and told Starr flat out he wouldn't rescue the motion picture without a good explanation for why he killed a fellow deputy. Starr's eyes darkened, but he would make no apologies as he set the record straight.

First, newspapers erroneously reported that Wilson was a deputy when, in fact, he was a "hired gun" of the Pacific Express Company railroad. Wilson had been a deputy US marshal at one time, but when he attempted to arrest Starr, he did not have a commission.[160] Wilson began his career as a deputy in 1880 and trained under Deputy Bob Dalton, who later murdered innocent civilians at Coffeyville. Ironically, Dalton was considered the more promising of the two since Wilson had a hot temper and was quick to shoot men for even the most trifling excuse. A US Army officer named Captain Scott related his experience meeting Deputy Wilson in January 1884. Wilson tried to arrest Scott on a trumped-up charge "without writ or warrant." When Scott resisted, Wilson brutally beat him with a pistol, leaving the captain badly injured. Scott reported the incident, describing Wilson as "malignant and despicable in the extreme."[161] In response, the court at Fort Smith stripped Wilson of his badge.

The facts of the case were revealed during Starr's trial for murder:[162]

On November 18, 1892, Henry Dickey, a railroad detective with the Pacific Express Company, traveled to the territorial court at Fort Smith, Arkansas, to get a warrant for Starr's arrest. He was suspected of robbing the Nowata train depot months earlier. Stephen Wheeler, commissioner of the US Court for the Western District of Arkansas, signed the writ. Dickey realized capturing a dangerous outlaw was out of his depth, and Starr agreed, writing, "You have my word for it, that it was no kind of work for a detective. Finding was easy, but the work had only just begun."[163] Dickey needed help, and by coincidence Floyd Wilson was skulking around Fort Smith looking for work. Wilson was a favorite of Judge Isaac Parker, but US Marshal Jacob Yoes refused to reinstate him as a deputy. Dickey wanted a deputy marshal to accompany him but settled on the 28-year-old Wilson as a hired gun instead.

When Dickey and Wilson arrived in Nowata during the second week of December, one of their first stops was the home of Starr's sister, Elizabeth "Lizzie" Lipsey. They pounded on her door at four in the morning, demanding Starr to come out. Lizzie came to the door in her nightgown and told them her little brother wasn't there. Wilson didn't believe her and pushed his way inside. Lipsey's two frightened children watched from their bed as Wilson ransacked the house. When he realized Starr wasn't there, Wilson told Lizzie to pass along a message: "If Starr didn't turn himself in, he'd shoot him on sight."

After Wilson and Dickey left, Lipsey contacted Starr and told him what had transpired. Starr's teenage blood boiled. He recalled, "In a dim sort of way, I knew that if chance should ever give us a meeting, there would be work for the graveman."

Wilson and Dickey's next stop was the XU ranch, where Starr had once worked as a hand. Arthur Dodge, a widower from Nova Scotia, owned the property and was raising four young children. Dickey and Wilson asked if he'd seen Starr, and Dodge said no. However, he expected Starr to come riding by on his regular route to town shortly. Dickey and Wilson knew their moment had come. Dodge testified that the men "fixed their guns up" and headed to the barn. Dickey and Wilson climbed up to the hayloft and took positions, preferring an

Figure 31 *A Debtor to the Law* (1920) lobby card. Floyd Wilson (P. S. McGeeney) and Detective Dickey (unknown actor) force their way into the home of Starr's sister, Lizzie (unknown actress). Courtesy of the Glenn D. Shirley Western Americana Collection, Dickinson Research Center, National Cowboy & Western Heritage Museum (RC2006.068.32.6.10).

ambush over a face-to-face confrontation. Dodge continued his chores, mucking the stalls, when he spotted Starr approaching from a distance.

"Here he comes fellas," Dodge hollered up to Dickey and Wilson.

Observing how trigger-happy Wilson was, Dodge asked them for a favor: "Would you mind hiding out in my smokehouse instead?" Dodge said. "It'd be safer for my children."

Annoyed, but with no time to argue, Wilson scrambled down from the hayloft and trotted toward the outbuilding. Dickey followed close behind.

"Now, don't kill this boy, if possible, to get along without it," Dickey said. "We'll call on him to surrender."

As Starr approached from a distance on his horse Sleepy Tuck, Wilson grew frustrated that he didn't have a clear shot. He decided not to wait and

Figure 32 *A Debtor to the Law* (1920) lobby card. Starr, playing himself, shoots Floyd Wilson (P. S. McGeeney). Starr was twice sentenced to hang for the murder but was ultimately charged with manslaughter. Courtesy of the Glenn D. Shirley Western Americana Collection, Dickinson Research Center, National Cowboy & Western Heritage Museum (RC2006.068.32.6.8).

jumped on one of Dodge's horses, which was already saddled. As Wilson took off, Dickey called out for him to wait.

Starr, on horseback, was a hundred yards from the ranch when he saw a horse and rider galloping full speed toward him. Starr was perplexed. He didn't recognize the man but knew the buckskin horse belonged to the XU ranch. Starr assumed one of Dodge's ranch hands was headed his way in earnest. *But why?* Starr admitted he had become complacent about being captured, describing himself as almost "foolhardy" in his carelessness. "I had greatly relaxed my watchfulness, and they had me to rights almost before I was aware that danger lurked."

Starr dismounted from Sleepy Tuck and pulled his Winchester from the saddle scabbard. Wilson reined his horse fifty yards away and dismounted in

134   Reel Three

kind. Starr stood with his rifle cradled in the crook of one arm and his reins casually looped around the other.

Wilson shouted to Starr. "I'm taking you to Fort Smith."

"For what?"

"Train robbery."

"You have a warrant?

"Not on me," Wilson admitted. He brought his rifle to his shoulder and said, "You'll just have to trust me."

"Hah!" Starr laughed. He was unflappable.

"Here's what's gonna happen," Starr said. "I'm going to let you shoot first. After you miss, I'm going to shoot you dead, and it will be self-defense."

A shot rang out.

Every witness to the confrontation testified that Wilson fired first.[164]

But he missed.

"That ball was not past my ear till I had my Winchester out and was pumping it for all I was worth," Starr said.

Starr's bullets struck home, knocking Wilson backward. But the hired gun kept firing. "Wilson took five shots at me, hitting my clothes twice," Starr said. "I took four at him and every shot went into his body."

As the smoke from the gunpowder cleared and the crack of gunfire echoed away, Starr could see Wilson lying on the ground, motionless. Starr sheathed his Winchester. "I was content to quit and ride off," Starr said.

But Wilson had been playing possum. He rolled over and fired once again at Starr. The shot zinged wide. Starr drew his pistol and charged at Wilson. Witnesses said Starr held his gun high as if he intended to club Wilson. But instead of striking a blow, Starr lowered the barrel of his gun down to Wilson's chest and fired two kill shots.

Just then, another bullet whistled past Starr's head. He turned and saw Dickey, a "detective sort of a chap," galloping toward him from across the plain. Starr fired at Dickey, intending to wing him, but he missed. The railroad detective jumped down from his horse and lay flat on the ground. "I honestly believe he fainted," Starr said, "he was so scared." In the distance Starr saw two new riders headed his way. "I was afraid the whole damned country was alive with marshals," Starr remembered.

Henry Movie Starr

His horse Sleepy Tuck had bolted amid the gunfire, so Starr mounted Wilson's horse and rode away.[165]

The men riding up were Dodge and his ranch hand. They dismounted next to Wilson to check on him. He was dead.

In later years Starr wrote of Wilson, "He was, perhaps, a good sort in his way and brave he was, beyond a doubt. Yet . . . he had so little judgment as to border on a fool."[166]

Reshoots and Rewrites

After the Muskogee sit-down, McGeeney was satisfied with Starr's version of the deadly Wilson standoff. Even Hobsbawm's fourth point in his Robin Hood / Gentleman Robber rubric allowed for killing in self-defense. More than a convert to Starr's side, McGeeney became a cheerleader. After Starr's death McGeeney wrote of the outlaw, "Henry Starr was a Robin Hood. He took from the rich and gave to the poor. He was a lovable chap who had many friends."[167]

Starr was often reviled by those who only knew him from what they read in the papers. Those who met him were charmed by his intelligence. Former US Marshal E. D. Nix, of Three Guardsman fame, wrote, "I do not wonder that he was always able to interest influential people and number them among his host of friends," Nix said. "He talked like an intellectual."[168]

Starr, McGeeney, and P. J. Clark chatted into the night. McGeeney agreed to take over the production but insisted on wholesale changes that dramatically shifted the direction of the film. First, he wanted to "bring out a moral—to show the fair-minded what greed will do to men who have lost their Christianity." Next, McGeeney thought the film should place more focus on the Floyd Wilson saga and had the perfect person for the role—himself.[169] As a short story writer and photoplaywrite, McGeeney knew the scenario needed a dash of romance. Starr recommended adding a character based on the outlaw's teenage sweetheart, May Morrison. In *Thrilling Events* Starr described himself as "daffy" over the real Morrison, who was of Welsh and Irish descent. She had naturally curly auburn hair, large hazel eyes, and a fair complexion. Starr wrote, "I might add that she was as good as she was

136   Reel Three

beautiful."[170] Director George Reehm's wife, Lillian Gaynor Reehm, a diminutive brunette, was cast in the role.[171]

McGeeney also felt Starr's character needed a sidekick with an experienced actor in the role.[172] He recruited Hollywood actor William Karl Hackett to play Starr's partner in crime. The 26-year-old Hackett (born Carl E. Germain in Carthage, Missouri) was a Broadway actor before being drafted in the Great War. He served in the 313th Engineering Regiment before returning to acting. Lauron Draper, a veteran from Triangle Pictures in Los Angeles, became the new cameraman. Draper cut his teeth as a US Army Signal Corps aerial cinematographer. After the war he shot moving pictures for Essanay, Universal, and Triangle.[173] At the time Triangle had the biggest directors (Thomas Ince, D. W. Griffith, and Mack Sennett) and the biggest stars (William S. Hart, Douglas Fairbanks, and the Gish sisters, Dorothy and Lillian). Draper had the professional chops to avoid a repeat of what happened at Stroud.[174]

One last hurdle remained before the production could relocate to San Antonio. As a condition of his parole, Starr wasn't allowed to leave Oklahoma. Doing so also increased the risk of capture and subsequent extradition to Arkansas. McGeeney, P. J. Clark, and Starr hatched a plan. Instead of Starr traveling with the cast and crew where Arkansas agents might be following him, he would depart on an earlier train with the cow ponies. A few days later, Starr rode in the cattle car with set wrangler Claude Smith.[175] The ploy worked magnificently. Starr and Smith became fast friends along the journey and decided to become "roomies" at the downtown San Antonio Gunter Hotel. Their room was on the mezzanine floor, allowing them to look down on the ground floor lobby and people watch.

Starr and Smith were early risers and would grab breakfast at the coffee shop at 6:00 a.m. One day they slept until noon. They joined other late-rising cast and crew at the coffee shop. When it came time to pay the bill, Starr and Smith were stunned to learn that everyone else had been putting their food bill on the Pan-American company tab. From then on Starr and Smith signed tabs for meals, the barber, the laundry, the tobacco counter, and any place that would take them. What a boon!

After arriving in San Antonio, Starr found himself with a lot of free time. Filming was delayed for three weeks because the railroad lost the trunks carrying the costumes. The postponement gave Starr the opportunity to gamble. One evening Starr borrowed twenty dollars from Smith and went out to play cards. When he returned at 2:00 a.m., a giddy Starr woke Smith up and said, "Look at my leg!" Starr typically kept his socks safety-pinned to his long underwear. He removed the pin, revealing his poker winnings wrapped around his leg. "He had $1,000 and gave me a hundred-dollar bill," Smith remembered.[176]

Some of the reshoots took place at McGeeney's second studio in Sabinas, Mexico, two hundred miles southwest of San Antonio. While across the border, Starr fantasized about buying a plane. A bandit, he theorized, could hit a bank in the United States and then fly to safety in Mexico. The gears of Starr's outlaw mind were always turning.

Reel Four

Start Picture

In late February and early March of 1920, the production returned to Oklahoma to shoot pickups in Stroud and Boynton.[1] When filming wrapped Starr showed his gratitude to McGeeney by giving him his Bisley .45 Colt.[2]

Unfortunately, *A Debtor to the Law* is a film lost to history. Film historians and cinephiles will never know precisely what Starr and Pan-American put on film. However, through surviving posters, lobby cards, on-set photos, a press book, and newspaper advertisements, an approximation of the motion picture experience can be imagined.

The film was advertised as a six-reel feature with a running time of over ninety minutes.[3] A group photo shows the main cast: Starr, Hackett (as the sidekick), Lillian Gaynor Reehm (as May), McGeeney (as Floyd Wilson), an unidentified woman (as Lizzie Lipsey, Starr's sister), and four unidentified male actors wearing suits, ties, and flap caps. (Oddly, McGeeney is standing center front as if he were the star of the film.) Black-and-white lobby cards reveal the film covered Starr's life from 1890 to 1915, when he was 17 to 42 years old. The costumes worn by Starr indicate which era he's re-creating. The scenes with him wearing a cowboy hat, red scarf, white shirt, and cowboy boots re-created events before 1900. Those with Starr wearing a Homburg, three-piece suit, and long wool coat covered the 1900s.

Figure 33 *A Debtor to the Law* (1920) cast photo. *Left to right*: Henry Starr, Lillian Gaynor Reehm (likely in the role of Starr's teenage love May Morrison), P. S. McGeeney (Floyd Wilson), unknown actress (Lizzie), William Karl Hackett (unnamed sidekick); rest of the cast unknown. Courtesy of the Glenn D. Shirley Western Americana Collection, Dickinson Research Center, National Cowboy & Western Heritage Museum (RC2006.068.32.6.9).

A cast list was not included in the press book, so it's unclear who in Starr's life Hackett was meant to represent. Like Starr, he is shown wearing a cowboy outfit in some photos and a suit and tie in others, indicating his character participated in heists over two eras. Factually, Starr had one set of gang members before entering the Colorado State Penitentiary at Cañon City in 1909 and a different set after. While John "Kid" Wilson participated in the People's Bank of Bentonville robbery (1893) and the Amity, Colorado, robbery (1906), the mustache Hackett wears in the film makes it unlikely his character would be called "Kid." Another on-set photo shows Hackett's character being helped from the ground after being shot in the chest. Most likely that scene is a re-creation of the Stroud bank robbery when Curry shot Lewis Estes. Estes was shot in the neck/collarbone area, not the chest, but the dark blood stain on a white shirt may have been a better cinematic choice. The Stroud heist was Estes's first and last robbery, so he would not have had the era-bridging history the Hackett character represents in the photographs. Hackett was an amalgamation of different Starr sidekicks.

Many credible historians have advanced a rumor that Starr was such a terrible actor that Pan-American hired Hackett to replace him. Oklahoma film historian Jack Spears wrote, "Starr, despite his striking Indian good looks, was hopelessly inept as an actor." He continued, writing that the producers demoted Starr to a technical consultant when the production moved to the Shamrock Studios in San Antonio.[4] Glenn Shirley, a 1981 inductee to the Oklahoma Journalism Hall of Fame, added to the confusion when he wrote in his 1989 biography of McGeeney, *The Purple Sage*, "To avoid his presence in San Antonio, Starr was kept under wraps at the Gunter Hotel and appeared 'incognito' until needed as an advisor."[5]

Spears's assertion has been repeated in other historical accounts. In *The Real Wild West: The 101 Ranch and the Creation of the American West* (1999), Michael Wallis writes, "Starr stayed on as a technical consultant, but William Karl Hackett, a noted screen actor, replaced him in the lead role."[6] Wallis cited Spears as the source.

In *Shot in Oklahoma* (2012), John Wooley also repeated Spears but added, "The film was advertised—at least in its premiere screening—as having Starr himself in the lead role."[7]

Spears cites author Richard Slotkin as his source for Starr being replaced. Slotkin, Olin Professor of English and American Studies at Wesleyan University, wrote a fictionalized version of the outlaw in *The Return of Henry Starr* (Atheneum, 1988). When told he was the source for Spears's assertion, Slotkin wrote, "I never found evidence that he was replaced."[8]

As if anticipating any confusion, a 1920 advertisement in the *Muskogee Times-Democrat* offered a "$1,000 Reward for Anyone Proving That Henry Starr Did Not Personally Appear in 'A Debtor to the Law.'"[9] In 1965 *A Debtor to the Law* pony wrangler Claude Smith wrote to Glenn Shirley, "They had weaved in some romance, and the leading man was a Mr. Hackett." While that phrasing may have led to some confusion, the preponderance of photographic

142   Reel Four

evidence of Starr and Hackett appearing side-by-side in scenes demonstrates that Hackett played Starr's sidekick, not the role of Starr.[10]

The final repudiation of the false narrative comes from the man in charge of the movie set, McGeeney, who told the *Newton Journal*, "A few years ago, I directed Henry Starr, who played the leading role in 'A Debtor to the Law.'"[11]

The *A Debtor to the Law* lobby cards and on-set photos reveal the plot along five storylines: Starr's false arrest for transporting liquor, the Nowata Depot train robbery, the killing of Floyd Wilson, the failed Cherokee Bill jailbreak, and the Stroud double bank robberies. Re-creating the 1892 Nowata Depot robbery was significant to the narrative because it eventually led to the Pacific Express Company hiring Detective Henry Dickey and the ill-fated Floyd Wilson.

Since many of the photographs come from the McGeeney family collection, they disproportionately feature him in the role of Wilson: leading a posse, gathering intelligence from farmers and train employees, and lying dead in an open field. Two lobby cards show Wilson (McGeeney) at the home of Starr's sister, Elizabeth. In one photo Wilson leers from the window as Elizabeth is in bed with her two sons. In the other photo, Elizabeth, in her housecoat, blocks the door as Wilson and Detective Dickey push their way inside. In *Thrilling Events* Starr angrily reflected on the moment: "The night before the shooting, these fellows . . . acted in a manner unbecoming to officers and gentlemen. The insults to my sister made me nearly crazy, and their threats to shoot me on sight brought about the killing."[12] The inclusion of this scene shows the sympathetic angle Director McGeeney had regarding the incident.

Two lobby cards demonstrate that *A Debtor to the Law* was a first-rate production. In a gorgeous wide shot, the cinematographer Lauren Draper reveals his talent for storytelling in a single frame. Starr stands at the left edge with a rifle to his shoulder. At the far-right edge, McGeeney reacts to the bullet's impact. A silhouette of horseback riders draws the viewer's eye to the horizon line. A second lobby card features a close-up of Starr during a melancholy moment in his jail cell. Amateur productions such as *The Passing of the Oklahoma Outlaws* locked down the camera in a wide shot and never varied their shot selection. McGeeney and Draper understood the language of cinema.

Start Picture

Figure 34 *A Debtor to the Law* (1920) lobby card. Starr, playing himself as a teenager, re-creates the time US deputy marshals (unknown actors) framed him for bringing liquor into the Indian Territory. The deputy marshal (*right*) shows Starr a liquor bottle he found hidden in a valise. Courtesy of the Glenn D. Shirley Western Americana Collection, Dickinson Research Center, National Cowboy & Western Heritage Museum (RC2006.068.32.6.4).

Only one photo exists showing what led to Starr's life of crime. On the lobby card, Starr sits on the buckboard of his horse and wagon with his hands raised. Two US deputy marshals train rifles on him. Starr's face registers surprise and confusion as one marshal shows him a whisky bottle. Although he said Teddy would be playing him as a teenager, it's clearly Starr in the photo. The scene captured Starr's 1889 false arrest by scheming marshals for bringing liquor into the Indian Territory.

McGeeney felt so deeply about this unfortunate incident that he later wrote about it in a short story. As McGeeney told it, Starr was driving a wagon into town to pick up mail for his boss when two men approached him. He offered them a ride, but instead they asked him to deliver two bags to a restaurant owner in town named Curley. Starr knew Curley and was happy to help. He said,

"Sure, put them under my seat." Starr rode off "daydreaming about what he would do when he should become a big cattleman."[13] McGeeney noted that Starr already had a good start with a small spread and a few cattle.

Just as Starr reached the outskirts of town, two mounted US deputy marshals blocked the road. They searched his wagon and found whisky bottles inside the two bags. The deputies hauled Starr to the town jail and locked him up. A lawyer told him he could have the case dismissed if he paid a fee. Starr had no cash, so he signed over his cattle to pay the lawyer. His little ranch was no more.

Later, Starr heard that the deputies and the lawyer were playing cards and laughing about what they had done to him. Starr "saw red," and his first instinct was to kill them. However, while he craved revenge, Starr wasn't a killer.

Instead, "Despair entered his soul," McGeeney wrote. "And drove him on and on to a life of crime."[14]

The Murderers Row Lobby Card

The most intriguing of the *A Debtor to the Law* lobby cards shows the re-creation of Cherokee Bill's bloody escape attempt from Murderers Row at Fort Smith prison. The art department at McGeeney's Shamrock Studios built a realistic prison set on one of its lighted stages. On the lobby card, an actor playing a prison guard lies dead on the floor. To his right, an actor portraying Cherokee Bill and Starr, playing himself, wrestle over a gun. Although it was a beautifully detailed set and the action dramatic, the lobby card had a multitude of historical inaccuracies. More importantly, in retrospect, it reveals a great deal about the state of the film industry and the racial tensions simmering beneath the surface of the country.

The actual Fort Smith prison layout differed significantly from the Shamrock Studios set. McGeeney's crew built a wide passageway with a bank of cells on each side facing each other. Murderers Row at Fort Smith had twelve cells placed back-to-back. Instead of Shamrock's cells with sliding doors made of bars, at Fort Smith each cell had a single, left-hand outswing door covered in woven strap metal. The style of the door was significant because it played a factor in the escape.

Figure 35 *A Debtor to the Law* (1920) lobby card. Starr, playing himself, wrestles a handgun away from Crawford Goldsby (a.k.a. Cherokee Bill, unknown actor), who has shot and killed a guard. The scene was filmed on the prison set built at Shamrock Studios near San Antonio, Texas. The set bears no resemblance to the prison layout at Fort Smith, Arkansas. Goldsby, who was mixed race, is portrayed by a white actor. Courtesy of the Glenn D. Shirley Western Americana Collection, Dickinson Research Center, National Cowboy & Western Heritage Museum (RC2006.068.32.6.7).

Instead of a broad, central passageway like in the Shamrock conception, the actual Fort Smith cells and catwalks were wrapped in a lattice of strap metal—a three-story cage nested inside the prison walls. The iron straps were 3/8 inches thick and 1½ inches wide. Woven diagonally, the straps formed diamond-shaped openings 3½ inches wide. The cells and wrapped catwalk area was called the "bull ring." The guards patrolled safely along the 6-foot corridor outside the cage while prisoners had the freedom to lounge along the catwalk.[15] "This gave them a chance to roughhouse, to swap dirty stories, and to cheat each other at craps and poker," wrote historian Fred Harvey Harrington.[16]

The day re-created for *A Debtor to the Law* was July 26, 1895. Fort Smith prison was overcrowded. It was designed to house 144 inmates, but jailer Capt. J. D. Berry tabulated 181. Typically, the inmates were "a jolly set of vagabonds and rogues,"[17] but on that summer day, it was extremely hot, humid, and stuffy. The heat had turned the smell of feces, urine, and body odor into a visible sheen, rising three levels—from Murderers Row at the bottom to Larceny, level two, and Minor Offenses, level three. Fifty-two-year-old US Marshal George Crump, who resembled Father Time, oversaw the prison. He understood he was sitting on a tinder box, so he allowed the inmates extra time outside their cells to stay cool.

Twenty-one-year-old Starr sat on the catwalk at the widest spot on the south end, next to the shallow water basin. He examined his playing cards, plucking them and arranging them in suits. On that evening, for a brief, tarnished moment, Fort Smith held the vilest killers, rapists, and thieves in the Oklahoma and Indian Territories on one prison floor. Starr looked up from his cards to see most of them sitting across from him—his cellmate Bill Cook, leader of the Cook Gang; Rufus Buck, leader of the Buck Gang; and arranging their own hands, brothers George and John Pierce. The men shifted about, scratching their armpits and crotches. Body lice were prevalent.

The part-Cherokee Cook ran a large gang of seventeen men, and for six months in 1894, they went on a major crime spree, robbing banks, stagecoaches, and stores. Cook had a flair for fashion, wearing a flat-brimmed, round crown bolero hat, a matching black vest, and a Western ascot. George and John Pierce were on Death Row for murdering their traveling companion, William Vandever, and taking his wagon, horses, and mules. Twenty-year-old Rufus Buck, half Black, half Creek, led a gang of Indian and Black teenage boys on a thirteen-day crime spree of robbery, murder, and gang rapes. Buck's whole gang was with him on Murderers' Row, waiting their turn at the gallows.[18]

That day, the most dangerous man in the facility wasn't playing draw poker; Cherokee Bill was sitting in cell no. 20, holding a pistol. The 19 year old was raised in Fort Gibson, like Starr and Cook, but was four years younger. He was rangy, standing half a foot taller than most men, and was an intimidating presence. Although he had killed eight men in his young life,

Cherokee Bill was going to hang for just one—Ernest Melton. The painter and wallpaper hanger from Paris, Texas, had the misfortune of peeking in the window as Cherokee was robbing the H. C. Shufeldt & Son store in Lenapah. Cherokee Bill shot Melton through the window just below the eye, killing him instantly.[19]

Marshal Crump's oversight of the prison was notoriously lax. Justice Department investigators discovered empty whisky bottles under the stairwells, and Crump admitted to allowing prisoners and guards to order spirits. His guards made two dollars a day and were easily susceptible to bribes. Hence, one of the guards, Ed Shelley, arranged for his wife to sneak in a gun under her shawl, and that's why Cherokee Bill had one in his hands on July 26.[20]

At 6:00 p.m. the guards sounded the bell for the prisoners to return to their cells. Starr folded his cards and stood up. Since he'd be locked up overnight, he joined the men lined up at the corner urinal. The prison had no running water, so the urinals were merely access holes cut into a pipe at the corner of the catwalk. The pipe ran from the ground floor to the roof, and as Starr peed, he could hear the urine raining down the pipe from two levels above. Finished, he dipped his hands in a shallow pan of murky water to the side of the urinal to rinse them.

Starr entered cell no. 24, a 5 × 7½ foot brick room without windows. His cellmate, Cook, was lying on one of the two metal bunks. The thin mattresses and bedding were "filthy beyond all reason" and infested with bed bugs. The cell was hot, and the chamber pot called a night bucket reeked of stewed feces. Starr pulled the strap metal cell door closed behind him. He heard the clang of doors echoing throughout the three floors of the building.

On each floor the guards worked in two-man teams to lock the twenty-four cells, arranged back-to-back, twelve east side and twelve west side.[21] For Murderers Row, night guard Lawrence Keating and turnkey R. C. Eoff drew the assignment. They wore matching uniforms: a baggy gray suit and a white dress shirt with the collar clasped by a string tie and topped by a kepi cap. Wearing uniforms was a new requirement. Fort Smith civilians complained that the guards were so slovenly and unkempt they couldn't distinguish them from the prisoners. The guards grumbled about the uniforms, especially since the cost was docked from their pay. The 41-year-old Keating was a popular

Figure 36 Restored section of the Fort Smith prison comprised of brick and steel. A full-sized mannequin, clothed in the guard's uniform, stands on the metal catwalk inside the "bull ring." Urinals are visible in the corner of each floor. Courtesy of Fort Smith National Historic Site, Fort Smith, Arkansas.

guard among the inmates, including Cherokee Bill. He wore his hair closely cropped and sported a bushy mustache and goatee. His job was to remain on the landing outside the bull ring while his partner, Eoff, went inside and locked the cell doors individually. If Eoff encountered trouble, Keating was armed and safely out of reach of the prisoners.

After the prisoners returned to their cells, Eoff unlocked the door on the east side of the bull ring and entered. He dutifully locked the cage door behind him. Eoff left his pistol behind, per policy. On the wall hung a sizeable scythe-shaped lever. Eoff threw it, and a flat iron bar the length of the corridor clanged into place above the odd-numbered cell doors. Thick iron tabs forged along the bottom of the bar prevented the cell doors from swinging open. Fort Smith employed a two-stage security system. In addition to the tab bar, each cell was locked individually. While Eoff progressed along the catwalk, locking each cell, Keating mirrored his movements from outside the bull ring.

Once the east-side cells were secured, Eoff made two rights, placing him on the west-side catwalk. He threw the west-side lever, and once again the iron bar slammed home, this time above the even-numbered prison cell doors housing Cherokee Bill and Starr. George Pierce, normally housed on the east side with his brother, was in Cherokee Bill's cell that evening. It was not unusual for prisoners to switch cells if they desired. Neither Eoff nor Keating noticed that Cherokee Bill had pushed the cell door ajar five inches so the metal tab passed behind the door, leaving it unblocked.

Eoff locked Starr's cell door on the corner first, then moved to no. 22. He inserted his iron key into the hole of the black lockbox, but it met resistance.

"Something's not right with this lock," Eoff called out to Keating, bending down to take a closer look. "Looks like the hole is stuffed with paper."

Keating stepped to the cage for a closer look, placing him directly across the catwalk from Cherokee Bill's cell no. 20. As the guards were distracted by the lock, Cherokee Bill burst from his cell armed with a pistol. Suddenly, Keating had a .38 double-action Colt revolver pointed at his face through the mesh.

"Throw up your goddamn hands, or I'll kill you!" Cherokee Bill growled.

The killer didn't wait for a response. He fired point-blank at Keating's face—but missed.

150   Reel Four

Eoff watched helplessly as Cherokee Bill pulled his gun back from the iron lattice, crouched down, and poked his Colt through a gap two spots lower. He fired two more shots. These struck home.

Keating grabbed his side, and a red stain spread on his white shirt. He staggered backward and threw out his hand, reaching for the radiator behind him for support. As this was happening, George Pierce launched from Cherokee Bill's cell brandishing a broken table leg. Pierce sprinted toward Eoff threateningly. Eoff scrambled around the southwest corner. Cherokee Bill fired at Eoff, bullets pinging off the metal cage behind his head.

Day guards William "Uncle Bill" McConnell, Brass Parker, and George Lawson were on the prison lawn when they heard the first shots and raced inside. McConnell arrived in time to see Keating stumble down the corridor and collapse face-first. The day guard turned him over. Keating's cheek was powder burnt from the shot that just missed his face. He mumbled a few unintelligible words to McConnell, and then the father of four died. Keating's gun had never been drawn in his defense, and McConnell pulled it from its scabbard.

Meanwhile, Eoff turned the southeast corner and sprinted up the east-side catwalk to the north bull ring exit. Since he'd secured that corridor, no inmates were outside their cells. To his horror, Eoff realized he'd left his keys in the lock of cell no. 22. Just then, bullets pinged above his head. Eoff looked back, and Cherokee Bill was firing at him from the southeast corner and George Pierce was advancing. He was pinned down. Day guard Lawson arrived at the bull ring exit where Eoff was cowering. He drove Cherokee Bill and George Pierce back to the west side with a hail of bullets.

With the coast clear, day guard Arch Stockton arrived with keys and unlocked the east-side bull ring door, freeing Eoff.

When Cherokee Bill reappeared back on the west side, McConnell was waiting for him. Bullets ricocheted wildly due to iron latticework. Then, day guard Lawson arrived at McConnell's side. Thirty rounds were exchanged in the fusillade before Cherokee Bill and George Pierce were forced to seek cover back in their west-side cells.

When Marshal Crump arrived, day guard Stockton unlocked the east-side bull ring door for him. As Crump maneuvered through the low-hanging gun smoke on the catwalk, the acrid smell of black powder bit at his sinuses. He turned at the southeast corner and squatted near Starr's cell. The *AHTA Weekly News* described the moment: "The jailer, the United States marshal, and deputy marshals were all brave men, but not one of them fancied the task of entering the steel cage and trying to disarm Cherokee Bill."[22]

Marshal Crump called out to Starr, "How much ammunition do you think Bill has on 'im?"

"Enough to kill all of your men if you give him a chance," Starr answered frankly.[23]

Marshal Crump swallowed hard, picturing his prison littered with the bodies of dead guards.

Hang 'em High!

While Crump grimly considered the bloody consequences of advancing on Cherokee Bill's cell, the outlaw fired a bullet down the catwalk.[24] Cherokee Bill followed the gunshot with a throaty turkey gobble.

"What in tarnation is that?" Crump asked, shuddering.

"Some say it's a Creek War Cry," Starr said. "And death is imminent."

"I don't want any more of my men killed," Crump said, his Father Time eyebrows knitted with worry.

"Want me to try and get the gun?" Starr offered.

"You'd do that, Henry?"

"You got to promise not to kill Bill when he's disarmed."

"You have my word."

Marshal Crump unlocked Starr's cell door, and he gingerly stepped out onto the catwalk. As he eased his way closer to Cherokee Bill's cell, he called out, "Bill, it's Henry. I'm coming your way."

Cherokee Bill fired another round down the catwalk and gobbled. Starr swallowed hard. He'd known the outlaw since they were both kids— when he still went by his birth name, Crawford Goldsby. Still, Starr knew Cherokee Bill was desperate and wouldn't hesitate to put a bullet through his head.

"I ain't got nothing on me," Starr called out. "I just want to talk."

When Starr reached the cell, his heart was pounding. Through the bull ring cage, he could see the jittery guards on the landing, ready to fire at any moment.

"I'm at the door, Bill, and I'm coming inside."

Starr did as he said and entered the dark cell.

Marshal Crump anxiously checked his pocket watch. Minutes ticked by with no sound from the jail cell. He looked at the tense faces of the guards on the landing. They kept watch on the prison cell, fingers tight on the triggers.

Then, the cell door slowly swung open.

Starr emerged carefully.

"I've got the gun," he announced, holding it aloft.

The Murderers Row lobby card showed Starr wrestling the gun from Cherokee Bill in a dramatic confrontation. It wasn't until Starr wrote *Thrilling Events* that the public knew what really took place inside Cherokee Bill's cell: "I told him that he could not possibly get out—that he might be able to kill a few more guards, but that would avail nothing, and to take my advice and give his gun to me, which he did, loaded all round."[25] While the facts were less dramatic, the impact of Starr's heroism was profound.

Crump would later say Starr's heroism was exaggerated. He said Cherokee Bill was ready to surrender and had given up the idea of killing more guards. "Starr simply took the gun in an orderly fashion," Crump told the *Boone County Headlight*.[26] One wonders, if it was so easy, why didn't Crump do it himself?

Whether or not *A Debtor to the Law* had any scenes showing the demise of the men and boys on Murderers Row is not known—but it would have been cinematic. Following the failed Cherokee Bill jailbreak, Starr watched from his cell door as each of his fellow poker players marched to the gallows. The parade played out to the somber scratching of Cherokee Bill's bow across the strings of his violin. On the day of his hanging, March 17, 1896, Cherokee Bill rose at 6:00 a.m., whistling merrily as he dressed. He knew he had an audience. Marshal Crump had invited reporters and privileged members of Fort Smith society to gather along the guard's landing to watch the killer's last day on earth. Cherokee Bill's mother and another woman who raised him as a child visited him in his cell. They found him sitting in the dark on a low chair, his ankles in chains. Cherokee Bill told them about the numerous visitors he'd had that week, including a man who paid him a dollar to take his photo. Another man asked Bill's permission to film the hanging on his motion picture Kinetoscope. Cherokee Bill didn't mind having someone film his death, but he felt he should be paid. At 2:00 p.m. the guards came for him. After kissing his mother on the cheek, Cherokee Bill was escorted from his cell and down the catwalk in shackles.[27]

Outside, at the northwest Fort Smith sally port, a crowd formed a gauntlet from the prison to the gallows fence. Scheduling the hanging to coincide with St. Patrick's Day created a festival atmosphere. Fort Smith residents buzzed with excitement; many were reportedly "deep into the cups." When Cherokee Bill stepped outside, he filled his lungs and then exhaled with a smile. "Today is a fine day to die," he proclaimed for all to hear. Cherokee Bill was determined to appear unrepentant and unafraid to meet his maker. He walked boldly toward the gallows and stepped through the gate. Once inside the fenced-off area, Cherokee Bill caught his first glimpse of the gallows, painted white and gleaming in the sunlight. He thought the gibbet was sturdy enough to hold eight men his size.

Cherokee Bill climbed the twelve steps to the top of the scaffold. The crowd craned their necks upward in unison as the gangly killer rose eight feet above their heads. Cherokee Bill turned and saw a dozen three-foot trap doors arrayed directly below the gibbet. Only one had an eight-inch diameter hemp rope—oiled and stretched—dangling above it. Cherokee Bill walked to his spot and placed his large feet on the wooden square. It was hinged on two sides and poised to drop open in the middle. Marshal Crump asked if he had any last words. Cherokee Bill said simply, "The quicker it's over, the better it is."

Then, it was time for the hangman, George Maledon, to begin his duty. He was a fussy little man who wore his best suit with a pistol belted tightly over his jacket in plain view. An exclamation point between his dark, furry eyebrows gave Maledon a stormy expression attesting to the seriousness of the occasion and his fastidiousness in orchestrating the hanging. Maledon's shiny, bald pate stretched from his eyebrows to the top of his head. The lack of hair was offset by a voluminous white mustache and beard spraying from his nostrils as if his nose were a spigot.[28]

Maledon stepped forward and tugged a black bag over Cherokee Bill's head. Before everything went dark, his last vision was of his audience— the electric thrill of anticipation arcing through the crowd, vendors hawking treats, and deputy marshals serving as ticket takers. Late arriving spectators were hustled through the high gate. The curtain was about to rise as the trap door was about to drop.

Maledon looped the noose around Cherokee Bill's neck, then fussed with the big knot so that it lay under the left ear in the hollow behind the jawbone to ensure it would snap cleanly.[29] The crowd held its breath. The US marshal flashed a signal to the hangman, who sprung the trap door mechanism. Cherokee Bill dropped through. The gibbet caught the slack, and his neck cracked. The crowd gasped and then watched in silence. The rope squeaked as his suspended body twirled slowly. Guards above loosed the rope and lowered Cherokee Bill's body into a cart below. The scaffold was backstopped to a stone wall. A wooden door in the center opened up. The cart bearing Cherokee Bill's corpse disappeared through the door, the body to be delivered to his mother.

The brothers George and John Pierce met their fate on April 30, 1896— dying as they lived—together.[30] They took the same path from the prison to the gallows as Cherokee Bill but with much less fanfare. When the siblings arrived at the gallows gate, their sister was waiting with a small boy. John Pierce asked the guard to remove his handcuffs for a moment. He then picked up his 4-year-old son and kissed him tenderly, tears streaming down his face. Women dabbed their eyes at the scene. George and John Pierce were then led to the scaffold. The brothers kneeled on their individual trap doors and repeated after the priest, "Merciful Jesus, have mercy on me and forgive me my sins." Then the brothers stood up, feet firmly placed on their wooden squares. Maledon performed his ritual duties, concluding with throwing the trap door spring.

On July 1, 1896, Starr observed a man pass his cell wearing a simple black cassock and carrying a small suitcase.[31] He was Father Pius of the Fort Smith German Catholic Church. That morning the priest had visited Rufus Buck and each member of his gang. One by one, in every cell, he unpacked his case and laid out a chalice, vials of water, and oil of catechumens, among other sacred paraphernalia. Father Pius began by asking each of them to

Start Picture   155

renounce Satan and confess their sins. They described their vile acts carried out over thirteen days.[32] Their bloody crime spree began with the armed robbery of a grocery store in Okmulgee. They shot and killed town Marshal John Garrett when he tried to stop them. Next, they overcame a wagon driven by Mrs. Wilson and her 14-year-old son. The gang sent the boy on ahead while they kept his mother and raped her.

Two days later the gang invaded the home of Mr. and Mrs. Henry Hassan and ordered her to cook them dinner. Then while holding the husband at gunpoint, they gang raped and murdered his wife. Afterward, they dragged Mr. Hassan into the woods and forced him and another man at gunpoint to wrestle in a mudhole. Later, the gang accosted a man on the road and took his horse, saddle, and gold watch. They took a vote on whether to kill him. His life was spared 3–2. A stockman, Bent Callahan, had all his clothing taken at gunpoint, and they shot at him as he fled naked. The farmhand with him—some reports said he was a boy—was killed in cold blood. In the town of Natura, Oklahoma, they came upon a woman still weakened from a recent childbirth and gang raped her. They pillaged another grocery before they were captured by lawmen and one hundred Creek citizens armed to the teeth.

Father Pius ended his visit by perfuming each member of the Rufus Buck Gang with scented oil as a symbol of the gift of the Holy Spirit. Newly baptized, they were forgiven all previous sins, original, venial, and mortal. The public later learned that the Rufus Buck Gang kept a strange and heinous oath. Any act one committed, the others had to perform as well upon punishment of death—thus, the gang rapes.[33] Now, they would continue that wretched vow in their final act.

Rufus led the procession to the gallows. He and the boys ascended the steps without trepidation. Each took their position on a trap door, a noose dangling above their heads. The young men listened quietly as their death warrant was read. Then, trap doors opened, the condemned dropped, and their necks snapped—except Rufus Buck. He fought and spun for several minutes before finally strangling to death. Unlike the Cherokee Bill spectacle, fewer than two dozen people showed up to watch the Rufus Buck Gang depart from the earth.[34]

A Black-and-White Peacock

In January 1920, while *A Debtor to the Law* was being edited, P. J. Clark and Pan-American sought a company to handle the marketing. They hired T. E. Larson, head of Peacock Productions, who had experience as a film promoter and controlled the exchange for Equity Pictures.[35] Larson had recently opened Peacock's offices in Tulsa's Drexel building at 319 S. Main Street and fitted the space out with new office furniture and finishings.[36] The four-story building was distinctive for its three large arched windows with white stone eyebrows. A year and a half later, the building would become infamous as the spark for the Tulsa Race Massacre.[37]

To entice exhibitors to order a particular film, companies like Peacock Productions produced press books with photos of the film's stars and scenes from the film, ready-to-clip articles to supply newspapers, and suggestions for promotional stunts.[38] For *A Debtor to the Law*, Peacock's book was a slick four-sided newspaper with a sample poster made of cardboard called a herald tucked inside. The headline for Starr's press book read, "A Debtor to the Law, The Man Who Stole a Million." Below that was a note to exhibitors: "It was an instinct for showmanship that brought you into this business—whether you realized it or not. Here's your chance to let out on a showman's show."

A clever promotional "Super Stunt" tailored explicitly to Starr's story was the inclusion of a faux "wanted" poster featuring a glamor photo of him wearing a white Stetson and a suit and tie. Theatre owners were encouraged to post them around town on busy streets. The public would see "WANTED" at the top and "REWARD" at the bottom in all caps and think it was real. A closer look revealed it was an advertisement: "WANTED, Henry Starr, Last of the Great Western Outlaws wants every man who dreamed when he was a boy of becoming a bandit—and every woman who knows such a man—to know what an outlaw's life really is and what it leads to. See 'A Debtor to the Law' at the _____ Theatre on _____, and more thrills than you've ever had packed into one evening will be your REWARD."

Clip-ready articles touted the former outlaw's acting prowess: "[Starr's] work in the picture is a revelation. Never is there a touch of the amateurish.

Figure 37 *A Debtor to the Law* (1920) press book featuring clip-ready articles, advertisements, and a "super-stunt" featuring an ersatz "Wanted" poster. Note the heavy makeup on Starr (in the white hat) in the group lobby card photo (*right*), making him appear white. Author's collection.

158   Reel Four

He acts with the authority of a veteran of the big screen." Other articles
compared Starr to top Hollywood talent, arguing that his real-life story
made the imaginary exploits of "Bill Hart, Tom Mix, et al., fade to a pale
pink." Starr was old friends with Mix since their days working on the Miller
brothers' 101 Ranch in 1907. While Starr didn't like actors pretending to be
cowboys, he had the utmost respect for Mix, who had been a ranch foreman,
Texas Ranger, and Rough Rider. "He rides like thunder, knows how to use
a gun, can use a rope," Starr said. "In fact, he's Western stuff all over."[39]
One article suggested that had Starr not been forced into outlawry, he might
have become as big a star as Douglas Fairbanks.[40]

In case exhibitors doubted the quality of the film, the campaign book
reassured them: "There's a regular Los Angeles director on the job, with
puttees and megaphone and all the rest of it." In addition, Starr, the King of
Bank Robbers, choreographed the robbery scenes, assuring their authenticity:
"The big scenes which he took a hand in directing are remarkable for their
fidelity, though the men in them are not experienced extras casually hired, but
largely those who were his friends and his enemies in the years when Starr
and society were at war." Articles touted Starr's bona fides as an outlaw with
headlines like "Greater Than Jesse" followed by "head and shoulders above
Jesse and Frank James, the Daltons, Al Jennings and the rest."

The press book provided articles to head off a backlash from women's
organizations. One article suggested that city governments supported Starr:
"Public officials in Oklahoma who have developed the most whole-hearted
respect for Henry Starr since he 'turned square' are watching the building
of 'A Debtor to the Law' with the deepest interest." They believed Starr's
biography would prove "a mighty strong warning for the youngster and man
who doubts that the straight path is the best." The article, conveniently, did
not name those supportive public officials.

In case people thought Starr was cashing in on his infamy, the article
"Oil Strike Makes Outlaw Wealthy" said he didn't need the money
because he'd recently struck oil on his Osage allotment. "If the gushers
keep flowing at the rate they've started, Starr soon will have put more
money back into banks of the West than he ever took out of them," the
article suggested. Another article stated that because of the oil well,

Start Picture 159

"The outlaw soon will be in possession of an income running into the hundreds of thousands annually."

The press book was filled with half-truths and, occasionally, bald-faced lies. One headline stated, "Never a 'Killer'"—an odd claim considering the murder of Floyd Wilson is featured in the film. Another article, "The Rope Was Ready," blurs the matter further, suggesting Starr was going to be hanged for stealing Charles Eaton's horse. The truth was Judge Isaac Parker twice sentenced Starr to hang for Wilson's murder.

The first trial began in 1893, at Fort Smith, home to the First District Court of the Western District of Arkansas. Starr called Parker the "Nero of America,"[41] referring to Nero Claudius Caesar Augustus Germanicus, the fifth emperor of Rome, who burned Christians alive in the service of perverted justice.[42] Most people called him "Hanging Judge" Parker because he sent seventy-nine men to gallows.[43]

Starr's defense attorneys felt confident the jury would only convict him on the lesser charge of manslaughter. However, the defendant wasn't so optimistic. "What chance had I, a noted outlaw, of a different race, before a jury in the town where Wilson had lived for years?" Starr asked rhetorically.[44] On November 4, 1893, the jury returned a verdict of guilty of murder in the first degree, which Starr knew "meant the rope." Judge Parker sentenced him to hang four months from that day on January 20, 1894.[45] Starr's lawyers immediately filed an appeal to the Supreme Court in forma pauperis, meaning he had no money to pay for it.[46] Seven months later, Parker's death sentence was reversed in *Starr v. the United States*. The justices found Parker's jury instructions prejudicial, particularly regarding Starr's claim of self-defense. Chief Justice Melville Weston Fuller wrote, "This Cherokee when riding across the country was entitled to protect his life, although he may have forfeited a bond, and been seeking to avoid arrest on that account."[47]

During the first trial, Starr had no witnesses for his defense because Fort Smith was too far to travel. For his retrial Starr's sister Lizzie testified that Wilson and Detective Dickey broke into her house by force and threatened to shoot her brother on sight.[48] Other witnesses stated Wilson didn't produce a warrant to Starr and fired first. Starr was hopeful for a reduced conviction on manslaughter charges. The jury convened for only one hour before returning

160 Reel Four

another guilty verdict for first-degree murder. Starr called them "a pack of idiots."[49] Judge Parker ordered Starr to hang a second time. "He sentenced me twice to the hemp, but I never batted an eye," Starr wrote. "I was young and foolish in the head in those days."[50]

Starr appealed to the Supreme Court a second time and, once again, the justices reversed Parker's decision. Justice Edward Douglass White questioned Parker's jury instructions stating Starr's flight from an arrest warrant constituted guilt.[51] The case was remanded, and the court was ordered to conduct a new trial.

By the time Starr's third trial came around in October 1898, Judge Parker had died of Bright's disease at 58 and the gallows had been taken down.[52] Under a new judge, John R. Rogers, Starr pleaded guilty to manslaughter, and the court sentenced him to serve fifteen years at the Ohio State Penitentiary. Starr later reflected on his gunfight with Dickey and Wilson: "I had promised myself never to shoot unless it was to save my own life and have never had any qualms of conscience over that occurrence. It was simply a case of their lives or mine. They started the fireworks."[53]

From the age of 19, Starr would never take another life.

Two Coats of Whitewash

Surviving *A Debtor to the Law* lobby cards and movie posters help piece together what audiences would have seen in the theater, but viewed through a contemporary lens, they also reveal how the production was strongly influenced by racial unrest. In two very important instances, Pan-American whitewashed history—once with the casting of "Cherokee Bill," and second with the marketing of Henry Starr.

The First Coat: Casting Cherokee Bill

Tina Harris, PhD, professor and endowed chair of Race, Media, and Cultural Literacy at Louisiana State University, defined whitewashing as the casting of performers without accurately reflecting the physical, racial, ethnic, and cultural markers of a group to which the character belongs. Doing so "reinforces the belief that whiteness is superior to all other groups

Start Picture   161

and renders BIPOC (Black, Indigenous, [and] People of Color) invisible and voiceless."[54]

Crawford Goldsby (nicknamed Cherokee Bill) was born in San Angelo, Texas, on February 8, 1876. Goldsby's father, George, was mixed race, including white and Sioux. He had family from Mexico and served as a Buffalo Soldier in the 10th Cavalry. Ellen Lynch, his mother, had mixed Black, Cherokee, and white ancestry.[55] "Cherokee Bill" presented as Black, but Pan-American cast a white actor in the role. To understand President P. J. Clark's decision, one must look at the sociopolitical landscape of Oklahoma and Texas during the time *A Debtor to the Law* was filmed (1919 to 1920) and recognize that casting a Black actor in a film meant for white audiences was illegal and potentially deadly.

Despite the passage of the Thirteenth Amendment to the Constitution in January 1865 abolishing slavery in the United States, Southern states enacted Black Codes to deny Blacks access to hotels, schools, and theaters. Over time these restrictions became legislation and were colloquially called Jim Crow laws.[56] "Jim Crow" entered the lexicon as a derogatory name for black people in 1820 when a white actor named Thomas Rice performed in blackface. He danced and sang a song with the lyric "Every time I wheel about, I jump Jim Crow." Rice's concept was a hit, and minstrel shows mocking Black people became the rage.[57] Under Jim Crow laws, train cars, water fountains, restrooms, building entrances, elevators, and cemeteries were all segregated.[58] White actors and Black actors were not allowed to appear together on stage, so if a play, such as Harriet Beecher Stowe's *Uncle Tom's Cabin*, written in 1852, was performed, Black characters were played by white actors in blackface.

The advent of motion pictures didn't alter how society viewed Black performers. In the film adaptation of *Uncle Tom's Cabin* (1903), directed by William S. Porter, Uncle Tom was portrayed by a white actor in blackface. Over a decade passed before a Black actor, Sam Lucas, played the Uncle Tom role in the 1914 remake of *Uncle Tom's Cabin* directed by William Robert Daly.[59] Lucas's achievement was an anomaly. A year later, in D. W. Griffith's *Birth of a Nation* (1915), white actors in blackface portrayed characters representing stereotypes ascribed by historian Donald

Figure 38 Notorious outlaw Crawford Goldsby (a.k.a. Cherokee Bill) with his mother, Ellen Lynch. On July 26, 1895, he attempted a violent escape from Fort Smith prison, killing one guard. Starr, a fellow death row inmate, negotiated his peaceful surrender. Goldsby was hung on March 17, 1896. Courtesy of the Oklahoma Historical Society.

Bogle as "toms, coons, mulattoes, mammies, and bucks." Audiences lacking sophistication to cinematic manipulation believed these stereotypical representations of Black Americans were accurate.[60] Griffith, as director, perpetrated the norm that an actor had to be a white person in blackface if a Black character and a white character appeared together on-screen—especially if the Black character shared the screen with a white woman. Demonstrating that whites and Blacks were kept separate on motion picture sets was especially important to producers seeking to mollify racist audiences in the Jim Crow south.[61]

Four years following the release of *Birth of a Nation*, racial tensions had exacerbated. At the close of World War I, Black soldiers returning from France and Black families who had worked for the war effort at home expected that whites would accept them with a new level of appreciation and equality.[62] Instead, from April to November 1919, racial violence erupted across the United States from Texas to Nebraska and from Connecticut to California. Twenty-five riots led to fifty-two lynchings of Black people, hundreds of additional Black and white deaths due to other violence, and countless injuries. Thousands of Black people fled their homes seeking shelter in safer locations. As historian Cameron McWhirter explained in his book *Red Summer: The Summer of 1919 and the Awakening of Black America*, "In almost every case, white mobs—whether sailors on leave, immigrant slaughterhouse workers, or southern farmers—initiated the violence." The racial tensions of Red Summer would continue to percolate and finally explode in 1921 with the Tulsa Race Massacre, "the deadliest outbreak of white terrorist violence against a black community in American history."[63]

A Debtor to the Law began filming in November 1919 at the tail end of Red Summer when the weather cooled but tensions still simmered. There is no evidence producer P. J. Clark or Starr ever debated the casting of Cherokee Bill. However, the racial unrest and Jim Crow laws make it unlikely they had any options. Despite the *A Debtor to the Law* press book stating Starr "has the right to get things done before the camera as they really were done in life,"[64] Pan-American opted for casting a menacing-looking white actor with a five o'clock shadow to portray Cherokee Bill, ignoring both racial identity and accuracy.

The Second Coat: Marketing Henry Starr

The second case of whitewashing involved the manipulation of Starr's ethnicity. In *Thrilling Events* Starr identified himself as having "Scotch-Irish Indian" ancestry. "My father, George Starr was a half-blood Cherokee Indian; my mother, Mary Scott, is one-quarter Cherokee," Starr wrote.[65] Based on photographs and descriptions of Starr, he presented as Native American. In *Thrilling Events* Starr joked, "It don't take the second look at me to see that I'm not a Swede."[66] Alexander Huling, who held a dinner for Starr and his gang following the Caney Valley bank robbery, sketched Starr as "every inch an Indian with his high cheekbones and dark swarthy skin."[67] The *Bartlesville Daily Enterprise* wrote, "He is plainly Indian. Any Oklahoman who has lived here long enough to distinguish the howl of a coyote from that of a spaniel couldn't be fooled over the question of Starr's ancestry."[68]

Yet Peacock Productions and Pan-American muddied Starr's ethnicity. The *A Debtor to the Law* press book only mentions his heritage jokingly: "You've got to be something of a mathematician to figure out the exact proportion of aboriginal blood that runs in his veins."[69] In a black-and-white on-set photo, Starr wears so much light pancake makeup he looks ghostly.[70] In the early silent era, the main characters often wore lighter makeup so they stood out from the rest of the cast.[71] That could be the case since Starr's skin tone appears natural in other black-and-white publicity photos, including the faux wanted poster.[72] However, the goal of whitewashing his ethnicity becomes apparent in one full-color poster for *A Debtor to the Law*. The image is a head and shoulders painting of Starr wearing a cowboy hat and pointing a gun directly at the viewer. Starr appears fair-complexioned, rosy-cheeked, and with light, sandy hair.

Why were Peacock Productions and Pan-American intent on hiding Starr's ethnicity? Native Americans on film hadn't always been a risky proposition. Eight years before *A Debtor to the Law,* self-proclaimed Winnebago James Young Deer ran Pathé's West Coast studio in Edendale (now Silverlake, four miles north of Los Angeles).[73] Young Deer directed two films, *The Cheyenne Brave* (1911) and *The Red Girl and the Child* (1911), and produced others that addressed Indian assimilation, miscegenation, and racism. His wife and writing/producing partner Lillian Red Wing (a.k.a. Lillian St. Cyr), a member of

Figure 39 *A Debtor to the Law* (1920) movie poster. In full color Starr is shown with a fair complexion, rosy cheeks, and light, sandy-colored hair, whitewashing his Cherokee heritage for motion picture audiences. Author's collection.

the Nebraska Winnebago reservation, would act in her husband's one-reelers while headlining *In the Days of the Thundering Herd* (Selig, 1914) with Tom Mix; *The Squaw Man* (Lasky, 1914), directed by Cecil B. DeMille; and *White Oak* (Paramount, 1921) with William S. Hart.[74]

There was no segregated infrastructure for Native American films, so Young Deer's productions were seen by mainstream audiences. In 1912, having a cast of in-house "full blood" and "half-blood" Native American talent was a reason for Vitagraph, Thanhouser, and Selig's motion picture companies to boast.[75] Slowly, the depiction of Native Americans on film devolved. Scenarios no longer characterized them as the "noble savage" but simply as savages. Louis Reeves Harrison, a top film reviewer for the national publication *Moving Picture World*, summed up the opinion of many white viewers toward Native Americans: "The average descendent of colonial families has little use for the red man, regards him with distrust and, with poetic exceptions, considers him hopelessly beyond the pale of social contact."[76]

Simultaneous to Peacock Productions and Pan-American marketing *A Debtor to the Law*, Pathé released *Lahoma*, a melodrama about the Oklahoma Land Rush.[77] A *Moving Picture World* review characterized the settlers as "hardy citizens" and the Indians as "murderous." The poster showed a white family in a covered wagon being attacked by Indians wearing war bonnets and carrying rifles. The era of Young Deer and Red Wing was over. Pathé, no longer concerned with authenticity, cast Will Jefferis as Red Feather and Yvette Mitchell as Red Fawn. The *Lahoma* poster showed the Native Americans as a violent threat to white settlers, but in the scenario, its white men dressed as Indians who massacred the innocent women and children in the wagon train. The poster took advantage of anti–Native American sentiment and fear to sell tickets.

Starr's feet were planted in two worlds. In *Thrilling Events* he wrote, "I have more white blood than Indian, and with my knowledge of both races, I fervently wish that every drop in my veins was R.E.D."[78]

The marketing of Henry Starr as white in *A Debtor to the Law* was a financial decision. In the noxious climate of Jim Crow laws and films like *Lahoma*, Pan-American and perhaps even Starr took the pragmatic approach and opted for whitewashing.

Shameless Exhibitionists

In April 1920 Pan-American Motion Pictures Corporation sent out printed invitations for a private screening of *A Debtor to the Law* at Lawrence Brophy's New Yale in Muskogee. The original "Old" Yale had been primitive and seedy. Over the years, Brophy improved the theater experience by expanding to 230 seats, pitching the flooring so seats in the rear had a better view, and installing an electric piano. In 1915 he built a new theater at 208 West Broadway, adding an elegant lobby that gave patrons the immersive feeling of entering a grand experience. Five years later the New Yale theater had 1,000 seats and electric lights framing the marquee. At 10:30 a.m. on April 8, Starr, local investors, and special guests passed beneath the grand archway and took their seats to watch the outlaw's life unspool on screen.[79]

After the screening the scene that stuck in viewers' minds was the reenactment of Floyd Wilson's murder. Bridget Wilson, the bounty hunter's widow, had died the prior week, so the name was fresh in people's minds. Mrs. Wilson's life as a widow had been difficult. At 55 she was declared insane and committed to the state asylum in Vinita. Her sons said she'd been suffering from hallucinations of an impending disaster. In 1917 the *Muskogee Times-Democrat* reported, "Mrs. Wilson never fully recovered from her husband's tragic death, although her physician stated during the sanity hearing that he didn't think Wilson's murder was the cause of her present affliction."[80] She died in the asylum three years later.

A reporter asked Starr if the murder of Wilson had been a revenge killing because the deputy marshal had arrested him as a boy for horse thievery. Starr clarified, "I had never been arrested by Wilson, and there was no hatred between him and I at the time of the shooting." Starr said he wouldn't have shot Wilson if the hired gun hadn't fired upon him first. "As soon as they started shooting, it was plain to me that there was no alternative."[81]

The *Muskogee Times-Democrat* reported that the premiere screening of *A Debtor to the Law* "made an excellent impression." Within days Pan-American planned a wide release of the film. P. J. Clark was confident that theaters would be willing to risk showing a quality bandit picture with a moral message. He boasted that *A Debtor to the Law* was already booked

168   . Reel Four

in several theaters in Oklahoma and didn't expect any trouble securing dates
months in advance.[82] Clark may have been putting on a brave face. Towns like
Nowata had already refused to show *A Debtor to the Law*.[83] The city still held
a grudge against Starr because he'd robbed the train depot in July 1892—
twenty-eight years earlier.[84]

Due to the self-censorship agreement TOMA had made with state and
federal lawmakers, *A Debtor to the Law* was shut out of the largest theaters in major cities. Small theater owners, however, weren't beholden to
TOMA and could decide for themselves which motion picture to screen.
Clark hoped to capitalize on the disgruntlement small time exhibitors felt.
They were routinely treated as second-class citizens by film distributors—
called exchanges—because they had fewer seats and charged less. Times had
changed, and not in favor of the little guy.

At the dawn of motion pictures there was no need for film exchanges
to manage distribution. Nickelodeon owners (exhibitors) purchased films
by the foot directly from manufacturers (producers). No matter the genre
or quality, early motion pictures were priced based on the running time.
Exhibitors owned the film and could show it as often as they wanted.[85]
However, the mania for movies meant "motion picture fans" were going
to the theater "once a day, if not two or three times a day."[86] Hence, exhibitors churned through the offerings quickly and audiences demanded
fresh films weekly. Suddenly, exhibitors found themselves with stacks of
one-reel motion pictures customers were no longer interested in watching. To add variety to their programs, theater owners started trading the
films they'd purchased like baseball cards. Sharing films soon morphed
into a new business model. Ambitious theater owners who had capital
began purchasing films from manufacturers and then renting them to
smaller theaters. Under this exchange system, film reels kept moving and
not collecting dust.

A few years later, studios such as Universal, Goldwyn, Essanay, Vitagraph, Mutual, Pathé, Metro, and Fox cut out the middleman and opened
their own exchanges, handling the delivery and distribution of their films.
Initially, the big studio exchanges operated on the coasts (New York
and San Francisco) or in major cities like Chicago. Paramount Pictures
founder W. W. Hodkinson brought order to the distribution system by

Start Picture 169

prioritizing cities by size and their theaters by capacity.[87] Consequently, the latest motion pictures took months to arrive in Oklahoma, especially in rural areas. A theater owner in Cordell, Oklahoma, keenly observed, "The exchange has not got the time to fool with us 'little folks' as they call us in small, country towns."[88]

In March 1920 Fred Pickrel from the Pathé exchange remarked in *Moving Picture World* that Oklahoma was "the richest little piece of ground in the entire country."[89] The Dallas exchanges were sending two hundred films a day through Oklahoma City, bringing in $4 million in business annually.[90] However, shipping from Texas meant long delays for exhibitors in eastern Oklahoma and Arkansas. Recognizing the financial benefit of rapid expansion, in the fall of 1920, Vitagraph Film Company, Universal, Fox, Mutual, and Metro opened offices on South Hudson Street in Oklahoma City.[91]

A Debtor to the Law was being released in the spring of 1920, meaning there was an opportunity for P. J. Clark to appeal to the "little folks" running a small-town theater before the new exchanges got up and running. To survive financially Pan-American would have to go "old school," as Tilghman had done in 1916, driving film cans of *The Passing of the Oklahoma Outlaws* from city to city, state to state, sometimes combining his travels into a camping trip with his wife Zoe and their two young boys.[92]

P. J. Clark knew *A Debtor to the Law* would still face opposition from every small-minded city council, ministerial leader, and women's organization who had read in the newspapers how bandit pictures corrupted children. Pan-American would need a choir boy as a sales agent.

Of all places, they found him in the town most closely associated with Starr as a notorious bandit—Stroud.

The Choir Boy

His name was George Dewey Peck, usually just called Dewey. He'd been a precocious public speaker since he was 12 and was the star performer in Stroud High School plays. During war drives Peck would do impersonations, sing popular ditties, and tell jokes, taking jabs at the kaiser.[93] He was the exact type of bright young man women's groups and religious leaders yearned to protect from the corruptible influence of bandit pictures.

170   Reel Four

At 19 Peck and his pal Roy White opened the Rialto motion picture theater in a vacant building along Stroud's business district—the same street Starr and his gang rode in on the day before the double bank robbery. The *Stroud Messenger* reported that Peck and White had obtained "a fine motion picture machine" and pitched the flooring "to create a more agreeable viewing angle."[94] For the grand opening on July 22, 1919, Peck asked the Stroud High School band to play during the ribbon cutting.[95] The Peck and White enterprise was so successful that six months later they remodeled the space, adding dressing rooms and expanding the stage to include vaudeville acts as part of the program.[96]

By April 1920, the Rialto screened "high class" pictures, including *Heart o' the Hills*, produced by and starring Mary Pickford. Never mind that due to film exchanges, the film had been a stale release from six months earlier.[97] But that same month, over two nights—Friday, April 30, and Saturday, May 1—the Rialto would have the honor of hosting the worldwide debut of *A Debtor to the Law*, just as P. J. Clark and Starr promised. "Many Stroud citizens will be shown in this picture," the newspaper reminded readers. The Rialto newspaper advertisement promised "scenes of the surrounding country, where the outlaw band camped the night before the double bank robbery at Stroud, giving a reproduction of both gangs up until they were marching away with the money when Henry Starr was shot."[98]

The following week, *A Debtor to the Law* screened at Tulsa's Royal for a four-night run. The local newspaper featured a photo of Starr on horseback holding a rifle, with William Karl Hackett standing next to him. The text read, "A story with a moral showing the utter futility of crime and its outcome, based upon the life of Henry Starr, who after 30 years, half of the time an outlaw, half the time in prison—speaks to the world and says the law must be obeyed."[99]

Peck's amiable personality and business acumen made a good impression on P. J. Clark and Starr. Shortly after the Rialto screening, they hired him as their advance man. His first assignment would be a tough one. Members of the Okemah City Council, the mayor, and town pastors prohibited *A Debtor to the Law* to be seen by its residents.[100] Undaunted, Peck jumped into his Ford runabout and drove forty miles from Stroud to the Okemah City Hall to meet with them. Although only a teenager, Peck mustered the same mixture

Start Picture   171

of charm and sincerity that would later help him be elected a state legislator. His task wouldn't be easy. Colonel James E. Burke, owner of Okemah's Crystal Theatre, was a member of TOMA and had signed on to the resolution in March to show "no more Al Jennings and Henry Starr pictures." He agreed that bandit pictures had a bad influence on the young and declared boldly that no "beating back class of pictures" would be displayed in Okemah in the future.[101] Peck told Burke that as a fellow theater owner, he, too, initially had grave misgivings about showing *A Debtor to the Law*. His friends and neighbors trusted him to provide wholesome entertainment, and Henry Starr's bandit picture might break that bond. However, Peck said he was thoroughly impressed with the moving picture, and its message of moral uplift was clear. Peck repeated the words from the Rialto advertisement copy: Starr's capture at Stroud was "the cause of his change for a better life." He added that even the citizens of Stroud didn't hold a grudge against Starr for the robberies and clamored to be in his moving picture. Peck didn't win his audience over completely, but Burke and the other civic leaders agreed to watch the film and judge for themselves.

That evening Burke escorted the Methodist and Baptist ministers and influential business leaders to their seats for his special preview.

"Gentlemen, thank you for coming," began Burke. He wore a three-piece suit, and his favorite bird dog stood beside him. "If you find anything in this motion picture that you would deem a bad influence on boys, I will refuse to show it."[102]

One of those boys was potentially Woodrow Wilson Guthrie, born in Okemah on July 14, 1912. He would become better known as folk singer Woody Guthrie.[103] As the Crystal Theatre's lights dimmed and the projector rolled, the men watched Starr's life story on celluloid.[104] Starr likely found it quite ironic that these men sat in pious judgment of his actions. Did they recall their own behavior nine years earlier when Okemah's "finest citizens," including Woody's father Charley, broke into the town jail and dragged into the street a 35-year-old Black woman named Laura Nelson, her 13-year-old son Lawrence, and her nursing infant?

The white mob raped Laura, and then she and Lawrence were hung from the middle span of a bridge across the North Canadian River.[105] George Henry Farnum, Okemah's only professional photographer, whose cheerful ad in the

172   Reel Four

Okemah Ledger read, "That Man Farnum and Wife, Photographs, Kodaks, and Supplies," launched his boat in the river below the bridge and found a perfect position for his camera. Fifty Okemah residents—men, women, and children (some waving)—stood on the bridge and posed for Farnum as the bodies dangled below. Not seen in the photograph was Laura Nelson's infant, who was left in the grass beside the bridge, wailing for its mother. Farnum snapped wide shots and ghoulish close-ups of the bodies and turned his ghastly images into money-making souvenirs and postcards. Nearly a decade later, Okemah city leaders closely watched *A Debtor to the Law* to determine if Starr's life story might be "detrimental to public morals."[106]

Following the screening, local journalists button-holed viewers for their response. An *Okemah Ledger* reporter wrote, "There were about thirty that dropped in to see the picture and all pronounced it good." *Okfuskee County News* quoted a member of the audience declaring, "It might have a good influence on the minds of boys for the reason that every scene emphasized the lesson that there is no escaping the penalty of crime." Okemah town officials granted Burke their imprimatur to show *A Debtor the Law* to the public, and he cleared $600 during its run—a satisfying sum.[107]

Encouraged by his first success, Peck revved his runabout and criss-crossed the state. On May 20 *A Debtor to the Law* opened at a different Rialto in Starr's birthplace, Fort Gibson.[108] The Mammoth in Dallas showed the film two days later, advertising it as "A Special Western Attraction Featuring Henry Starr Oklahoma's and Texas' greatest of all Outlaws—AL JENNINGS, JESSE JAMES, and all the rest have nothing on HENRY STARR."[109] The show on May 29, at Henryetta, Oklahoma's Morgan, sold out, turning away customers.[110] Competition was fierce for quality entertainment. The rival Yale showed *A Debtor to the Law* on June 3, and then the film returned to the Morgan on June 5.

At Tulsa's Wonderland Starr shared the bill with Charlie Chaplin in *Some Nerve* and Roscoe Arbuckle in *Fatty the Mermaid*.[111] The nearby Lyric showcased an Ohio State Penitentiary alumni reunion featuring Starr and fellow outlaw-turned-actor Al Jennings in *A Highway Romance*. The Guthrie ran a salacious teaser for the upcoming *A Debtor to the Law* screening, disclosing Starr had secretly married a woman in New Orleans and that "Pictures of his

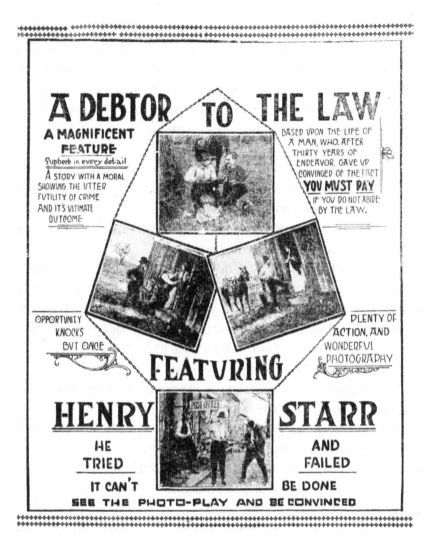

Figure 40 *Dallas Express*, May 22, 1920, newspaper advertisement for *A Debtor to the Law* that emphasized the film's message of "moral uplift." Scenes from the film include (*top*) Starr and his partner William Karl Hackett counting money; (*left*) Detective Dickey (unnamed actor) and Floyd Wilson (P. S. McGeeney) forcing their way into Starr's sister Lizzie's home (unnamed actor); (*right*) Lizzie telling Starr that Dickey and Wilson will shoot him on sight; (*bottom*) Starr captured by two police officers (unnamed actors) at the Bouse, Arizona, post office after being betrayed by a friend.

174 Reel Four

old and new wife are flashed on the screen."[112] In a humorous coincidence, Starr's motion picture appeared on the same bill as the musical comedy *Too Many Wives* at the Newkirk Cozy.[113] The Dazy in Lindsay advertised *A Debtor to the Law* as "Not a Feature without Justice. Nor with crime reigning Supreme."[114] Advertisements for a two-day run at the Mission in Ponca City promoted the film as a "historical masterpiece."[115]

After a screening at Lawton's Orpheum on June 19, a reviewer wrote, "Besides Henry Starr himself, the cast contains a group of excellent screen artists, who fit in their roles perfectly."[116] At the Guthrie Starr's film appeared on the same bill with a different fellow Ohio State Penitentiary inmate with O. Henry in *A Car Loan*. Former heavyweight boxing champion-turned-actor Jack Dempsey was also featured in *Daredevil Jack*.[117]

June ended with shows at the *Happy Hour* in Hominy[118] and two nights at the Liberty in Drumright.[119] During a special four-night return run at Brophy's New Yale in Muskogee, P. J. Clark and his team conducted audience testing.[120] They handed out pencils and paper and asked viewers to write their opinions of the picture and give pointers "as to where they would have had it different." The *Muskogee Times-Democrat* was full of suggestions, writing, "The photography of this picture is good, and as an actor, Henry Starr is quite at home. The rest of the cast is poor, and the whole production is not a very good ad for Oklahoma." Despite the negative review, 1,500 moviegoers paid to see Starr's life on screen.

On July 10 *A Debtor to the Law* showed at Jenk's Majestic,[121] then had a two-night run in Starr's adopted prison hometown of McAlester at the Kozy.[122] An advertisement in the Bartlesville *Examiner* claimed that on the night of July 20, the Yale had to "turn 'em away," but customers had a second chance on July 21.[123]

Following the July 1 screening at the Liberty in Marietta,[124] Peck returned home to Stroud for a much-needed rest.[125] Starr had also grown weary of being on the road. "My picture is not making as much money for me as it would if I would go around with it and stand up and let people see me," Starr said. "But I can't see that kind of life."[126]

Starr said he'd like to make one more picture and then start farming. At least he wasn't considering a return to bank robbery—yet.

Personal Potholes

Within days of the *A Debtor to the Law* screening at Muskogee's New Yale, Starr stepped into several personal potholes. Hearing that the film was completed, Starr's ex-wife Ollie filed a petition for child support with the Muskogee Superior Court.[127] She only earned $90 a month as a stenographer at the Indian agency—an insufficient income to support herself and the now 15-year-old Teddy. Ollie claimed Starr had received a $20,000 royalty check from Pan-American and she sought the garnishment of $150 monthly for their son. Starr settled out of court, agreeing to pay Ollie $2,000.[128]

The second pothole occurred in May when Muskogee police spotted a 23-year-old Cherokee woman on the street behaving strangely.[129] An officer looked into her half-lidded brown eyes and asked who she was.

"I'm Lucille Starr," she slurred. "Henry Starr is my husband."

The police searched the pockets of her dress and found a packet of cocaine. The officers thought her claim of marriage to Starr was the "dream" of a drugged mind. They hauled her to the Muskogee police court on charges of being a "dope user."

"You told the officers you are the wife of Henry Starr?" the judge asked.

"Yes, your Honor," Lucille Starr answered. "We were married in San Antonio while he was filming a motion picture."

"And how do you explain the narcotics in your possession?"

Lucille Starr said she'd been in the Baptist Hospital for several weeks receiving treatment "to break her drug habit." She had only been out a few days, and Starr was going to take her to a private sanitarium for treatment.[130]

"Mrs. Starr, I am remanding you to the custody of our jailer for you to sober up. In the meantime, my bailiff will place a call to the San Antonio Justice of the Peace and get an answer on this."

Within days the Muskogee Police Court received the marriage certificate from Bexar County, Texas.[131] The official document identified the groom as 46-year-old Henry Starr, a member of a motion picture company, and his wife as 23-year-old Lucille Starr. Her maiden name was also Starr because she was his distant cousin. Lucille Starr, who was called Hulda, was born in 1896 to Ellis and Martha Starr. At 21 she married John L. Sullivan (not the famous

176   Reel Four

boxer) in McAlester.[132] Hulda filed for divorce seven months later, saying Sullivan subjected her to cruelty, cursing her in public and beating her when he was drunk.

Two years later she met Starr, and they married in February 1920. Starr asked the Bexar County, Texas, justice of the peace to delay the filing of the marriage certificate, explaining that an announcement in the newspaper would draw undue attention to him because he was a movie star. Not knowing Starr was a famous outlaw, Fisk agreed to the request. In truth, Starr likely asked for the delay because he didn't want to alert lawmen or bounty hunters that he'd left Oklahoma. The certificate wouldn't be officially recorded until March 3, after Starr and his new bride had returned home.

Back at the Muskogee County Jail, Doctor Claude Thompson, Starr's friend, had Hulda released into his custody to transfer her to a sanitarium.[133]

The Great Miss Kate

In June 1920 Starr told the *Oklahoma News* he was disappointed with the money *A Debtor to the Law* had earned. He phoned his old friend Kate Barnard, former commissioner of charities and corrections.[134] She stood barely five feet tall and weighed only eighty-five pounds, but newspapers called "Miss Kate" a dynamo and a "veritable live-wire of wholesome doing."[135] In 1909 she was instrumental in building the Oklahoma State Penitentiary in McAlester, making it her mission to provide Oklahoma's inmates with a humane facility.[136] A year later Barnard helped to enact the Juvenile Court Law, ensuring minors weren't treated like adults in the court system. She stated, "No boy or girl should be placed in a jail where hardened criminals are kept. Jails are breeding grounds for crime."[137]

Over the next five years, Barnard took up and won many more battles. With stirring speeches she advanced the cause of compulsory child education, helped enact child labor laws, and established state support for widows. By 1914 Miss Kate had made numerous enemies among the rich and powerful by championing the cause of Indian orphans and protecting the rights of Indians against grafters stealing their allotments. The state legislature, unable to eliminate her office, slashed her budget, choking off

Start Picture   177

the oxygen to her reform efforts. Instead of running for reelection, Barnard cited ill health and retired.[138]

In 1915 Barnard decided to write a profile of the prisoners in the Oklahoma State Penitentiary. She was instrumental in having it built and now she wanted to return to McAlester to conduct interviews. "This pamphlet will contain the heart's story of these fifty-two men, stripped of the romance and glamor and leaving nothing but the teeth and claws and I want the whole population of the state to read their stories."[139] One of the men she interviewed was Starr.

Barnard listened to his story and had tremendous sympathy for his journey. She understood the corrupt nature of the law during the territorial days, especially toward Native Americans, and the abusive legal and penal system for juveniles. Unfortunately, her Juvenile Court Law was enacted too late to prevent Starr's life-changing experience of being locked up in the Fort Smith prison in 1891 at age 17. Barnard and Starr bonded and became lifelong friends. "I know things about him no one else on earth knows," she later explained.

Five years later Starr called Barnard at the Cadillac Hotel in Oklahoma City, where she was now living. He asked to borrow $100 to get back on his feet. He told her Pan-American had cheated him out of $15,000 in proceeds. The loan would allow him to "carry on the fight to get what was due him from the company." She gave him $20, and he delivered his raincoat as collateral on the loan. Barnard phoned her attorney, Roy Hoffman, to help Starr recoup his money from Pan-American. Hoffman was the same man who wanted Starr to join his National Guard troops to fight Pancho Villa and later battle the kaiser in World War I. Hoffman was a Starr supporter and told Kate he'd ask Governor Robertson to revoke Pan-American's license if they didn't settle fairly.[140]

Starr was in desperate financial straits. His mother, Mary, had just divorced her third husband, Tulsa Police Detective Raymond D. Gordon. When he bumped into Gordon on the street he had to swallow his pride.[141] Gordon noticed Starr appeared out of sorts.

"What's the matter, Henry?" Gordon asked.

"Nothing much," Starr replied. "Only, I could use a hundred bucks if you've got it to spare."

"That so?"

"I'll hand it back to you in a few days. I promise."

"I'm a little light right now, Henry," Gordon answered, walking away. "Good luck to you."

Starr immediately cursed himself.

Starr's finances continued to take a hit the rest of the summer and into the fall. There were no recorded screenings of *A Debtor to the Law* in August and only one in September at the Grand in Cherokee.[142] In October Starr shrugged off his dislike of personal appearances and took the risk of crossing the border into Missouri. Over the weekend of October 23 and 24, *A Debtor to the Law* had five showtimes at Renraw Park.[143]

The Chillicothe Constitution alerted filmgoers that Starr's personal engagement at the Liberty in Kansas City, Missouri, might not happen, writing, "He intended to appear on the streets in Kansas City that day in the company of an Oklahoma sheriff but finds there is an indictment against him in Kansas which he has not answered and unless he can have it squared he will have to stay in Oklahoma to avoid arrest."[144] The sheriff referenced in the article was Bill Tilghman. The retired deputy marshal was still peddling *The Passing of the Oklahoma Outlaws* when they crossed paths in Kansas City.

During a personal appearance at the Gayoso, Starr spoke about his release from the Oklahoma State Penitentiary: "I came out with less than $50, a game leg, and the desire to tell the world what my life of crime had taught me."[145] Starr traveled to Grenola's Gem on November 8 and Iola's Elite on November 15.[146] While in a hotel, Starr penned his obligatory letter to the Oklahoma State Pardon and Parole Office, writing that he was "getting along all right in a motion picture venture."[147]

Meanwhile, Tilghman thought something was off with Starr. "Henry has got that wild look in his eye," he wrote. "He's getting ready to rob another bank."[148] Tilghman planned to visit Oklahoma's Governor Robertson and suggest revoking Starr's parole before it was too late.

Buffalo Ray and Radium Water

Based on the moderate success of *A Debtor to the Law*, Starr received interest from production companies in Hollywood. Starr wrote a letter to Al Jennings expressing his interest in joining him there.[149] Working in California's film industry could be the solution to his financial troubles.[150] However, Starr didn't know if the state's governor, William Stephens, would grant Arkansas's request for extradition.[151]

Starr couldn't take the chance. If he wanted to make motion pictures, it would have to be in Oklahoma—but it wouldn't be with Pan-American. P. J. Clark had moved on from Starr and was developing two new pictures, *Legend of the Osages*, written by Vivian Woodcock Kay, and the supernatural romance *Trails of the Serpent*.[152] Clark was negotiating with Gloria Swanson to play the role of a femme fatale leading a dual life for the latter film.[153] Despite his hiccups shepherding *A Debtor to the Law*, George Reehm was tapped to direct the picture with a budget between $75,000 and $100,000—double that of Starr's biography. Even with only one picture under his belt, Starr understood the fuel that powered the motion picture engine—financing.

As a condition of his release from the Oklahoma State Penitentiary, Starr was required to write a letter every month to Governor Robertson to provide an update on his adjustment to society. In a March 1919 letter, he wrote that he was feeling "run down from incarceration" and had traveled to Claremore to try the healing radium water baths.[154] Radium water was discovered in 1903 when oilman George Washington Eaton struck an artesian aquifer instead of crude oil. The rotten egg–smelling geyser wasn't believed to really contain radioactive and cancer-causing radium, but the name sounded exotic, and Eaton decided to market its dubious healing properties.[155] Soon, bathhouses, spas, and hotels with hot and cold running radium water sprang up everywhere. The business district became known as Radium Town, and "bathhouse boosters" mobbed passengers at the depot with flyers and pitches for their products.[156]

The Mendenhall Hotel and Baths touted radium water as "That Wonderful Cure for Rheumatism, Eczema and All Stomach Troubles." If that wasn't wondrous enough, they added: "Removes the most obstinate cases of dandruff."[157] Andrew Lerskov, MD, in his report for the Journal of the Oklahoma State Medical Board, called radium water "quackdom." Lerskov's report, however, didn't dissuade the public; the radium bath business kept bubbling.[158] By 1930 Claremore's favorite son, the cowboy-philosopher-humorist-actor Will Rogers, offered radium water baths at his eponymous hotel and jokingly called it a liquid "that will cure you of everything, even presidential ambition."[159]

In 1919 Starr had his choice of bathhouses, including the Mendenhall Hotel and Bath House, a two-story red brick building with decorative iron-work.[160] After checking in Starr was escorted to a private room. The moment had a quasi-religious aura as he undressed and stepped into a steam cabinet. After developing a copious sweat to draw out toxins, Starr stepped into a soaking tub of tepid mineral water pumped in from two on-site tanks. Hot water was slowly added by an attendant—"usually a colored man or woman, as they seem to stand the gasses of the water best."[161] While soaking in the rotten egg–smelling stew, Starr noticed the decor was new. The sulfurous fumes discolored wallpaper and furnishings and corroded plumbing quickly, requiring frequent renovation. The attendant gave Starr a massage, kneading out knotted muscles, their fingernails blackened by the radium water. Finally, he was taken to a cooling room, where he was gently placed between blankets on a cot. The stained towels, he was told, were evidence that toxins had been cleansed from his body. While Starr rested, the attendant began cleaning the custom-made glass tub with an acid bath.[162]

On December 16, 1920, Starr returned to Claremore, not to soak but to pitch his motion picture venture to the Claremore Commercial Club (CCC).[163] Starr sat in the ballroom of the Mason Hotel as President F. E. Keith gaveled the weekly luncheon meeting to order. Starr sat through the club's mundane business, such as authorizing an extra five dollars for janitor services at the high school for a concert and paving updates on nearby roads. Then they welcomed new members, including John R. "Buffalo Ray" Spurrier.

Spurrier was a thin, blue-eyed man who wore a Western sombrero with a brim wide enough to cover his shoulders in the rain and an oversized bison fur coat. After his swearing-in, he pitched his business proposal. Spurrier told the CCC he was bringing the largest bison herd in Oklahoma to his new

Start Picture 181

property on the western edge of town. He wanted to start an annual cowboy round-up in Claremore like the one that filled the Dewey coffers every year. All he needed from Claremore was free water for the herd and permission to paint the Buffalo Ray Ranch logo on the city's water tower so that people diving along the highway or on passing trains could see it. After Spurrier finished his pitch and returned to his seat, Keith authorized a committee to consider the matter.

Then, Keith invited Starr to come forward. Unlike Spurrier, he was not sworn in. Starr ignored the slight. He stood at the front of the room, flashing a "whimsical smile," and began his pitch:

"Fellas, I propose filming my next motion picture in Claremore. But there's good and bad news. The good: the storyline will promote Claremore's radium water baths. The bad, I'll be the star."

The crowd chuckled.

"My motion picture will be a gripping Western story where men live hard, fight hard, love strong and die with their boots on."

Starr described the scenario: He would portray a wounded outlaw on the lam after a train robbery. Fleeing a fast-pursuing posse, Starr finds shelter with an aged physician friend in Claremore. The doctor restores the outlaw's health with its curative radium water. Starr told the men he would hire a director, cameraman, and a professional actress from Hollywood to play his love interest. "Buffalo Ray" would play his sidekick and provide the use of his bison herd. Starr said the Miller brothers' 101 Ranch had already agreed to ship horses, saddles, cowboys, and all motion picture equipment whenever he got the funding. The picture would be four reels, take three weeks to shoot, and cost $8,000 to $10,000—which Starr hoped the CCC could provide.

"My reputation as a badman will bring the production into instant prominence in the public eye," Starr said, "and Claremore and radium water along with me."

The plot of Starr's next film revealed the exciting next phase of his cinematic career. He was no longer bound to his biography but would be playing a character—although certainly not a stretch dramatically—an outlaw who is set on the road to redemption by the love of a good woman. Starr's character arc took a page, or several, from the William S. Hart "good" badman playbook that had successfully appealed to middle-class theatergoers. However, as a part-Cherokee matinee idol, Starr would have the opportunity to reverse a growing white supremacy and anti–Native American agenda in Hart's films. In *The Aryan* (Triangle, 1916), Hart plays Steve Denton, a miner whose heart is broken by a white dance hall girl. Embittered, Denton begins consorting with fierce outlaws. Only after a white woman reminds Denton of his responsibility to his race does he turn on his gang of "half-bred greasers and Indian cut-throats" who intended to rape the white women. Two years later Hart appeared in *Blue Blazes Rawden* (Triangle, 1918), playing a virile lumberjack who seduces a "half-breed" woman with a "savage strain from an Indian mother." Once again, Hart's character is redeemed through the influence of white women and Christianity.[164] Unlike Hart's characters, Starr would not be drawing his six-guns "to establish racial order."[165] Instead, as Starr told the CCC, the good woman at the heart of the picture would be Native American.[166] With his second picture, Starr could change the negative perception of Native Americans and control the whitewashing of his image.

In the audience listening to the proposal was Starr's friend State Senator E. E. Woods, an heir to the O. E. Woods Lumber Company with yards across Oklahoma and Kansas. As a member of the CCC, Woods was happy to introduce his friend Starr to the group.[167] Keith thanked Starr and said they would consider his proposal. Woods thought Starr had made a good impression and was optimistic. "The recollection of this Chamber of Commerce meeting can never be obliterated by those who were present, and met with Henry," Woods wrote.

Later, in a private meeting, however, Woods said one of the bankers was "cool on the proposition." Rumors were that Starr guaranteed that no Claremore banks would be robbed if the CCC provided the funding. To some members this may have sounded like blackmail. No final decision was made during the meeting.

Meanwhile, Starr continued to hustle for money, making a personal appearance at a screening at Tulsa's Lyric on December 5 and back in Kansas City at the Maple eleven days later.[168] Neither would bring in the $10,000 Starr needed to make his next motion picture or pay off his mounting debts.

Financial pressure was building like a capped radium water well.

Reel Five

Pushed to the Brink

A Debtor to the Law had a two-night pre-Christmas run at the Lyric in Tulsa. The advertisement read: "It is more crowded with thrills and incidents—re-enactments of things that actually happened—than any 'bad man' play that ever came out of a scenario writer's head or director's imagination."[1] That same week Starr was already writing a sequel—a heist at the Bank of Seligman in Missouri.

Despite what Starr had told the CCC, the Miller brothers had no interest in helping him with his moving picture.[2] "When Starr got ready to film his outlaw picture, he made every effort to get us to go in with him, but his proposition was turned down by us," said Col. Joseph C. Miller. They were very familiar with Starr. They'd hired him as a bronco buster for their 1907 Wild West show in Kansas City, Missouri. "He could bust 'em all right," Miller concluded. "But he traveled too fast a gait for us." The Miller Brothers had to let him go because he always wanted to "smoke up" the town. Nevertheless, the Millers had been kind to Starr over the years, welcoming him to stay for a meal when passing through. However, they had no intention of going into business with him.

183

In July 1920 Starr convinced Hulda to rent out thirty acres of her Sallisaw allotment.[3] In August she sold a portion of her land for $8,150.[4] Al Jennings, who stayed in touch with Starr off and on, believed he had put her property up as collateral for a loan he wouldn't likely be able to pay back.[5] By December the eight grand had been gambled away. Starr took out several small loans at exorbitant rates to stay afloat, but he was sinking fast.[6] He needed financial relief—the type only available at the end of a blued-metal gun barrel.

Once again, Starr had to assemble a gang. He found 29-year-old Rufus Rollens (a.k.a. Rowlands), a champion cattle roper out of Winnipeg, Canada.[7] Rollens had recently moved to Claremore with his wife and two children to find better prospects. He thought he'd found the perfect opportunity when he bumped into Starr and "Buffalo Ray" Spurrier. They told him they were launching a motion picture Western and were hiring real cowboys. "There was to be considerable horseback riding, and my reputation as a good rider is well known," Rollens said. Starr hired Rollens on the spot, and the champion cowboy was thrilled to begin an exciting career in the motion picture business. Then, something changed. "About two months later, Starr began talking about raiding a bank," Rollens said. Starr, Jennings, and Dalton were outlaws who became motion picture stars—which was strange enough. But Starr initiated an unprecedented cinema metamorphosis, turning an actor into a bank robber.

Starr recruited another Claremore local, Charles Brackett, and World War I veteran Dave Edward Lockhart, who hailed originally from St. Joe, Arkansas. Brackett was a violent man with his fists and his pistol.[8] At a stomp dance he got into an argument with his brother that escalated into a gunfight. Another time he assaulted a World War I vet and paid a heavy fine. During yet another altercation, he was shot five times and lived. Lockhart would be especially useful to Starr since he knew the banks near his home, including those at Seligman, Cassville, Missouri, and Harrison, Arkansas. Lockhart was "a good country boy" who served in the 36th division with the American expeditionary forces in France.[9] He'd fought in six major engagements, and friends say Lockhart returned from Europe a changed and bitter man. At 30 he was with his second wife, had four children, and had another due in four months.

In mid-December 1920 a woman was stuck at the side of the road with a flat tire outside of Cassville, Missouri.[10] She was in despair until a motorcar

Pushed to the Brink

pulled up behind her and a man matching Starr's description alighted from the car, offering help. Three men with Starr lifted one end of the car while the outlaw put on the spare. Starr tipped his hat, and the four men climbed back into their car and continued. Later that afternoon, the Bank of Cassville was robbed.

Two days before Christmas, *A Debtor to the Law* screened at the Attica Opera House in Attica, Kansas, featuring "Henry Starr (The Great Outlaw)." "A few years ago," the advertisement explained, "Starr was leading the life of a criminal." Now, "He is giving his life in pictures. Come see the pictures."[11]

The day after Christmas, *A Debtor to the Law* screened at the Grand in Springfield, Missouri, eighty miles from Seligman. An advertisement in the *Springfield News Reader* announced: "6 Reels—6,000 Feet—Over a Mile of Real Adventures of a Real Outlaw. It Teaches the great lesson—Go Straight, It Pays Best!" In this case, the Seligman robbery paid Starr best, as he and his gang drove away with $1,200.[12]

Between the holidays, Tulsa Police Captain George Blaine spotted Starr leaning against the side of the Security State Bank building. He thought nothing of it until thirty minutes later he passed Starr again leaning against the National Bank of Commerce building down the street.[13]

"Which of these two banks are you planning to make, Henry?" the captain asked.

Starr smiled. "Nope, I'm off that stuff for good. No more bank robberies for me."

Starr's one-time vow that he'd gone straight and "beat back" was now an outright lie. He bemoaned the heavy automobile traffic along Main and Second Streets. "There was a time when it was dead easy," Starr said. "Just a little gun play and a little rough talk and the money was yours."

Captain Blaine agreed that a man would be "a big fool" to try to rob a bank in Tulsa. Starr seemed to have put a lot of thought into making an escape in an automobile in a big city rather than on horseback like the old days. "Look at those automobiles," Starr mused. "They'll go like hell when they're going, but they're liable to break down right when you need them most."

January saw a sprinkling of out-of-state *A Debtor to the Law* screenings. There were two four-day runs at the Queen in Fort Worth. In Texas, outside

Oklahoma's negative opinion of Starr, his film was garnering good reviews.[14] The *Fort Worth Star-Telegram* wrote that *A Debtor to the Law* had the "fastest kind of action in every foot of it" and added, "There's love and laughter to relieve the tension. And happily, there's the kind of ending picture patrons like best." Unfortunately, Starr's happy ending was now make-believe, but the public didn't know it—yet. The review's closing paragraph was painfully ironic, given Starr's financial straits: "Oil discovered on a lease he holds in the Osage field is making him rich, and if the gushers keep flowing a few months will see him crowned as one of Oklahoma's greatest petroleum kings." The *Star-Telegram* had used marketing language directly from the Peacock Productions press book. A year later, the rich oil man story mocked Starr.

Starr spent the short winter days of January with Hulda on her Sallisaw homestead, fixing fences and tending their livestock.[15] Starr was sick at heart knowing they were likely to lose it all because of him. Starr told Hulda, "We can't live here. We've got too many enemies. When we get the money, we will go to Mexico."[16] Hulda thought he meant the income from *A Debtor to the Law*. She didn't realize he was planning to rob the People's Bank in Harrison, Arkansas. "If I had known, I could have talked him out of it," Hulda said.

Starr was despondent. "I thought about killing myself rather than do the thing I've just done—starting back on the scout," he said.[17]

Starr's thoughts might have strayed to another melancholy outlaw, Jim Younger.[18] He was Cole Younger's little brother, and both were members of the James-Younger Gang. On September 7, 1876, Jim and Cole were shot and captured attempting to rob the Northfield Minnesota bank. The brothers spent the next twenty-five years at the Minnesota Territorial Prison in Stillwater. (A third brother, Bob, died while incarcerated.) In 1901 Jim was 53 and Cole 57 when the Minnesota Board of Pardons granted them their release.[19] Both men said they were happy to live the rest of their days honestly and without violence.

To help them land on their feet, the government provided Cole and Jim jobs as traveling monument salesmen; "monument" was a euphemism for tombstones.[20] Their new profession was a cosmic punchline, considering the number of people the brothers had sent to early graves. Monument sales were difficult for Jim. A bullet had shattered his jaw during the Northfield Raid,

Figure 41 *A Debtor to the Law* (1920) lobby card. Starr, playing himself, contemplates his life decisions while inside a cell on the Fort Smith prison set built at Patrick "P. S." McGeeney's Shamrock Studios near San Antonio, Texas. Courtesy of the Glenn D. Shirley Western Americana Collection, Dickinson Research Center, National Cowboy & Western Heritage Museum (RC2006.068.32.6.3).

and he didn't speak clearly. Six additional bullets had lodged in his body, including one in his neck, caused him chronic pain. While Cole was boisterous and a born salesman, Jim was described as "smiling, blue eyed, and mild of voice, as gentle as he is genial."[21]

As a condition of Jim and Cole's parole, they were forbidden from signing a legal contract, including, oddly enough, a marriage license. While Jim was in prison, Alix Muller, a charming journalist and St. Paul socialite, interviewed him. Over time they developed a relationship and fell in love. When the Board of Pardons approved Jim's release, he and Alix began to plan their wedding. Then, Jim learned they wouldn't be allowed to marry. He grew despondent. His declining health and inability to make a living sent him on a downward spiral.[22]

Jim befriended a street corner socialist who deeply influenced his view of society's responsibility to its citizens. On his last day on earth, Jim sat on the bed in his hotel room. He set his empty coin purse on the nightstand and placed his last dime on top of it. Then, Jim raised a .35 "bulldog" revolver to his temple and pulled the trigger. The following day the housekeeper discovered the body. Jim left a suicide note declaring himself "A Socialist and decidedly in favor of women's rights." A year after his release from prison, Jim Younger was dead. [23]

Starr knew he could easily put a bullet through his own head and end all of his money troubles.

He had a gun loaded and ready.

The Final Betrayal

Ultimately, Starr didn't let depression get the best of him. "I believed in fighting the thing through," he said.[24]

On February 2, 1921, Starr drove his motorcar northwest from Claremore to the Miller brothers' 101 Ranch in Ponca City to visit Milt Hinkle, a veteran rodeo rider he knew. Unbeknown to Hinkle, Starr was looking to add a new member to his gang.[25]

Starr parked and waved Hinkle over.

"I'm going to Fort Worth, then to Arkansas," Starr said. "Come along and I'll pay you well for the trip."

"Okay," Hinkle replied. That sounded good to him.

Zack Miller, Joseph's brother, saw Starr pull up at the ranch. He "had a fondness for the rascally Starr," but suspected the reformed outlaw was up to no good. As Hinkle was packing his bag to join Starr, Miller pulled him to the side.

"You are headed for trouble," Zack said. "You know you missed getting into trouble a few years ago, so take my advice and don't go."

Hinkle respected Zack's opinion. He returned to Starr's car and begged off. "I forgot I promised Zack I would go up to Kansas with him," Hinkle said. "But thanks for the offer, Henry."

Annoyed, Starr gunned the motor and drove away kicking up dust. Witnesses claimed they saw Starr checking out the Ponca City banks on his way out of town.[26]

Pushed to the Brink 189

In mid-February Starr and Hulda spent more time in Claremore near Mary Gordon. They enjoyed having meals in the Mecca Cafe and had become familiar faces around town. After completing his night shift, Chief of Police Lew Rutherford stopped by Starr's booth to make small talk.[27] Starr mentioned he was starting "a Wild West picture company." Rutherford had also heard Starr was spending his time at the poker tables and losing badly, but he didn't mention it in Hulda's presence. Forgotten were Starr's words to Governor Robertson in his monthly parole letter: "I have played cards for money, but it holds no fascination for me now."[28]

Starr had been edgy lately, impatiently awaiting a decision from his pal E. E. Woods and the Claremore Commercial Club. In the newspapers he read about two new censorship bills being considered in the Oklahoma state legislature. Starr wasn't alarmed. The situation had become old hat. Censorship legislation always cropped up as a fundraising stunt for politicians and then disappeared. The first was from Democratic State Senator Charles McPherren, who proposed a bill explicitly designed to punish "theatres depicting Henry Starr and Al Jennings, former outlaws, in action."[29] The content of the second piece of anti-Starr legislation didn't surprise Starr, but the author of the bill left him stunned. He read that Republican state senators M. F. Ingraham and E. E. Woods—his pal from the CCC—had submitted a bill banning the making of films depicting a crime, mob violence, lynchings, and other "blood curdling" scenes.[30] Starr felt a blade sink between his shoulder blades. E. E. Woods had betrayed him.

Starr's hot temper—long-simmering—began to boil.

The week of February 14, Hulda watched as Starr prepared for a mysterious trip. Before walking out the door, Starr called his bride to him; their first anniversary was just six days away. He put his arm around her and asked, "Honey, if I should die, would you have me buried?" She said she would, of course. Starr said he'd been thinking it over. "I have a horror of being dumped into the ground. I want to be cremated."[31] Hulda didn't ask him why he'd brought up the morbid topic or where he was going. Starr kissed her good-bye and walked out the door without looking back.

On February 17, if one wanted to watch Starr rob a bank, there were two choices: *A Debtor to the Law* was screening at the Rex in Commerce,

190   Reel Five

Oklahoma,[32] or one could wait a day and witness Starr do it live at the People's Bank in Harrison, Arkansas. Sometime after midnight on Friday, February 18, Starr rode in a stolen four-cylinder Nash five-passenger motor car driven by Dave Lockhart.[33] The plates had been switched, the engine number filed off, and the windshield wings removed. The other passengers were the same crew from the Bank of Seligman robbery the previous December: Charles Brackett and Rufus Rollens. They stopped in Berryville, Arkansas, on the way and filled the Nash's tank at the Carroll County Hardware Company. Starr poked around inside the store and purchased a campfire coffeepot. When they arrived northeast of Harrison at an area known as Cotton Woods, Starr ordered Lockhart to pull to the side of the road.[34] The gang set up camp by the light of the headlamps. They built a fire to fight off freezing overnight temperatures and put on a pot of coffee.

At sunrise on February 19, Harrison, Arkansas, mail carrier Ethel Holman loaded her one-horse leather-topped mail buggy with letters, packages, and her faithful dog, Ol' Peg, who rode shotgun.[35] The Saturday morning fog was thick. It felt like "snow weather," and a record blizzard was expected later that day. While making her deliveries near Cotton Woods, she saw a fancy black Nash with bright yellow rims parked along the roadside.[36] "It was unusual to see a car that nice in the area," she recalled. The windows were frosted, but she could see the silhouettes of men sleeping inside.

"What do you think, girl?" Holman asked Ol' Peg. "Should we alert the sheriff?"

Ol' Peg tilted her head as if considering the question.

As Starr and his gang slumbered unaware, they faced capture before even opening their eyes.

The Heist

Ethel Holman decided the men weren't suspicious enough to notify the authorities. Besides, an extra stop at Sheriff Sibley Johnson's office would only set her back further. She snapped the reins and continued on her mail route with Ol' Peg.

At 10:00 a.m. Ruth Wilson stood outside People's Bank, waiting for it to open.[37] She was the bookkeeper for the Harrison Grocery Company and

Pushed to the Brink   191

had early-morning business. Wilson clasped the upturned collar of her coat
tightly against the cold. The clouds hung low like a quilt of dark cotton wool,
making her feel claustrophobic. She noticed the first snowflakes as they
landed on her shoulders.

At the same moment, Lockhart arrived with the Nash in the Harrison
business district.[38] He puttered the car counterclockwise around the courthouse square. The expanse of grass on the courthouse lawn had turned winter
yellow. White flakes landed on his windscreen and began to stick. Lockhart
engaged the wipers. In the passenger seat, Starr pulled a county map from
the breast pocket of his gabardine overcoat. He reviewed his notations on the
various escape routes and the conditions of the highways.

Finally, People's Bank President J. Marvin Wagley unlocked the front
door and welcomed Wilson inside.[39] She felt the warmth of the wood-burning
stove in the corner and was grateful. Wilson stepped to the open teller
window occupied by cashier Cleve Coffman, a thin, bookish man wearing
a neat three-piece suit. Behind him, in the counting room, two young clerks,
Edith Thistlewaite and Naomi Moore, sat at a table, scissor-cutting currency
sheets and placing the bills into piles. They wore matching dark dresses with
navy middie tops.

To the right of the clerks, Wilson could see the door to the steel vault was
wide open. The shelves were empty because the bank didn't use it anymore.
Instead, the bank's money was kept in a three-foot-high combination safe
on the floor to the far left of the counting room. Wilson recognized the bank
board president, William J. "Bill" Myers, next to the clerks, reviewing ledgers.
His small spectacles and white mustache made him appear like a doddering
old man, but she knew better. On the right side of the foyer was the bank
director's room, where Al Davis, a former bronco buster, sat across the desk
reviewing a car loan application from an insurance salesman named Baker.

Lockhart parked the Nash across from People's Bank along South Willow
Street and pointed toward their intended escape route across Crooked Creek
Bridge. Starr wrapped a pair of costume spectacles over his ears while Brackett
and Rollens checked their weapons. Since Lockhart was from nearby St. Joe,
Starr didn't want to risk him being recognized. Starr told him to stay behind
the wheel and keep the car idling. Brackett, Rollens, and Starr stepped out of

Figure 42 Staff photo from the People's Bank of Harrison, Arkansas, taken days after the failed bank robbery on February 19, 1921. *Left to right*: Edith Thistlewaite (clerk), Naomi Moore (clerk), President J. Marvin Wagley, and (*seated*) Cleve Coffman (cashier). Photo courtesy of the Boone County Heritage Museum, Harrison, Arkansas.

the Nash. The cold air immediately bit at their ears, and puffs of breath rose from their nostrils and mouths. They flipped up the collars of their long coats and pushed down their hats. Starr wore a stylish homburg with a silk hatband. Each of their gloved hands was shoved deep in their pockets, tightly gripping pistols. Their getaway by automobile would be modern, but Starr eschewed an automatic for the reliable double-action .44 Colt New Service revolver.[40] Starr led the way, walking stiffly across Willow Street, his bum hip tightening up in the cold.

Wilson was still at Coffman's teller window when the three robbers burst into the lobby, weapons drawn.[41]

"Hands up, everyone!" Starr barked.

Rollens slipped behind Wilson and hooked his left arm around her waist. With his right hand, he pointed his gun in Coffman's face through the bars.

Pushed to the Brink

"Up with your hands, Mr. Cashier!" he yelled.

"That means you too," said Brackett, pointing his weapon at President Wagley behind the second teller window. "Up with your hands!"

Starr quickly crossed to the bank director's room, slipped past a startled Baker and Davis at the desk, and entered the counting room by a hidden rear entrance. He'd done his homework. "Don't worry, everyone," Starr said. "We're just going to do a little business together."[42]

Wilson studied the three men: Rollens, holding her tightly, wore cowboy garb and a white hat; Brackett had a scar on his face; and Starr, she thought, was "a rather good-looking man."[43]

Inside the counting room, Starr demanded, "Who's the cashier here?"

The tongue-tied Wagley could only sputter and blink. Starr jabbed him hard in the ribs with the barrel of his gun and put it another way: "Who can open the safe?"

Wagley quickly pointed to Coffman. Starr spun his pistol on Coffman.

"Open it," Starr ordered.

Brackett followed Starr's route through the bank director's office, herding Davis and Baker into the counting room. Rollens remained in the foyer with Wilson.

Starr trained his gun on Coffman as the man knelt before the safe.

"Work fast," said Starr. "You are not working for the bank now; you're working for me."[44]

The cashier licked his fingers and then spun the ridges on the combination dial. He knew $30,000 was inside, but he was helpless to stop the bandits.

Starr noticed the hands of the clerk, Moore, were trembling as she held them aloft. She was terrified.

"It's okay," Starr said. "You can put your hands down." Moore lowered her arms. He pointed to a stool with his gun. "Sit still and you won't get hurt."[45]

After Coffman turned the crank and opened the safe door, he stood up and stepped back. Starr moved into position and genuflected. He pulled a pillowcase from his belt and hooked it open over one knee. Bank Board President Bill Myers watched helplessly and with silent anger as he stood in the vault room doorway.[46]

194   Reel Five

At that moment the bank's front door banged open. J. D. "Bud" Eagle,[47] an elderly Harrison resident, stepped into the foyer and looked around. Rollens released Wilson and snatched Eagle by the collar.

"What are you fellers up to here this morning?" Eagle asked. "This some kind of gag?

Rollens ordered Eagle to join the others in the counting room.

"What's that you say?"

The old man was hard of hearing. When he didn't move, Rollens gave him a "severe punch in the ribs" with his gun.

In the counting room, Myers suddenly remembered something. Twelve years earlier, he'd hidden a Winchester Model 1873 rifle in the vault in case of just such an emergency. Eagle's unexpected entrance had distracted Brackett and Rollens long enough to allow him to slip into the open vault unnoticed. Once inside, he found the Winchester hidden among the iron rods thatched across the ceiling to keep the walls of the vault together. He quickly pulled down the rifle, not knowing what to expect after the gun had sat for over a decade unnoticed and untouched. *Is it even loaded?* He saw there was no bullet in the chamber. Quietly and gently, Myers eased the lever action downward. A small smile of relief pulled at his mustache as a brass casing popped into place.

Myers stepped quickly to the vault's proscenium and brought the steel-cased Winchester to his shoulder. He sighted down the barrel and found his target—the bandit leader on one knee in front of the safe. Moore, the clerk, saw Myers with the rifle. She flinched, thinking Myers was aiming at her. Coffman also saw the Winchester and "cringed back." Starr noticed the cashier's reaction but didn't understand what was happening.

"Look me in the eye," Starr snapped. "If anyone gets hurt here, you'll be the first one to get killed."

Starr spun and hit the wall.

The crack of Myers's shot rang out milliseconds later. Black powder filled the room with acrid smoke. Everyone's eyes darted. Their brains tried to piece together what had happened. Then, shrieks and shouting penetrated muffled eardrums.

Brackett saw Starr writhing on the ground in pain. Fire flared from his eyes, and he whipped his pistol toward Myers. "You're gonna pay!"[48] Rollens swept his gun from person to person ready to fire.

Wilson shrieked, "They're going to kill us all!"[49]

Will He Live?

Brackett's finger was tightening on the trigger when he heard:

"Don't shoot!"

The order came from Starr.

"They got me," Starr groaned. "Beat it!"[50]

Brackett looked to Rollens, whose eyes read, "Let's go!" Brackett raced back through the director's office and grabbed Wilson on the other side. He used her as a shield as he headed for the door. Rollens was already out. When Brackett reached the entrance, he flung Wilson to the floor and fled.

On the counting floor, Starr looked up and saw Myers advancing on him with his Winchester.

"Don't shoot again. I'm down," Starr promised.

Baker, the insurance salesman, snatched up Starr's Colt from the floor. Satisfied the outlaw had been incapacitated, Myers and Wagley ran to the front door. Wilson was still picking herself up, blocking their path. Myers would later tease her, "Ruth, I'd have gotten them if it hadn't been for you."[51]

Brackett and Rollens jumped into the idling Nash.

"Go! Go! Go!" they ordered.

Lockhart gunned the motor, and the three men sped off, past the Boone County Jail on the left and over Crooked Creek Bridge.

When Myers landed on the sidewalk, he shouldered his rifle again. He looked for a shot, but pedestrians were in his way. Myers finally found an opening and tugged off a few rounds at the shrinking Nash. As the *Boone County Headlight* reported, "Myers began pumping lead again, and his bull's eye aim was again attested by the shattered glass from the windshield that was found on the bridge."[52]

Back in People's Bank, Moore jumped from her stool and ran to Starr.[53] She took his head and rested it on her lap. Her blond locks draped down her face as she looked into his glazed eyes. Starr asked Baker to remove his costume specs and asked Thistlewaite for a drink.[54] The clerk filled the dipper from a barrel and brought it to him. Coffman kneeled beside Starr; his fear had turned to effrontery.

"What's your name?" Coffman demanded.

"Jim McCoy."

"Where are you from?"

"Joplin, Missouri."

Outside the bank the winter storm gathered. Naomi Moore's father ran five frigid blocks from their home to the bank. Marvin Wagley's wife received a telephone call and jumped in the car. Wilson's boss from the Harrison County Grocery Company called the bank, and she was handed the phone.

"What's taking you so long?" he demanded.

"The bank's been held up," she responded—then hung up.

Dr. Tildon P. Fowler, whose office was above People's Bank, came down the stairs with his medical bag. He kneeled next to Starr and brought out his scissors. Dr. Fowler carefully cut away Starr's clothing to get a better look at the wound.

"Please doc, give me a shot," Starr said, begging for a painkiller.

A few minutes later, Dr. Frank Kirby arrived, and he injected a painkiller. Dr. Fowler spoke to Starr soberly: "You are mortally wounded. If you have anything to say, you'd better say it."

Starr considered his situation for a beat, then announced, "My name is Henry Starr."

There was a collective gasp in the counting room. Henry Starr, the most notorious bank robber of the decade—wounded and dying right there in People's Bank!

Starr asked if someone could call his wife, Hulda, in Claremore, and his mother, Mary. By this time Mrs. Wagley had arrived. She looked around the counting room and found Starr's pillowcase heavy with cash and coins.

"Count it and return it to the safe," she said, handing the pillowcase to Coffman. In the chaos of people entering and exiting the scene, someone took Starr's gun belt. Moore kept the bloody pillowcase "prettily embroidered on the open end."

Dr. Fowler continued to monitor Starr's vital signs.

"You know, I've robbed more banks than any man in America," Starr whispered to him.[55] Then, Starr began writhing in agony, begging for someone to move his legs.

Coffman obliged.

"Dr. Johnson is going to operate and see if he can remove that bullet," Dr. Fowler said.

Starr was placed on a stretcher, and then a group of local men carried him to the Boone County Jail directly behind People's Bank at the corner of Willow and Central.

"Who shot me?" Starr asked.

Darley Callicott, one of the stretcher-bearers, told him, "It was old man Myers. There was a rifle hidden in the vault."

"A fella like that would make a better bank robber than a banker," Starr quipped through his delirium.[56]

The Boone County Jail was a red brick, two-story building built only seven years earlier. The facility more closely resembled a house, which it was in essence since the bottom level served as the sheriff's residence with bedrooms, a living room, and a kitchen. Upstairs were seven jail cells—one specifically for women—a water closet, and a narrow exercise area. The stretcher detail arrived at the side entrance along Willow Street. The jailer, Carter Curnutt, peered through the speakeasy window, saw who was there, and opened the door.[57] The steps to the upstairs cells were steep and narrow. Every bump caused Starr to cry out in pain. They brought him into one of the cells and transferred him from the stretcher onto a metal bed. Starr asked Callicott to remove his boots. He had no feeling in his legs, but if he was going to die, he didn't want to do so literally with his boots on like in the Old West. The man pulled them off, and Starr thanked him. Callicott would keep the bandit's blood-stained bandana as a souvenir.

Two miles southeast of Harrison, near Bellefonte, Lockhart braked the Nash to a stop. One of their tires had gone flat.[58] He, Brackett, and Rollens bailed out of the "machine" and set it ablaze. By the time the possemen arrived at the burning hulk, the bandits had melted away into the broken country of the Ozark Hills.[59] Officers attempted to cordon off the region, but the quickening snowstorm hampered their efforts. By nightfall they called off the pursuit entirely.[60]

"I knew he'd do it. I knew he'd do it if they didn't watch him," Bill Tilghman declared to the *Oklahoma City Times*, recalling his last encounter with Starr in Kansas City.[61]

Dr. J. J. Johnson administered chloroform to Starr and began his jail cell operation. He made an incision and removed the .38 ball. It had entered Starr's right side above the hip, torn away his right kidney, and lodged in his spinal cord, severing a piece of it. The surgeon turned the mashed bullet over to the prosecuting attorney, Karl Greenhaw.[62]

"The danger now is blood poisoning," Dr. Johnson told reporters following the surgery. "One of his kidneys was punctured, releasing uric acid."

"Will he live?"

"We'll know in three to nine hours."[63]

The Bedside Vigil

As the hours passed, Starr's doctors became more optimistic about his recovery.

"Whether I live or not," Starr told them, "My days of freedom are over. I don't expect to be able to convince anyone that I was excusable."[64] Starr was informed Oklahoma's governor had revoked his parole, and as soon as he could be moved, the governor of Arkansas would take custody of him to face charges for the Bentonville robbery.[65]

Harrison townsfolk collected outside the Boone County Jail, keeping vigil late into the night. They shivered at the sound of Starr's agonized cries. His nurse, Bud Wynn, provided them with periodic updates on his condition. One enterprising boy, 10-year-old Bill Jim Milum, snuck up the stairs to peek at Starr lying in his cot. He reported the outlaw was flat on his back, sleeping, with the blankets pulled up to his chest.[66] The cotton bandages around Starr's waist had become supersaturated. The blood soaked through the thin mattress "to fall, drip, drip, drip, in a shallow pool upon the concrete floor of his cell."[67]

The next day, jail staff helped 80-year-old former US Marshal George Crump up the steep steps to the Boone County Jail's second floor. Thin and

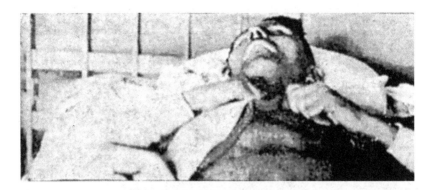

Figure 43 Starr on his deathbed in the Boone County Jail. Dr. J. J. Johnson removed the .38-caliber bullet lodged in Starr's spine. Harrison residents kept a vigil in the streets, listening to cries of pain and awaiting updates on his health. He died on February 22, 1921. *Harrison Times*, February 26, 1921. Courtesy of the Boone County Heritage Museum, Harrison, Arkansas.

frail, with a long white beard, Crump looked down upon Starr lying in his bed and identified him as the same person who talked Cherokee Bill into giving up his gun twenty-six years earlier. Through his delirium Starr could easily have mistaken Crump for Father Time, only missing his scythe and hourglass—but coming for his due nevertheless.[68]

When Myers, the "grizzled old banker," came to his bedside, Starr told him, "I don't blame you. The only blame I've got in my heart is against myself. It was an open fight, and the best man won."[69] According to Myers's boyhood friend W. H. Wilson, the banker was always good with a gun and "cool as a cucumber."[70] Born in 1852 in Fredonia, Kentucky, William Johnson Myers was the eldest of three boys. Wilson said back then young people viewed justice differently and would right wrongs with firearms. He gave an example: "Negroes had become almost unbearable to the inhabitants" of Princeton, Kentucky, by hanging out inside the Illinois Central depot. They were "making themselves at home and all white people miserable with their impudence and made it almost unsafe for a white woman to go about." One day Myers gathered his younger siblings and arrived at the depot with their rifles. He demanded to know what right the "negroes" had for being there. Myers got an "insolent reply" in return, so he and his brothers opened fire. According to Wilson, "Negroes began pouring out like molasses from a

Figure 44 The Peoples Bank, Harrison, Arkansas. The sign for Dr. T. P. Fowler's office, the first to treat Starr, can be seen in the window on the second floor. Across the rear alley is the Boone County Jail, where Starr died on the second floor. Courtesy Western History Collections, Special Research Collections, University of Oklahoma Libraries, Box T-4, item 45. *Inset*: William J. "Bill" Myers fatally shot Starr while the bandit-turned-actor-turned-bandit attempted to rob the bank on February 19, 1921. The wily former bank president used a Winchester Model 1873 rifle he'd hidden in the vault. Courtesy of the Boone County Heritage Museum, Harrison, Arkansas.

bunghole." From then on Black people would poke their heads in through the back door of the depot and ask the first white person if the Myers boys were around. If not, they would continue their business quickly and not linger. In Myers's view, the best way to curb "negro impudence" was with a rifle.

The anecdote was meant to compliment Myers, but it revealed a lot about Harrison's mindset at the time. In 1921 Harrison was a "sundown town," meaning Black people could not be in the city limits after nightfall or they would face fines, jail, beatings, or death.[71] Overt racism and violence had thrived for over sixteen years in Harrison. On September 30, 1905, over two dozen white men armed with guns and clubs attacked Black residents. They tied them to trees, whipped them, and demanded they leave Harrison.

Many Black families fled the town after their homes were burned to the ground in the mob violence. Some Black people stayed, mostly to work in white households. The first episode of mob violence proved unsatisfactory, so white residents started another round four years later, chasing away the remaining Black families.

Cleve Coffman also visited Starr. When the patrician cashier arrived at his bedside, Starr asked for Coffman's forgiveness, reminding him he'd saved everyone's lives by telling Brackett and Rollens to leave and not to shoot anybody. The point was important to Starr, who reminded the cashier he had "conducted the affair in the whitest manner possible, and appealed to Coffman to witness that it was so."[72] Starr insisted that Coffman should have his gun if he died. The cashier joked that he deserved it since he had to look down the barrel in fear for his life.[73] Coffman, "like so many who came under the personable outlaw's spell,"[74] developed a warm regard for Starr and spent the next seventy-two hours caring for him.

Starr granted an interview with J. W. Perry, a staff correspondent from the *Daily Oklahoman*.[75] Starr lay flat on his back, only able to hold an intermittent conversation between spasms of pain.

"Why did you do it?"

"The only excuse I have is that I was in debt," Starr confessed. "I couldn't stand to permit my friends to bear the burden of my financial delinquencies, and some of the banks I owed were threatening to sue. The only way I knew to get quick money was to rob a bank." .

"Wouldn't your friends have preferred you to default on your debts rather than return to bank robbery?"

Before answering, Starr asked for water for his parched lips. The nurse, Wynn, handed him a glass. After sipping and taking a moment to gather his strength, Starr answered the question:

"I've not only failed in my attempt to make good my debts, but I've betrayed their trust. God knows I meant to make good, when I promised to go straight; and now I can't even convince them that I meant it."

"What about your family?"

"I broke my vow to my wife Hulda and my boy Teddy," Starr said. "That's the worst part of it. You don't know how that hurts; you can't understand."

Starr said he owed Pan-American $1,200 and had borrowed money from five different banks.[76] His total indebtedness had increased to $5,000. Other newspapers reported Starr had $2,000 in gambling debts alone. There is no explanation for why Starr would owe Pan-American money unless he'd borrowed from them based on future revenue. He'd told former Oklahoma Commissioner of Charities and Corrections Kate Barnard the opposite: Pan-American owed him money.

Newspaper reporters descended upon Ollie Starr's home, seeking her reaction. She had grown weary of Starr's recidivism. "Of course, I feel this deeply and always will," Ollie said. "But I can't seem to care so much now since he has brought this on our boy. My only desire is to shield him from the taunts and whisperings that are sure to follow him now."[77] Asked about her relationship with Starr's new wife, Ollie responded, "I don't know Hulda Starr, but I believe I wouldn't object if she'd come to see him now if she wants to."[78] Ollie didn't leave immediately to be by Starr's side. Instead, she sent Teddy to ride along with Starr's mother, Mary Gordon, now 72.

Not needing Ollie's or anyone else's permission, Hulda boarded the Missouri & Northern Arkansas in Claremore.[79] She arrived Saturday at midnight. Starr had been moaning throughout the evening and calling out her name. However, when she entered his cell, the opiates had kicked in, and he was unconscious. By morning the drugs had worn off, and he was writhing in pain again. Hulda watched as the doctors administered laudanum, and he closed his eyes. Hulda leaned over and kissed his cheek.

"Honey, don't bother me now," he said gently. "Let me sleep."

As he slowly drifted off, she returned to the waiting room of the Boone County Jail and gazed out the window. The blizzard had brought a foot of snow. "Oh, if this snow had only come a day earlier, then he couldn't have done it," Hulda said, weeping.[80]

Later that day, Walter Stapleton, the cashier from the Bank of Seligman, was escorted into Starr's cell and positively identified him as the leader of the December 20, 1919, armed robbery.[81]

In the afternoon, the train carrying Mary Gordon and Teddy pulled into the Harrison station. Hundreds of people gathered at the depot, standing in the snow and cold to peek at the older woman and the tall young man who resembled his father. At the Boone County Jail, Mary and Teddy were asked to wait while the nurse made Starr "presentable." When they were allowed to enter, Starr was half-conscious and heavily sedated. A witness said, "He recognized her and held out his enfeebled hand, then the normally stout mother burst into tears."[82] Teddy offered his father a hopeful smile. The doctors advised them to return when Starr felt stronger and more himself.

Teddy, now a high school senior, told a reporter that his father had visited him two weeks ago in Muskogee. "I had no idea then that he would go back to his old habits," he said. "The appeal of outlawry was too strong for him and had a strong grip on him."[83]

When Ollie arrived, she was asked about her relationship with Starr. "It is not that I have much love left for Henry," she said, "but I can't forget that he is the father of my son."[84]

Kate Barnard sent Starr a telegram: "Put your faith in God, and He will save you. Be brave and pray."[85] She provided a vague update on Roy Hoffman's effort to investigate whether Pan-American had cheated Starr. "I suppose Hoffman's efforts failed," she said. "It's enough to make heaven weep that he was literally driven back to crime because those who had entered into a contract with him robbed him."[86]

Hulda remained hopeful. "I am going to do everything I can for Henry if only he lives. I think he could serve out his twenty-five years and have some of his life left for me," she said. Dr. Johnson informed her that her husband would be paralyzed from the waist down, even if he managed to pull through. Hulda hoped the prison would take pity on him and let him remain free.

"They couldn't be so hard on him as to force him to live the rest of his life in the penitentiary," she stated naïvely.[87]

Fade Out. The End

On Starr's final day, a tall, heavyset man came to Starr's bedside with a shocking revelation. He introduced himself as Toney, Starr's long-lost son. No family member had ever heard of him, including Mary Gordon. Looking to be in his early 30s, he seemed too old to be the son of 47-year-old Starr, although it wasn't impossible. Upon hearing his father was dying, Toney Starr said he caught the first train out of Homer, Louisiana.[88] The family suspected he was a grifter and opportunist but didn't make a public fuss. "Privately, they referred to him derisively as 'Goldie' because of several gold teeth which gleamed prominently in his mouth."[89]

"So, he's dying with his boots on?" responded Tilghman when apprised of Starr's condition. "Well, that's the way he always wanted it, and heaven knows he took plenty of chances to make it come true."[90]

Author and historian Fred E. Sutton had interviewed Starr decades earlier and warned him he'd come to a violent and bloody end one day.

"They'll corner you and tear the flesh from your bones with bullets," Sutton told him.

"I know it, but what of it?" Starr countered. "It will be over in a flash, and I won't feel it."[91]

But Starr's death wasn't over in a flash. By day three Starr's jail cell echoed with pleas for drugs to relieve his unbearable pain. Drainage tubes ran from his pierced kidney to prevent uric acid poisoning.[92] He knew he was dying. Dr. Fowler increased his laudanum dosage.[93]

"It's all right for these doctors to encourage me by telling me I have a chance to get well," Starr said. "But I am the man wounded, and I know the nature of my wound. It is all off with me. I am paying the penalty, and I hope God will forgive me."[94]

Initially, Starr gave the police fake names for his accomplices. Then he clammed up entirely. The police continued to badger him, and under extreme pain and in a drugged stupor, Starr relented. The sheriff, two witnesses, and Karl Greenshaw, the prosecutor for the Fourteenth Judicial District, gathered around his deathbed. Greenshaw recorded Starr's confession:

I, Henry Starr, realizing that I am fatally wounded and believing that I am soon to depart this life and that I cannot possibly recover, do hereby make this as my dying statement, that the persons who assisted me in robbing or attempting to rob the People's National Bank of Harrison, Arkansas, on February 18th, 1921, were Dave Lockhart of St. Joe, Arkansas, and Rufus Rowland and Charley Brackett of Claremore, Oklahoma. Lockhart was driving the car and remained on the outside so he would not be seen and identified while Charley Brackett and Rufus Rowland and I went in the bank to get the money.[95]

Starr also implicated Lockhart and Rollens in the Bank of Seligman robbery but not Brackett. The *St. Louis Globe-Democrat* printed the headline "Henry Starr 'Squeals' On His Confederates."[96] Mr. C. W. Grimes, a Tulsa resident who'd been in Harrison, related, "It was common talk in Harrison that Starr, under the influence of the anesthetic, muttered the names of his companions in the robbery."[97]

While Starr faced the prospect of death, the press insisted on framing his final moments as a religious epiphany. In *Thrilling Events* Starr responded to people curious about him. "What is your politics? Haven't any," he wrote. "Your religion? Same."[98] Harrison Sheriff Sibley Johnson made a point of saying in the press that Starr's confession was probably a lie because "despite the talks of several ministers, Starr has manifested little interest in religion."[99]

The *Dresden Enterprise* reported Starr refused to speak to a minister who called on him, saying he already knew about the hereafter.[100] Yet the *Tulsa Tribune* insisted that Starr, lying on his deathbed, began thinking of religion and divine intervention. Under a headline reading "Divine Aid," Starr is quoted as saying, "I am going to die and am anxious to make my peace with God."[101] Starr understood how his deathbed conversion was being manufactured for public consumption. During a visit, two local ministers asked him about "his spiritual condition." Starr said he understood the choice between the Lord taking him into his bosom and eternal damnation, but he had no religion. He was willing to accept their prayers but nothing more. After they'd left, Starr thought about the conversation. He turned to Wynn, his nurse:

"Bud, chase down those preachers for me, would you?" Starr asked. "Make sure they know not to run around telling stories that I had a change of heart or anything of that sort."[102]

Starr held on until Tuesday, five days after the robbery, but sank rapidly.

"What must have been his feelings as his eyes sought the barred windows?" J. D. Eagle wrote for the *Harrison Times*. "Never again would he see the boundless sweep of the prairies, nor feel again the breath of Spring upon his cheeks as he thrilled to the canter of his cayuse upon the trackless plains."[103]

Hulda, Teddy, and Gordon stayed at his side, and "he said goodbye to them with a nod of the head and a smile just before consciousness left him." At 1:25 in the afternoon of February 22, 1921, Starr died.[104] A reporter from the *El Reno Democrat* conveyed the moment: "A hush had fallen on the town, for although Starr was shot down when he attempted to hold up a bank, his notorious escapades made him a popular figure, and sympathy here was with him in his final battle."[105]

Reminiscent of a Haiku, the *Ocala Evening Star* wrote: "Henry Starr, a western bandit, died at Harrison, Ark., Tuesday. His star has set."[106]

Volunteers from Harrison transferred Starr's body to the R. D. Cline Furniture and Undertaking Company along the courthouse square. Only days earlier Lockhart had giddily driven the Nash past the location where Starr would be embalmed. Cline placed Starr's corpse in his front window for public viewing. He placed Starr in a dark suit and stretched him out in quiet repose on a bier covered in a white cloth. His head rested on a pillow, and his hands were placed one above the other across his stomach.

The children of Harrison had been in a wild state of excitement since the robbery.[107] When the lunch bell rang at the nearby elementary school, Ruth Kirby McCoy and her little pals raced to the upstairs mortuary. They circled the bier, gawking at Starr's corpse for the whole lunch period. When the bell rang again, they raced back for fourth-period class.[108] Starr's mother, Mary Gordon, and sister Adna Benge were appalled that Starr's body was on public display for a day and a half. They berated Cline, and the mortician sheepishly removed the body from the window.[109]

Starr's family thanked the people of Harrison for their hospitality during Starr's illness, especially "the sheriff, attending doctors and newspaper men for kindness and courtesies shown."[110] William J. Myers received hundreds of letters of congratulations for stopping the robbery and killing Starr. One letter, however, had a decidedly different tone. The paper was plain but heavily soiled. The penmanship was good but scrawled with lead pencil. The message was clear and unsigned: "You got Starr, but we'll get you yet!"[111] Gordon assured the public that her family would not seek revenge on Myers. The *Ozark Daily Times* phrased her response in a particular manner: "We want him to know that we will not hold it against him. If he had shot

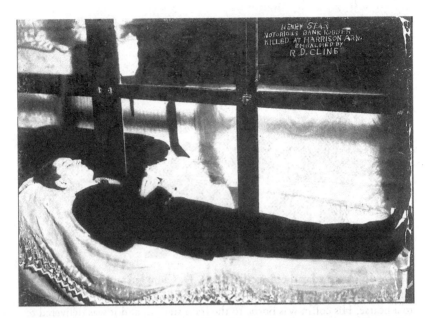

Figure 45 Starr's body was laid out for public display on the second floor of the R. D. Cline Furniture and Undertaking Company in Harrison, Arkansas. Children from the local school spent their recess gazing at the corpse. Starr's mother, Mary Gordon, and his sister Adna Benge demanded the body be taken out of the window. Courtesy of the Boone County Heritage Museum, Harrison, Arkansas.

Henry more than once, it would have been different, she said, with her dark, piercing eyes full of meaning."[112]

Hundreds of people came to see Starr's body at Cline's while it was on view, and a hundred more gathered in the street the day his corpse was brought down from the second floor and loaded into a white hearse.[113] Some spectators arrived in horse-drawn wagons and others in automobiles—an inadvertent reflection of the eras Starr had bridged. Then, the crowd followed the caisson to the train station. Porters loaded Starr's coffin on the Frisco bound for Joplin, where his corpse was transferred to the Santa Fe at Cherryvale, Kansas.[114]

Starr's body arrived in Dewey on Thursday morning, February 24, and the family had his casket transferred to Burt's funeral parlor. Starr's desire to be cremated wouldn't be honored. Toney said his father had told him a year earlier he wanted to be buried in the open, without trees nearby.[115]

Figure 46 A crowd gathers outside the R. D. Cline Furniture and Undertaking Company in Harrison, Arkansas, as Starr's body is transferred to a hearse. His coffin was borne to the train station, and it was delivered to Dewey, Oklahoma, on February 24, 1921, where Starr was buried. Photographer: Charles G. Jones. Courtesy of the Boone County Heritage Museum, Harrison, Arkansas.

"Father always loved the prairie, and he spent most of his life there," Toney explained.

Hulda agreed. "Cremation sounds horrible to me, and when I die, I want to be buried beside him. Then, too, I want to be able to visit his grave," she said.

At 3:00 p.m., February 25, inside the Methodist chapel, a choir sang, "Nearer My God to Thee."[116] Starr's handsome black casket lay on a catafalque at the church's transept, flanked by floral arrangements. From the pulpit Reverend James Eldridge delivered the sermon, reminding Starr's friends and family that Jesus pardons "even unto the last minute of life." The small church was filled, and the overflow crowd spilled out onto the steps. Mourners craned to hear the reverend's final words. As the sobs of the women in Starr's life—Mary, Ollie, and Hulda—echoed in the church, a thousand mourners formed a procession to view Starr's open casket. Teddy walked up to his father and placed a pink rose in his clasped hands. Among the mourners were Lucy Auldridge and her husband, Allan. Starr had herded cattle for them when he was 18, and she remembered him as "an ideal young man."[117]

After the services, Hulda and Gordon led the cortege to the Dewey Cemetery, "where all that was mortal of Henry Starr was laid to rest beside the grave of his infant son."[118] The funeral procession, two and a half miles long, was the largest in Dewey history at the time and included automobiles and a horseback contingent from the 101 Ranch.[119] Although Starr's funeral expenses were already paid, Ollie and Gordon wanted to expose Toney's real intentions. They asked him to pitch in on the burial costs. Toney said he would help; however, after the funeral, he was "never seen nor heard of again by his relatives."[120]

With Starr in his eternal home, reflections on his life began: "Henry was as good a boy at heart as ever lived, and I loved him just as dearly as any mother loves her son, no matter what he had done," said Gordon.[121] She had a theory for her boy's criminal bent: "I believe his character was being molded even before his birth. There was a serious uprising in Oklahoma in those days, and those dark, dangerous days must have had a prenatal influence."[122]

Edith C. Johnson, a columnist for the *Daily Oklahoman,* in an editorial titled, "Quitter and Parasite Is Real Henry Starr," wrote that Starr was simply lazy: "If you know the inner thoughts of Henry Starr and all other safe-crackers, hi-jackers, hold-up artists and outlaws, you would find that they have hated work. Their ambition has not been to give something to society, but to be parasites and live off the labor of others."[123] Whether or not Starr was lazy is debatable. A more apt description of him as a serial bank robber and gambler would be "adrenaline junky." Author Kenneth Carter, in his book *Buzz! Inside the Minds of Thrill-Seekers, Daredevils, and Adrenaline Junkies* (2019), describes high sensation–seeking personalities as people who crave "exotic and intense experiences, despite physical or social risk."[124] When US Marshal E. D. Nix asked Starr what streak in his nature led to outlawry, he responded, "I must have excitement. I crave it, and it preys upon me until I just slip out and get into devilment of some sort."[125]

When attempting to go straight, Starr could only achieve a similar thrill by playing cards. A Tulsa coachman recalled spending four hours driving Starr to all the city's gambling houses. "And he done gave me a twenty besides my fare, too. He was a gentleman, was Henry Starr," declared the driver.[126]

210   Reel Five

For a while the excitement at winning a big pot or losing it all kept Starr away from banks. But playing cards with borrowed money to pay off debts wasn't fun. Starr kept losing, falling farther into debt, and it drove him to his fatal bank robbery in Harrison, Arkansas.

The *Durant Weekly News* offered a more nuanced summation of Starr's life and career: "Henry Starr, the last of the old-time bank robbers, has paid the price and has gone on the long journey West. . . . If there is anything in the character of Henry Starr that anyone would wish to emulate, we have never discovered it. He was weighted in the balance and found wanting. However, it can be said of him in comparison with the holdup men, two-bit robbers, and things who are now depredating on society promiscuously, Henry Starr was both a gentleman and a scholar."[127]

Two weeks later Oklahoma experienced another notable death: Senate Bill 6 for motion picture censorship. The *Oklahoma City Times* noted, "Some bills are murdered, others go to sleep from mere laziness and knockout drops are administered to a few." Like Starr, film censorship was sleeping peacefully—for the moment.[128]

Reel Six

Post-Credits Scenes

A nd life carried on.

The day after Starr's burial, a craven and opportunistic advertisement for Jackson & Geiser Groceries appeared in the *Creek County Democrat*:

Died in Jail

After a good many years of bandit life, and outlawry. Henry Starr quit the business. He died from the effect of a rifle bullet, fired by a bank official. Had he been living an honorable life, he would not have been shot.

It Does Not Pay to Be Crooked

We are taught that "Honesty Is the Best Policy."

We follow that Slogan at our store. We price our merchandise in accordance with the daily market quotations, regardless of cost to us. When the market comes down, our prices do likewise.

We Do Not Rob Our Patrons

Jackson & Geiser

GROCERIES[1]

A second advertisement for the Kozy Soda Shop appeared in the *Wetumka Gazette*. Though equally tasteless, it at least wasn't self-righteous:

Henry Starr

Didn't patronize us, but everybody else does. Why shouldn't they, when they can get those delicious Malted Milks, Ice Cream Sodas, and all the other good drinks that we serve from our fountain.

"Gee, but they're Good"

THE "KOZY"[2]

A reader of Arkansas's *Mena Weekly Star* didn't like the favorable profiles of Starr in the paper, writing to the editor, "The most important and vital feature is that he got what he deserved after long deserving it."[3]

W. E. Sharpe from the Fayetteville sheriff's office attended the Floyd Wilson murder trial at Fort Smith in the 1890s. He declared, "Starr was just naturally a bad Indian."[4] W. T. Yadon, who sat on the jury, thought Starr should have been hanged, stating, "The world would have been saved suffering from his later crimes."[5]

Starr continued to live on the silver screen. In March a Little Rock theater tied its promotion for *The Passing of the Oklahoma Outlaws* to his death less than two weeks earlier: "Henry Starr, the noted bank bandit who was recently shot and killed while robbing a bank in Harrison, Ark. will be seen in motion pictures at the Princess today."[6]

In April 1921 the Arkansas Bankers' Association honored William J. Myers at its annual meeting in Little Rock.[7] The audience applauded enthusiastically when his photo was projected on the screen with a stereopticon. Myers gave a brief speech after receiving a gold Elgin pocket watch honoring "his services to the banks of Arkansas." The award was followed by S. J. Doyle, who entertained the crowd "with amusing 'Wop' stories."[8]

Police used Starr's deathbed confession to hunt down Rufus Rollens, Charles Bracket, and Dave Lockhart. Two months after the Harrison robbery, deputies followed Rollens's wife, and she led them to her brother's house in Muskogee, where he was hiding. When offers burst in, Rollens attempted to escape by jumping out a window but was captured by Vinita Deputy Sheriff E. D. Ridenour. Rollens pleaded guilty to attempted robbery in the circuit court at Harrison and was sentenced to three years in the Oklahoma State Penitentiary.[9]

Post-Credits Scenes

On April 26, 2021, Charles Brackett surrendered to a sheriff's posse in Miami, Oklahoma, after a pitched gun battle. "Starr double-crossed me," Brackett whined. "He squealed!" Brackett pleaded guilty to a robbery in Locust Grove, Oklahoma, so he wouldn't face extradition to Arkansas.[10]

On March 26, 1924, three years and one month after Starr succumbed to his injuries, Lockhart was captured by police at a farmhouse outside of Sperry, Oklahoma. When Special Officer Mont Grady attempted to handcuff Lockhart, they fought over a gun. A shot rang out. The bullet pierced Lockhart's stomach below the kidney. "My God, you've killed me," Lockhart moaned before falling to the ground. The death of Lockhart marked the end of what Oklahoma's peace officers touted as the "big three," including Starr and Al Spencer.[11]

Starr's Stroud accomplice, Joe Davis, would spend fourteen years behind bars at the McNeil Island, Washington, and Leavenworth facilities. He was 40 when he was released on February 6, 1931. Davis would never be indicted for the Stroud robbery.[12]

Roy "Arkansas Tom" Daugherty, who visited Starr in his Chandler jail cell, toured briefly with William Tilghman as a guest speaker during *The Passing of the Oklahoma Outlaws* roadshow. On November 26, 1923, he returned to bank robbery, pulling off a bank heist in Asbury, Missouri. Eleven months later he was gunned down by Joplin detectives. Despite contemplating the career move, Arkansas Tom never went to Hollywood.[13]

Tulsa County Sheriff James Woolley had a checkered career and was often accused of being too friendly with outlaws like Starr. Woolley was a bad cop, allowing vigilantism to thrive in his jurisdiction, leading up to the Tulsa Race Massacre. He called the lynching of one white man and one Black man "more beneficial than a death sentence pronounced by the courts."[14] In 1931, at 62, Woolley was a detective with the Tulsa Police Department when he approached a vehicle with suspected stolen items inside. The driver fatally shot him in the chest.[15]

Naomi Moore, the People's Bank clerk who had cradled Starr's head in her lap, had a boyfriend named Fred Stewart who owned a hardware store on the courthouse square. After the robbery, Stewart went to Moore's home to check on her condition. She was fine, sitting safely in her living room with

214   Reel Six

her family. Stewart made a bold pronouncement in front of her parents: "You're not working anymore," Stewart said. "We're getting married." They did get married, and Moore spent the rest of her life as a homemaker.[16]

In 1927 George Dewey Peck, the incorrigible young advance man for *A Debtor to the Law*, earned his law degree and became the Thirteenth District State Senator for two terms.[17] He would become editor of the *Stroud Democrat*, the same newspaper on whose pages he'd appeared as a young man. His love of motion pictures never diminished, and he owned two movie theaters, the Rialto and the Ritz.

The last five years of Kate Barnard's life were spent at the Egbert Hotel in Oklahoma City.[18] "Miss Kate" never married or had children. At one time she'd advocated for all women to forego marriage until men learned how to treat children better. Barnard spent her last years flirting with a run for US Senate and worked on her autobiography. On February 24, 1930, exactly nine years from the day Starr had been buried, Barnard died of a heart attack in her bathtub at 54.[19] In her will she donated her home and library to the Catholic Little Sisters of the Poor. She directed them to establish the Barnard Home for the Friendless, so "the youth of the world may emulate me in dedicating their own lives to securing justice for the poor of their generation."[20] Instead, the will was contested, and her three half-brothers split the $24,000 estate. Even in death, Barnard's efforts to do good were thwarted.[21] Her contribution to Oklahoma's history went unrecognized for decades. On May 15, 2001, a bronze sculpture of Barnard was placed in the East Gallery of the Oklahoma State Capitol.[22]

Patrick (P. S.) McGeeney went on to direct *Perils of the West* (1922) with William Karl Hackett as his leading man. Hackett had a long career in Hollywood as the weaselly villain and appeared with Shirley Temple in *The Littlest Rebel* (1935). In addition to *Perils of the West*, McGeeney directed *Little Miss Bluebonnet* (1922) and *The Germ* (1923).[23]

William Tilghman had one final call to duty. In August 1924 the Cromwell Chamber of Commerce sought his help cleaning up their newly incorporated city.[24] The oil town had become overrun with "hop peddlers," illegal liquor joints, gambling houses, prostitutes, and bootleggers. That sounded like a challenge to the 70-year-old Tilghman, who accepted the position of chief of police.

Post-Credits Scenes   215

Tilghman traced the source of cocaine flowing into Cromwell to a plane from south of the border that made drops in the outlying oilfields. Tilghman faced one of the first Mexican drug cartels, a pox that would inflict the United States for the next hundred years. The local drug kingpin warned Tilghman that he was getting too "nosey," and Cromwell wasn't a good place for his health.

One evening Tilghman was sitting on a stool at a Crowell diner when he heard a gunshot and someone calling his name. Tilghman walked outside and saw federal prohibition agent Wiley Lynn waiting for him in the street. Tilghman believed Lynn was in the pocket of the drug kingpin and bootleggers. Tilghman met Lynn face-to-face. He grabbed the wrist of the prohibition agent's gun hand and called for assistance. With his free hand, Lynn pulled out a second gun, a short-barreled "belly gun," and fired two shots into Tilghman's rib cage at close range. Lynn hopped inside a getaway car as Tilghman collapsed to the street. Townsfolk gathered up the lawman and carried him to a couch inside a furniture store. "The grayness of death was already upon his face," a witness noted. Tilghman died fifteen minutes later.

Toney Starr posted an advertisement in the *Arkansas Democrat* six months after Starr's death, reading, "Tony Starr, son of the famous bandit, Henry Starr, will ride at the Wild West show, Forest Park, tonight."[25] Toney almost didn't make the horse show. A day earlier, the "happy-go-lucky" man wearing a spiffy Western hat adorned with beads was arrested for a bank robbery in Bauxite, Arkansas. After offering a legitimate alibi, he was released. Toney told reporters he was out of work but looking to enter the hotel business. Henry Starr never confirmed or denied paternity.

Loretta "Retta" (Wilkins) Elwick avoided the headlines after her divorce from Guy. She often referred to herself as Mrs. Henry Starr, although they never were married. In 1919 she moved to Rocky Ford, Colorado, and married Arthur Austin. They divorced in 1937. She died at 91.[26]

Hulda tearfully packed up the solid silver spurs Starr had made in the Oklahoma State Penitentiary and sent them to cowboy movie star Tom Mix, whom Starr worked with at the Miller brothers' 101 Ranch in 1907.[27] In April 2021 creditors swooped in with "quiet title and ejectment" lawsuits and she lost her Sallisaw property.[28] Hulda later remarried; her mysterious

Muskogee drug arrest in 1920 portended her future troubles. Four years after Starr's death, the new Mrs. Charles Murphy was returned to Fort Smith from El Paso, Texas, on charges of transporting narcotics.[29] She'd forfeited a bond several months earlier while awaiting an appeal to the Supreme Court and hoped to avoid a six-month prison sentence. In 1931 Hulda remarried John L. Sullivan, whom she had first wed in 1917. Mrs. Hulda Lucille Sullivan died on April 27, 1932, at the age of 34, of a gastric hemorrhage.[30] The manner of death was ruled a suicide after ingesting bichloride. She is buried at the Restland Memorial Park in Dallas, Texas.

Starr died intestate, meaning he didn't leave a will. Ollie Starr petitioned for a claim of his assets for Hulda (23), Teddy (16), and Toney (30).[31] In the Petition for Letters of Administration, her lawyer listed potential assets as an interest in oil leases in Muskogee County and a one-fourth interest in A *Debtor to the Law*, valued at $5,000. The document noted "that up to this date neither said decedent or his estate has received any income therefrom, so far as known to your petitioner." Two years later, on May 20, 1924, the administrator delivered a final report stating the court had "not received any money, property or anything of value of any kind or character belonging to said estate."[32] If P. J. Clark and Pan-American owed Starr money, they never paid up.

A year after Starr's death, Ollie married L. D. Nunyard, a Kansas City grocery salesman.[33] She lived in Muskogee for twenty years, working at the veteran's hospital and the agency for Indian affairs. Ollie relocated to Oklahoma City in 1936 and was employed at the Federal Building as a deputy clerk in the Internal Revenue Office. On November 23, 1951, she had a fatal heart attack at her desk at 69.[34] Ollie's obituary didn't mention Henry by name but said he was a "salesman and oil dealer" who died in 1921. Her tombstone at the Memorial Park Cemetery in Muskogee reads "Ollie Starr."

Theodore "Teddy" Quay Roosevelt Starr graduated from Central High School in Muskogee.[35] He competed in track at the University of Oklahoma, displaying his father's athleticism. Teddy earned his bachelor of arts in business in 1926 and later served in China as an Army 1st lieutenant during World War II. Teddy had one child named Barbara and died on April 3, 1979, at 74. He is buried at the Memorial Park Cemetery in Muskogee.

Post-Credits Scenes 217

At 88, three years before her death on August 2, 1938, Starr's mother, Mary Gordon, gave an interview at the Confederate Home in Ardmore. Of her son she said, "He would rob banks and give the money to farmers to pay off mortgages." A mother's blind love never dies.[36]

Dalton and Jennings

In 1919 Emmett Dalton moved his motion picture operations from North Carolina to Los Angeles, forming two new companies: the Great Western Pictures Corporation and the Standard Pictures Company of California.[37] Dalton dipped into the same biographical waters again in January 1931, writing another version of the Coffeyville raid titled *When the Daltons Rode*.[38] Despite getting rich by periodically stirring the ashes of his criminal career, he insisted crime doesn't pay. Since his early days touring with *The Last Ride of the Dalton Gang* in 1913, he had the foresight to purchase land in many parts of the country, including Hollywood and Florida. "I've made more money in two or three years of real estate deals than the Dalton gang ever made in all the years of our deviltry," Dalton boasted.[39]

In 1932 Dalton sued Columbia Pictures for $50,000 for copyright violation after the studio released *Beyond the Law*, a Dalton Gang drama using the same title as his autobiography. Dalton claimed that the studio tried to buy the rights to his book, but when they couldn't agree, Columbia took his life story anyway. He lost the case, and the legal ruling was a setback for Dalton, whose health was failing.[40] Dalton died on July 14, 1937, at 66 due to diabetes and a heart ailment. The bullet wounds he received at Coffeyville troubled him his entire life and required multiple surgeries. He is buried at Kingfisher Cemetery, Kingfisher, Oklahoma.[41]

Universal Pictures adapted Dalton's earlier book *When the Daltons Rode* into a film in 1940. The film starred Randolph Scott, future Best Actor Academy Award Winner Broderick Crawford as Bob Dalton, and Frank Alberton as Emmett.[42] The studio invited Dalton's widow Julia to visit the Coffeyville set where the facades of the First National and Condon Banks were re-created. She wept as she watched the Dalton Gang being shot down with blanks. Julia remarried and died in Fresno, California May 20, 1943. She was buried in Dewey Cemetery, where Starr resides.[43]

218   Reel Six

In January 1921 Al Jennings formed his motion picture production arm in Los Angeles, delivering "five thrilling stories" every four to eight weeks with budgets in the range of $8,000 to $30,000. According to Jennings, his film *Traffic in Souls* was produced for $10,000 and earned $3 million.[44] That same year Jennings published a second autobiography, *Through the Shadows with O. Henry: The Unlikely Friendship of Al Jennings and William Sydney Porter*.[45] The book's release followed a series of short films about their true-life misadventures, including *The Fugitives Who Came Back*, where Jennings played himself.[46] A decade later Jennings earned a living as a technical advisor for Westerns, including *The Oklahoma Kid* (1939) starring James Cagney and Humphrey Bogart.[47]

At 82 Jennings fought it out with the Lone Ranger. More precisely, in September 1945 he sued the producers of the Lone Ranger radio program for defamation. Jennings sought $100,000 in damages because in one episode the Lone Ranger easily disarmed him. "They made me mad. They had this Lone Ranger shootin' a gun out of my hand and me the expert," declared Jennings. He was also upset that the episode implied he recruited young men to join his gang.[48]

Jennings lost his lawsuit; however, the publicity paid dividends when Columbia Pictures cast Dan Duryea, a leading man in 1951, to portray Jennings in the film *Al Jennings of Oklahoma*, based on the book *Beating Back*.[49] With laughable hyperbole the lobby cards proclaimed, "The real and violent story of the last of the great outlaws!" and "15 years as an outlaw told by Al Jennings himself!" The movie trailer criminally exaggerated Jennings's impact, declaring, "They were all wanted . . . Dead or Alive: The Daltons, The James Boys, Billy the Kid, The Doolins, and Al Jennings of Oklahoma." Jennings provided Duryea with coaching on handling a six-shooter "straight from the horse's mouth."[50]

In January 1960, when Jennings was 96, United Pictures announced the filming of an Al Jennings TV series with Johnny Duncan in the role. Oscar Nichols, a former Columbia and 20th Century Fox writer, described the project as a "cowpoke" series on the life of Jennings—"at least the rootin'-tootin' portion of his life he likes to remember."[51]

Post-Credits Scenes

Jennings died in Tarzana, California, the day after Christmas 1961, at 98. His death prompted a desire from some to separate fact from fiction regarding his criminal exploits. An obituary in the *Record Searchlight* dubbed Jennings a "self-styled bantam badman from Oklahoma"[52] and questioned the veracity of his tales: "Was he really a desperado of the Jesse James and Dalton gang caliber? Or was tiny Al, only a lick and a split over 5 feet tall, a one-time loser, a luckless train robber, who cashed in on a legend he embroidered for naive movie folks in later years?" Jennings claimed to have killed more men than he could count, but always in self-defense. Wyatt Earp biographer Stuart Lake bristled at the outlaw's lies: "There's no record of Al ever killing anybody." And his gang's only proven train robbery "only netted about three bucks apiece."

Jennings was writing a third book, *Six-Shooters*, about his relationship with Starr, beginning at the Ohio State Penitentiary until his death while robbing the People's Bank in Harrison. The book was never completed or published.[53]

Alphonso Jennings, the raconteur, evangelist, silent film actor, and producer is buried at the Oakwood Memorial Park Cemetery in Chatsworth, California.[54]

Epilogue

Over the weekend of September 12 and 13, 1992, Stroud celebrated its centennial with a reenactment of Starr's daylight double bank robbery seventy-seven years earlier. Stanley Curry, 75, Paul's nephew, attended the event.[1] In 2022 Stroud City Manager Bob Pearman commissioned the erection of iron silhouettes to mark the historic double daylight bank robberies. Outside the former Stroud National Bank, tourists will find three figures: a cashier behind a teller window, a cowboy pointing at him with a gun, and a little girl holding a bag of pennies. Along Fourth Avenue, against the exterior of First National Bank, there are three more figures: another cashier and two cowboys with guns. At the intersection of Fourth Avenue and West Second Street, fleeing iron cowboys on horseback are mounted on a building. Pearman is considering reviving the robbery reenactment show to draw tourists to Stroud.[2]

In 2006 the Dewey Civic Association honored Starr with a new headstone, which quotes his famous boast: "I've robbed more banks than any man in America."

In 2009 business development leaders in Harrison, Arkansas, hoped to revitalize the Harrison Courthouse Square Historic District with a reenactment of the 1921 People's Bank robbery.[3] The Community Organization for Revitalization and Enhancement (CORE) looked at Tombstone, Arizona (site of the Gunfight at the OK Corral) as a model for how to monetize Western history. Currently, the OK Corral Historical Complex offers a "historama," the *Epitaph* newspaper history museum, and three gunfight reenactment shows a day at 11:00 a.m., 1:00 p.m., and 3:00 p.m.[4] At a September 2009 Harrison City Council Meeting, North Arkansas College Drama Department Chairman Michael Mahoney took the stage in "full Henry Starr" regalia. Mahoney retold the story of the notorious bank robber and said the historical reenactment would conclude with the shoot-out at the former People's Bank.

The reenactment idea never gained traction. CORE disbanded in 2014.

In a 1999 made-for-television movie, *You Know My Name*, Sam Elliott portrayed Bill Tilghman during his final days in Cromwell, Oklahoma.[5] In 2021 a Black actor from the United Kingdom, Idris Elba, portrayed Rufus Buck in the film *The Harder They Fall*. The role of Cherokee Bill was played by African American actor LaKeith Stanfield.[6]

In 2017 the Wild Bunch Film Festival awarded *The Outlaw Henry Starr*, written by Mark Archuleta, Best Modern Western Screenplay.[7] Archuleta continues to seek financing to film the life story of Henry Starr.

He's considering robbing a bank.

Endnotes

Notes for the Preface

1. Starr was approved for Dawes Rolls September 18, 1903, as a member of the Cherokee Nation per Department of the Interior Commission to the Five Civilized Tribes. Dawes Enrollment Jacket for Cherokee, Cherokee by Blood, Card #10329.

2. "En Route to Prison," *Franklin County Tribune* (Union, MO), January 28, 1898.

3. Jay Robert Nash, *Jay Robert Nash's Crime Chronology: A Worldwide Record, 1900–1983* (Facts on File Publications, 1984), 10.

4. "Robbery of Two Stroud Banks by Starr and His Bandits," *Stroud (OK) Messenger*, April 2, 1915.

5. Carl W. Breihan, "King of the Bank Robbers," *Frontier Times*, May 1964.

6. "Henry Starr Arrested For 1892 Robbery," *Muskogee (OK) Times-Democrat*, June 16, 1919. Henry Starr, *Thrilling Events: Life of Henry Starr, by Himself* (R. D. Gordon Publishing, 1914).

7. Colorado State Penitentiary at Cañon City, intake card, prisoner no. 7613, Henry Starr, November 28, 1909.

8. John J. Koblas, *The Great Cole Younger and Frank James Historical Wild West Show* (North Star Press of St. Cloud, 2002).

9. Dary Matera, *John Dillinger* (Hachette Books, 2005), 353.

10. Jeff Guinn, *Go Down Together* (Simon and Schuster, 2012), 339–41.

11. Michael Wallis, *Pretty Boy: The Life and Times of Charles Arthur Floyd* (W. W. Norton, 2011), 452–53.

12. G. Russell Girardin et al., *Dillinger: The Untold Story* (Indiana University Press, 2004), 222–23.

13. Mark Freedman, "The Dangerous Myth of Reinvention," *Harvard Business Review*, January 1, 2014, https://hbr.org/2014/01/the-dangerous-myth-of-reinvention.

14. "Hall of Fame Member Glenn Shirley," *Oklahoma Journalism Hall of Fame*, accessed June 7, 2024. https://okjournalismhalloffame.com/1981/glenn-shirley/.

15. Michael Wallis, *The Real Wild West: The 101 Ranch and the Creation of the American West* (St. Martin's Press, 2000), 385.

Notes for Reel One

1. Matthew Solomon, *Fantastic Voyages of the Cinematic Imagination: Georges Méliès's Trip to the Moon* (State University of New York Press, 2011). Billi Brass Quintet, "Le Voyage Dans La Lune (1902) - Georges Méliès - (HQ) - Music by David Short - Billi Brass Quintet," YouTube. April 9, 2018, https://youtu.be/ZNAHcMMOHE8?si=0ubcJ5BXA_KiFbjp.

2. "Thirteen Ask Pardon from Pen," *Cañon City (CO) Record*, September 11, 1913. "Starr Hopes for Pardon," *Daily Ardmoreite* (Ardmore, OK), September 25, 1913. "Henry Starr Is Paroled," *Independence (KS) Daily Reporter*, October 9, 1913.

3. "Henry Starr Pardoned," *Daily Chieftain* (Vinita, OK), January 17, 1903. "Mother's Appeal Successful," *St. Louis Republic*, January 16, 1903.

4. Starr, *Thrilling Events*, 66.

5. US Court, Western District, Indian Territory, Marriage License No. 1071, Mr. Henry Starr of Tulsa in the IT age 29 years and Miss Ollie Griffin of Starvilla in the IT age 21 years, 15th day of September 1903. "She Loves Starr Though a Bandit," *Muskogee (OK) Daily Phoenix*, February 19, 1921.

6. "Outlaw Turns Land Agent," *Fort Worth Record and Register*, October 7, 1906.

7. Fred Ellsworth Sutton and A. B. Macdonald, *Hands Up! Stories of the Six-Gun Fighters of the Old Wild West* (Bobbs-Merrill, 1927), 238.

8. Clara B. Kennan, "When Henry Starr Robbed the Bentonville Bank: 1893," *Arkansas Historical Quarterly* 7, no. 1 (Spring 1948): 68–80.

9. "Oklahoma Desperado," *Daily Ardmoreite*, March 20, 1908, 5.

10. "Robbed Bank at Tyro," *Coffeyville (KS) Daily Journal*, March 18, 1919.

11. Starr, *Thrilling Events*, 68.

12. "Not Starr Who Sent Message to Dewey," *Muskogee Times-Democrat*, March 21, 1908. "Death of Starr's Child," *Bartlesville (OK) Weekly Examiner*, March 21, 1908.

13. "Starr Will Die, Doctors Repeat; Suspects Freed," *Muskogee Times-Democrat*, February 21, 1921.

14. "Oklahoma Desperado," *Arizona Republican* (Phoenix), May 13, 1909. "Famous Henry Starr Brought to Pueblo for Safe Keeping," *Cañon City Record*, June 10, 1909.

15. "Starr Gets 25 Years," *Vinita (OK) Daily Chieftain*, November 27, 1909. "Bandit Admits Robbery," *Chickasha (OK) Daily Express*, November 17, 1909.

Notes for Reel One

16. Victoria R. Newman, *Prisons of Cañon City* (Arcadia, 2008), 100.
17. Henry A. L'Engle, "Prison Reform in Colorado," *La Follette's Weekly Magazine* 4, no. 2 (January 13, 1912): 7–8.
18. One of Starr's inlaid boxes can be seen at the Museum of Colorado Prisons located next to the old Colorado State Penitentiary, Cañon City.
19. L'Engle, "Prison Reform in Colorado," 12.
20. Starr, *Thrilling Events*, 92–93.
21. "'I Loved Him Just the Same,' Mother of Henry Starr Says," *Daily Oklahoman* (Oklahoma City), February 25, 1921.
22. "Henry Starr Finds His Wife Quit Him," *Wichita (KS) Beacon*, October 17, 1913.
23. "Henry Starr Is Paroled," *Independence Daily Reporter*, October 9, 1913. "Henry Starr on Parole," *Maysville (OK) News*, December 11, 1913.
24. Granada, Colorado, has a colorful history with notorious outlaws but also a darker one as the site of the Ameche Japanese Internment Camp during World War II. Kathy Alexandèr, "Granada, Colorado—Legends of America," *Legends of America*, accessed June 6, 2024, https://www.legendsofamerica.com/granada-colorado/2/.
25. "Once Noted Outlaw Paroled," *Daily Ardmoreite*, October 12, 1913. "Paroled," *Lamar Register* (Prowers County, CO), October 1, 1913.
26. Grant Foreman, *The Five Civilized Tribes: Cherokee, Chickasaw, Choctaw, Creek, Seminole* (University of Oklahoma Press, 1934), 414. John Downing Benedict, *Muskogee and Northeastern Oklahoma: Including the Counties of Muskogee, McIntosh, Wagoner, Cherokee, Sequoyah, Adair, Delaware, Mayes, Rogers, Washington, Nowata, Craig, and Ottawa* (S. J. Clarke Publishing, 1922), 267–68.
27. Starr, *Thrilling Events*, 8.
28. "It is said he may become a partner of Al J. Jennings, another of the few survivors of out outlaw days in Oklahoma, who is a successful attorney here." "One-Time Bandit Would Be Lawyer," *Chronicle* (Scottburg, IN), May 6, 1914. "Convict Studies Law," *Daily Ardmoreite*, November 3, 1910.
29. "Holly-Western Heritage," *Town of Holly*, accessed June 5, 2024, https://townofholly.com/western_heritage.html.
30. "Henry Starr on Parole," *Maysville News*, December 11, 1913.
31. *Kansan* (Jamestown, KS), April 10, 1919.
32. Ava Betz et al., *A Prowers County History* (Prowers County Historical Society, 1986), 139–42. "Fort Amity Colorado 1902," *Vintage City Maps*, 2020, https://www.vintagecitymaps.com/product/fort-amity-colorado-1902/.

33. "A Talk With Henry Starr," *Evening Star* (Independence, KS), April 3, 1915.
34. Betz et al., *Prowers County History*, 314.
35. Betz et al., *Prowers County History*, 314.
36. "Legends of the West," *Daily Sentinel* (Grand Junction, CO), January 8, 1980, 5.
37. "Henry Starr, Once Bandit, a Fugitive," *Muskogee Times-Democrat*, November 18, 1916. "Guy Elwick Buys Garage," *LaJunta (CO) Tribune*, August 12, 1913.
38. F. Scott Fitzgerald, *The Great Gatsby* (Charles Scribner's Sons, 1925).
39. James Mallahan Cain, *The Postman Always Rings Twice* (Grosset & Dunlap, 1934).
40. "Starr Admits His Guilt; 25 Years," *Tulsa Daily World*, August 3, 1915. "Talk with Henry Starr," *Evening Star.*
41. Sutton and Macdonald, *Hands Up!*, 263. "His Last Stand," *Stillwater (OK) Gazette*, April 2, 1915.
42. "Talk with Henry Starr," *Evening Star.*
43. *Tulsa Daily World*, July 25, 1914.
44. Starr, *Thrilling Events*, 14.
45. Patrick Sylvester "Purple Sage" McGeeney, "Henry Starr: A Debtor to the Law," in author's possession.
46. Starr, *Thrilling Events*, 17–19. "I should have been given a hearing before being put in jail, and the reason I wasn't was because the deputy got $125.00 for committing me to jail; he also got something like $40.00 for mileage, 50 cents for the sausage and 50 cents each for the breakfasts I was supposed to get, but didn't. Eaton received over $20.00 for milage and $1.50 per day while waiting for the trial, making a total of between $95 and $100.00 that the government was out."
47. Starr, *Thrilling Events*, 17.
48. "Starr's Career a Bad Man in Real Life," *Buffalo (NY) Courier*, April 17, 1921.
49. "Talk with Henry Starr," *Evening Star.* Family genealogy provided by Starr's sister Adna Benge on Eastern Cherokees Allotment application, Application Number 12364, January 24, 1907. Eastern Cherokee Applications of the US Court of Claims, 1906–1909, Department of the Interior, RG 123, National Archives, Washington, DC.
50. Glenn Shirley, *Belle Starr and Her Times: The Literature, the Facts, and the Legends* (University of Oklahoma Press, 1982), 78–85, 160–65; 234–37; 212–15.

Notes for Reel One 227

51. Sutton and Macdonald, *Hands Up!*, 269.
52. "Henry Starr's Reformation Cloak to Hide His Activities," *Arkansas Gazette* (Little Rock), February 27, 1921, 7.
53. Starr, *Thrilling Events*, 77–78. A copy of *Thrilling Events* is preserved at the Princeton University library. The book was a gift from Starr to A. B. MacDonald on August 13, 1915.
54. "It's All Wrong Says Hy. Starr," *Oklahoma City Times*, August 16, 1915.
55. Starr, *Thrilling Events*, 76–78.
56. Jerry Thompson, *Wrecked Lives and Lost Souls: Joe Lynch Davis and the Last of the Oklahoma Outlaws* (University of Oklahoma Press, 2019), 140–44. "Joe Davis Freed of Murder Charge," *Choctaw Herald* (Hugo, OK), November 16, 1914.
57. "Talk with Henry Starr," *Evening Star.*
58. Thompson, *Wrecked Lives and Lost Souls*, 167; (entitled) 97; (brands) 49–50; (bribes) 139.
59. "Crime Can't Win, All Who Play It Fail in End," *Muskogee Daily Phoenix*, July 4, 1920.
60. Thompson, *Wrecked Lives and Lost Souls*, 78. "Joe Davis Again Freed of Charge," *Daily Oklahoman*, November 11, 1913, 4.
61. "Trio Drive Cashier and Customer in Vault in Bold Daylight Robbery," *Daily Arkansas Gazette* (Little Rock), August 12, 1914.
62. "Bank Robbed," *Times-Democrat* (Pawnee, OK), September 10, 1914.
63. "On Trail Baxter Springs Robbers," *Columbus (KS) Weekly Advocate*, November 26, 1914. "Higgins and Kitterman to Be Tried in Pueblo Colorado January 18," *Sedan (KS) Times-Star*, January 6, 1916. Starr, *Thrilling Events*, 72–74. "Last of Starr Gang," *Cherryvale (KS) Republican*, January 3, 1916. "Requisition for Baxter Robbers," *Columbus (KS) Daily Advocate*, November 25, 1914. "Baxter Springs Bank Robbery," *Oklahoma Farmer and Laborer* (Sapulpa), September 25, 1914.
64. "Bandits Rob Bank," *News-Capital* (McAlester, OK), October 1, 1914, 8.
65. "Henry Starr a Fugitive," *Sequoyah County Democrat* (Sallisaw, OK), November 20, 1914.
66. "Henry Starr, Noted Outlaw, Lived for Months in the Heart of City of Tulsa," *Tulsa World News*, April 18th, 1915, morning edition. Author's note: A visit in 2022 revealed Starr's former bungalow was razed, but similar homes from the era are still standing on the same block, providing a sense of how it would have looked in 1915.

67. "Henry Starr, Once a Bandit, a Fugitive," *Muskogee Times-Democrat*, November 18, 1914.

68. "Our New Governor," *Coalgate (OK) Record-Register*, January 14, 1915. On January 14, 1915, Judge Robert L. Williams became Oklahoma's third chief executive since statehood.

69. "Henry Starr, Noted Outlaw," *Tulsa World News*.

70. "Henry Starr Again," *AHTA Weekly News* (St. Paul, KS), November 26, 1914.

71. "Outlaw Returns to Old Life of Crime," *Arizona Republican*, November 22, 1914. *Paint, Oil, and Drug Review* (Chicago), January 7, 1914.

72. "Henry Starr, Noted Outlaw," *Tulsa World News*. "How It All Began," *The Church Studio*, accessed March 20, 2025, https://thechurchstudio.com/about/. In 1972 the Grace M. E. Church located at 304 S. Trenton Avenue became the Church Studio when Tulsa native and 70s rock and roll legend Leon Russell converted the building into a recording studio.

73. Eileen Bowser, *The Transformation of Cinema, 1907–1915* (University of California Press, 1994), 2–4.

74. *Moving Picture World*, September 23, 1910, 658.

75. Richard Koszarski, *An Evening's Entertainment: The Age of the Silent Feature Picture, 1915–1928* (University of California Press, 1994), 10. "A stereopticon is a slide projector or 'magic lantern,' which has two lenses, usually one above the other. These devices date back to the mid-19th century and were a popular form of entertainment and education before the advent of moving pictures." "Stereopticon Pictures: 'Magic Lantern,' late 1800s–early 1900s," *Performing Arts Archive*, accessed May 30, 2024, http://www.performingartsarchive.com/Vaudeville-Acts/Vaudeville-Acts_S/Stereopticon-Pictures/Stereopticon-Pictures.htm.

76. "Starr Shows Up Curly-Haired 'Bad Men,'" Peacock Productions press book, (Oklahoma City, OK), 1920, 2.

77. Jay Robert Nash, *Bloodletters and Badmen* (Warner Books, 1975), 214. Nash, *Encyclopedia of Western Lawmen & Outlaws* (Da Capo Press, 2010), 189–91.

78. Al Jennings and Will Irwin, *Beating Back* (D. Appleton, 1915), 117–18.

79. Jennings and Irwin, *Beating Back*, 1.

80. Lisa Stein Haven, *The Early Years of Charlie Chaplin: Final Shorts and First Features* (Pen and Sword, 2023). James L. Neibaur and Terri Niemi, *Buster Keaton's Silent Shorts, 1920–1923* (Scarecrow Press, 2013).

Notes for Reel One

81. Glenn Shirley, *Temple Houston: Lawyer with a Gun* (University of Oklahoma Press, 2010), 215–17. Jennings and Irwin, *Beating Back*, 40–44. Temple Lea Houston was the model for the Yancey Cravat character in Edna Ferber's novel *Cimarron* (1929), which was adapted for the screen in 1931 and 1960. Houston was also a character in the TV series *Death Valley Days*, "The Reluctant Gun" episode (1959). *Temple Houston*, a Western comedy television series starring Jeffrey Hunter, ran for one season on NBC from 1963 to 1964. Boyd Magers, "Do You Remember . . . 'Temple Houston,'" *Western Clippings*, accessed June 6, 2024, http://www.westernclippings.com/remember/templehouston_doyouremember.shtml.

82. "US Senate: Marcus A. Hanna: A Featured Biography," Senate.gov, accessed June 8, 2024, https://www.senate.gov/senators/FeaturedBios/Featured_Bio_HannaMarcus.htm. Jennings and Irwin, *Beating Back*, 241.

83. Zoe A. Tilghman, *Marshal of the Last Frontier: Life and Services of William Matthew (Bill) Tilghman, for 50 Years One of the Greatest Peace of the West* (Arthur H. Clark, 1949), 310–11.

84. Bill Moore, "Kent, James B. 'Bennie': The Encyclopedia of Oklahoma History and Culture," *Oklahoma Historical Society*, accessed June 6, 2024, https://www.okhistory.org/publications/enc/entry?entry=KE017. Kent's camera is on display at the Lincoln County Museum of Pioneer History, 719 Manvel Avenue, Chandler, Oklahoma. "Red-Cheeked Britisher, He Filmed the Story of Oklahoma," *Bristow (OK) Daily Record*, March 14, 1938. "Bennie Kent, State's Pioneer Film Historian, Dead at 80," *Daily Oklahoman*, December 18, 1945

85. Jeannette Covert Nolan and Hamilton Greene, *O. Henry: The Story of William Sydney Porter* (Messner, 1945), 160–67.

86. Nolan and Greene, *O. Henry*, 227–28.

87. O. Henry, *Sixes and Sevens* (Doubleday, Page, 1911). C. D. Merriman, "O Henry: Biography and Works," *The Literature Network*, accessed 2013, http://www.online-literature.com/o_henry/. "The Gift of the Magi" and "The Ranson of Red Chief" are considered Porter's most celebrated short stories.

88. Jeff Nilsson, Will Irwin, and Al Jennings, "Romancing the Robber," *Saturday Evening Post*, December 11, 2014, https://www.saturdayeveningpost.com/2014/12/romancing-robber/.

89. "'Beating Back' Tells Thrilling Story," *Times-Democrat*, November 25, 1914.

230 Notes for Reel One

90. Nancy B. Samuelson, *The Dalton Gang Story: Lawmen to Outlaws* (Shooting Star Press, 1992), 154. "Dalton Gets Parole," *Coffeyville Daily Journal*, July 5, 1907.
91. "He Boosts Dalton," *Bartlesville (OK) Examiner*, July 2, 1909.
92. "Dalton's Good Sense," *Coffeyville Daily Journal*, November 8, 1907.
93. "Emmett Dalton Visits the City," *Coffeyville Daily Journal*, June 13, 1908.
94. Scout Younger, interview by Effie S. Jackson, "Scout Younger and His Cowman's Bar," August 26, 1937, Indian Pioneer Papers, University of Oklahoma Western History Collections, accessed June 9, 2024, http://digital.libraries.ou.edu/cdm/ref/collection/indianpp/id/6093.
95. "History of the Midland Theater," *Historic Midland Theater*, accessed June 4, 2024, https://www.historicmidlandtheater.com/history. "Dalton Gang, Coffeyville, Kansas," Kansas Memory, accessed June 4, 2024, https://www.kansasmemory.gov/item/723.
96. "Hoch Objects to Moving Pictures," *Coffeyville Daily Journal*, January 13, 1909.
97. "Dalton to Write Book," *Coffeyville Daily Journal*, December 4, 1908.
98. "Emmett Dalton Tells of the Raid," *El Reno (OK) Daily American*, September 28, 1909.
99. Samuelson, Dalton Gang Story, 114–19. Nash, *Bloodletters and Badmen*, 102. "Twenty Years Ago Today," *Coffeyville Daily Journal*, October 5, 1912. Emerson Hough, *The Story of the Outlaw* (Curtis Publishing, 1907), 381–92. "Seventeen Years Ago the Dalton Raid on the Coffeyville Banks Took Place," *Topeka (KS) Daily Capital*, October 10, 1909. The Tackett death photos show Bob Dalton's unbuttoned front shirt and the exact location of the bullet's entry. Grat Dalton's fatal neck wound is also visible, and the fake mustache he's still wearing. Souvenir hunters have already cut away the cuff area of Bob's pants.
100. "Hoch Objects to Moving Pictures," *Coffeyville Daily Journal*. "Will Not 'Stand for' It," *Sapulpa (OK) Weekly Democrat*, January 1, 1909.
101. "Raid in Moving Pictures," *Coffeyville Daily Journal*, December 17, 1908.
102. "Dalton Gets a Ducking," *Pawnee (OK) County Journal*, January 14, 1909.
103. Gem Theatre *Great Dalton Raid* advertisement, *Oklahoma State Capitol* (Guthrie), September 26, 1909.
104. "Dalton Raid Is Reproduced," *Bartlesville (OK) Morning Examiner*, September 14, 1909.

Notes for Reel One 231

105. "Coffeyville Version of Dalton Pictures," *Morning Examiner* (Bartlesville, OK), December 15, 1912.

106. *Bartlesville (OK) Daily Enterprise*, January 24, 1913.

107. *The Last Stand of the Dalton Boys* one-sheet poster features a painting of a scene from the film where Dalton receives his pardon, with the tagline across the top (1913); in the author's possession.

108. Kathy Alexander, "Henry Starr—the Cherokee Bad Boy," *Legends of America*, updated January 2024, https://www.legendsofamerica.com/we-henrystarr/. Banks robbed from August 1914 through January 1915:

08/11/1914	*Cove Bank, Cove, Arkansas $1,300
09/08/1914	*Keystone State Bank, Keystone, Oklahoma $3,000
09/22/1914	*First National Bank, Baxter Springs, Kansas $8,452
09/28/1914	*Keifer Central Bank, Kiefer, Oklahoma $5,400 – $6,400
10/06/1914	*Farmers National Bank, Tupelo, Oklahoma $800 – $2,240
10/14/1914	*Pontotoc Bank, Pontotoc, Oklahoma of $1,100 – $2,000
10/15/1914	Bank of Kensett, Kensett, Arkansas $2,000
10/20/1914	Byars State Bank, Byars, Oklahoma $425.25 – $700
11/13/1914	*Farmers State Bank, Glencoe, Oklahoma $2,400 – $3,500
11/20/1914	*Citizens State Bank, Wardville, Oklahoma $678 – $800
12/16/1914	*Price State Bank, Prue, Oklahoma $1,400 – $1,500
12/29/1914	*Carney State Bank, Carney, Oklahoma $2,000 – $2,853
01/04/1915	*Oklahoma State Bank, Preston, Oklahoma (no money taken, but $1,500 damage)
01/05/1915	First National Bank, Owasso, Oklahoma $1,200 – $1,500
01/12/1915	First National Bank, Terlton, Oklahoma $1,800 – $3,000
01/12/1915	Garber State Bank, Garber, Oklahoma $2,736 – $7,000
01/13/1915	Vera State Bank, Vera, Oklahoma $1,300 – $1,400

*likely robbed by Starr

109. "CPI Inflation Calculator," *In 2013 Dollars*, accessed June 4, 2024, https://www.in2013dollars.com/us/inflation/1915.

110. *A Debtor to the Law* press kit, Peacock Productions, 1920.

111. "Henry Starr on Bank Robbers," *Palmyra (MO) Spectator*, April 21, 1915. "Talk with Henry Starr," *Evening Star.*

112. "Walter Jarrett's Prey Again Touched by Yeggs," *Nowata (OK) Weekly Star-Times*, December 25, 1914.

113. "Daylight Robbers Secure Big Sum," *Daily Oklahoman*, December 30, 1914, 10.

232   Notes for Reel Two

114. "Another Daylight Bank Robbery," *Collinsville (OK) News*, January 14, 1915.

115. "Talk with Henry Starr," *Evening Star.*

116. "Back at His Old Game," *Coffeyville (KS) Journal*, January 1, 1915, 2.

117. "Governor Williams Offers Thousand Dollars Reward For Capture Of Henry Starr and Others Alleged to Have Been in Carney Bank Robbery," *Queen City Times* (Agra, OK), March 4, 1915. "Puts Price on Head of Starr," *Maysville News*, March 4, 1915. "Governor Places Signature to Bank Robber Bill," *Guthrie (OK) Daily Leader*, February 6, 1915.

118. "New Jesse James! Here's Wild West Romance of Today," *Tacoma (WA) Times*, April 7, 1915.

119. Sutton and Macdonald, *Hands Up!*, 263.

Notes for Reel Two

Epigraph. "Eye Witness Tells of Daring Holdup," *Tulsa Daily World*, March 28, 1915.

1. "Estes Tells Story of Stroud Bank Robbery," *Chandler (OK) News-Publicist*, August 6, 1915. "Estes Implicates Both Higgins and Johnson," *Osage Journal* (Pawhuska, OK), August 5, 1915.

2. Ashley, "These 24 Rare Photos Show Oklahoma's Oil History like Never Before," *Only in Your State*, December 30, 2016, https://www.onlyinyourstate.com/oklahoma/rare-oil-industry-photos-ok/. Micheal Wallis, *Oil Man: The Story of Frank Phillips and the Birth of Phillips Petroleum* (University of Oklahoma Press, 2014), 90–92.

3. Wallis, *Oil Man*, 95.

4. Jessica D. Harper, "Life in an Oklahoma Oil Town," *Tulsa Tribune*, December 18, 1921.

5. "Roughnecks," *Bullock Museum*, accessed April 2, 2025, https://www.thestoryoftexas.com/discover/campfire-stories/roughneck.

6. "Estes Tells Story," *Chandler News-Publicist.*

7. Thompson, *Wrecked Lives and Lost Souls*, 169–70.

8. The origin of the term "honky-tonk" is disputed. It originally referred to bawdy variety shows in areas of the Old West (Oklahoma, the Indian Territories, and mostly Texas) and to the theaters that showed them. "Honky-Tonk," *Merriam-Webster*, accessed April 2, 2025, https://www.merriam-webster.com/dictionary/honky-tonk.

9. "Estes Tells Story," *Chandler News-Publicist.* "Covered Wagons," *Hansen Wheel Wagon Shop*, accessed April 2, 2025, https://www.hansenwheel.com/covered-wagons/.

Notes for Reel Two

10. Matera, *John Dillinger*, 152. "Henry Starr Captured in a Bank Raid," *Shawnee (OK) Daily News-Herald*, March 28, 1915.

11. "Forestry Services," *Oklahoma Department of Agriculture, Food and Forestry*, accessed May 25, 2024, http://www.forestry.ok.gov/post-oak-blackjack-forest. In 1832 Washington Irving called the blackjack oaks "forests of cast iron." Later, cowboys driving herds along the Chisholm and Shawnee Trails gave this forest its existing name. The timbers snagged cattle as they attempted to cross.

12. "Stroud," *Oklahoma Historical Society*, accessed May 25, 2024, https://www.okhistory.org/publications/enc/entry.php?entry=ST053.

13. "Stroud, OK, October 10, 1908," photo by H. C. Chaufty, *Gateway to Oklahoma History* https://gateway.okhistory.org/ark:/67531/metadc 1593104/; "Photograph of Main Street, looking west, Stroud, Oklahoma Territory, c.1895–1911," photo by H. C. Chaufty, *Gateway to Oklahoma History*, accessed June 9, 2024, https://gateway.okhistory.org/ark:/67531/metadc1592887/.

14. "Henry Starr Re-Enacts Famous Bank Robbery at Stroud for Movies," *Indian Citizen* (Atoka, OK), November 20, 1919.

15. "Robbery of Two," *Stroud Messenger*.

16. "Robbery of Two," *Stroud Messenger*.

17. "Henry Starr Admits His Identity; Talks of Deed," *Daily Oklahoman*, March 28, 1915. "Starr Refuses to Give Names," *Kansas City (MO) Star*, March 29, 1915.

18. "Henry Starr Again Robs Two Banks at Stroud, As an Actor," *Tulsa Daily World*, November 2, 1919.

19. "Henry Starr, Bandit, Shot And Captured," *Guthrie Daily Leader*, March 27, 1915. "His Last Stand," *Stillwater Gazette*, April 2, 1915. "Henry Starr Re-Enacts," *Indian Citizen*. "Eye Witness," *Tulsa Daily World*. "Robbery Of Two," *Stroud Messenger*. "Stroud Banks Robbed, Henry Starr Captured," *Stroud (OK) Democrat*, April 2, 1915. Author's note: I visited the First National Bank and Stroud National Bank in 2017. First National is hardly recognizable because the second story has been completely removed. At the time it housed an employment center. The clerks were kind enough to allow me to see the safe in the back that had never been removed. Stroud National Bank is now a law office. The attorney graciously allowed me to look around. A large safe is still there in the entry, and down the hall a second safe door opens onto a red brick, barrel-vaulted room.

20. "Henry Starr, Bandit," *Guthrie Daily Leader*.

21. "Robbery of Two," *Stroud Messenger*.

234 Notes for Reel Two

22. "Henry Starr Re-Enacts," *Indian Citizen*.
23. "Robbery of Two," *Stroud Messenger*. "Lose Trail of the Bandits," *Kansas City (MO) Star*, March 29, 1915. "Eye Witness," *Tulsa Daily World*. "Undertaker Recalls Day His Brother Shot Outlaws," *Tulsa Tribune*, December 8, 1965. "Hero's Sister Lives Here," *Kansas City Star*, March 29, 1915. "Robbery of Two," *Stroud Messenger*. "Didn't Expect Boy to Get Me Starr Declares in Jail," *Muskogee Daily Phoenix*, March 28, 1915. "Henry Starr Captured in Stroud Bank Robbery," *Tulsa Democrat*, March 27, 1915. "His Last Stand," *Stillwater Gazette*. "Stroud Banks Robbed," *Stroud Democrat*. "Robbery of Two," *Stroud Messenger*. "Other Bandits Are Strangers," *Oklahoma City Times*, March 29, 1915. "Eye Witness," *Tulsa Daily World*.
24. "Gang of Noted Outlaws Rob Two Banks at Stroud," *Chandler News-Publicist*, April 2, 1915.
25. "Estes Implicates," *Osage Journal*.
26. "Bandits Raid Oklahoma Town," *Cameron Missouri Sun*, March 29, 1915. A handwritten contemporaneous and unsigned note is in the possession of the Stroud Chamber of Commerce, detailing the events of the day. The letter is written on letterhead reading, "Office of Hugh V. Corey, Clerk, Stroud Camp No. 7525 M. W. of A. Stroud, Okla." The letter is written in pencil. A different hand wrote in pen, "May 1915." "M. W. of A." stands for Modern Woodmen of America, which was founded by Joseph Cullen Root on January 5, 1883, in Lyons, Iowa. Root created the organization to protect families following the death of a breadwinner. "Modern Woodmen of America, a Fraternal Financial Services Organization," *Modern Woodmen*, accessed May 25, 2024, https://www.modernwoodmen.org/.
27. "Gang of Noted Outlaws," *Chandler News-Publicist*.
28. "Henry Starr Captured in Bank Raid," *Shawnee Daily News-Herald*, March 28, 1915. "Lose Trail," *Kansas City Star*.
29. "Saying 'Howdy' To Starr," *Kansas City Star*, March 31, 1915.
30. Michael J. Hightower, *Banking in Oklahoma, 1907–2000* (University of Oklahoma Press, 2014). Pressure from farmers continued to build, and the progressive Oklahoma legislature eventually defied the bankers. On March 4, 1916, the governor signed the Glasco Usury Bill limiting the maximum legal interest by banks to 10 percent per annum, or they'd forfeit twice the amount on loans that exceeded the statutory rate.
31. "Eye Witness," *Tulsa Daily World*. "Robbery of Two," *Stroud Messenger*.

Notes for Reel Two   235

32. "His Last Stand," *Stillwater Gazette*, 7.

33. Kalton C. Lahue and Terry Brewer, *Kops and Custards: The Legend of the Keystone Films: A Book* (University of Oklahoma Press, 1972), 47–51. Keystone Kops were humorously incompetent policemen featured in silent film slapstick comedies produced by Mack Sennett for his Keystone Film Company between 1912 and 1917. Stroud residents would be familiar with the Keystone Kops, whose frenetic style first appeared in *Hoffmeyer's Legacy* on December 23, 1912. The hyperactive movement was achieved by undercranking the camera at eight to twelve frames per second rather than at sixteen to twenty-four. When played at regular speed, the action would move rapidly.

34. "Henry Starr, Bandit," *Guthrie Daily Leader*, 5. "Starr Gives Doctors Horse and Saddle," *Muskogee Times-Democrat*, March 28, 1915.

35. Irwin Hurst, "Starr Gave Back Gem He'd Stolen," *Daily Oklahoman*, May 17, 1959.

36. "Eye Witness," *Tulsa Daily World*.

37. "Got Away with $4,500," *Kansas City Star*, March 29, 1915.

38. "Starr Gang Eludes Posse And Escapes," *Guthrie Daily Leader*, March 29, 1915, 1.

39. "Gazettes," *Stillwater Gazette*, April 2, 1915, 2.

40. "Girls Seek Out Boy Hero," *Kansas City Star*, March 29, 1915. "Saying 'Howdy,'" *Kansas City Star*.

41. "Starr Gang Eludes," *Guthrie Daily Leader*, 8. "His Last Stand," *Stillwater Gazette*, 2.

42. "Hero's Sister," *Kansas City Star*.

43. "Girls Seek Out Boy Hero," *Kansas City Star*.

44. Sutton and Macdonald, *Hands Up!*, 262.

45. Nancy B. Samuelson, *Shoot from the Lip: The Lives, Legends and Lies of the Three Guardsmen of Oklahoma and US Marshal Nix* (Shooting Star Press, 1998), 37–40; 94–100

46. "Starr Didn't Know His Pals," *Kansas City Star*, March 29, 1915.

47. Tilghman, *Marshal of the Last Frontier*, 216–17; 312–13.

48. *Moving Picture World*, April 4, 1914, 377.

49. "HITE, Charles J.," thanhouser.org, accessed June 4, 2024, https://www.thanhouser.org/tcocd/Biography_Files/9756m4.htm.

50. In a letter dated November 23, 1914, Jennings typed out a note to William Tilghman on stationery from the Hotel St. Francis, San Francisco. Jennings wrote that he'd heard Tilghman was making a picture "to strike back at me." He suggested they collaborate on a

236 Notes for Reel Two

moving picture focusing on "little episodes" from Tilghman's days as the Oklahoma City chief of police. "I will lay it bare as a clean swept floor, and, God, she will be a hummer." "The Collection of Jim and Theresa Earle," copy in author's possession.

51. "Items Of Interest In Southwest," *Moving Picture World*, January 23, 1915. In January 1915 the Eagle Film Company incorporated in Oklahoma City with a capital stock of $12,000. The incorporators were former US Marshal E. D. Nix (St. Louis, MO) and his previous underlings, Deputy Marshals Bill Tilghman (Oklahoma City) and Chris Madsen (Guthrie). Former Deputy Marshal Chris Madsen was also a part of the company. Tilghman, Madsen, and Heck Thomas (who died in 1912) worked under Nix and were known as the Three Guardsmen. Samuelson, *Shoot from the Lip*, 110. Tilghman, *Marshal of the Last Frontier*, 316–17. Tilghman did not capture Cattle Annie and Little Breeches in real life, and the film had many other inaccuracies. Samuelson, *Shoot from the Lip*,115. "Other Bandits," *Oklahoma City Times*.

52. "'Well, That's the Way He Wanted It,' Says Bill Tilghman of Henry Starr," *Oklahoma City Times*, February 19, 1921.

53. "Stroud Visited by Robbers," *Chandler (OK) Tribune*, April 1, 1915. "'Starr' Pictures," *Tulsa Daily World*, May 30, 1915.

54. "His Last Stand," *Stillwater Gazette*, 2. "Morning Star," *Chandler News-Publicist*, April 2, 1915, 7. "Sheriffs, Good and Bad," *Prague (OK) Times-Herald*, October 30, 2008.

55. "Henry Starr Is Dying," *Evening Star*, April 3, 1915. "Wounded Outlaws Improving," *Chandler News-Publicist*, April 9, 1915. "The Week's Doings," *Chandler News-Publicist*, April 30, 1915, 5.

56. "Saying 'Howdy,'" *Kansas City Star*.

57. "Talk with Henry Starr," *Evening Star.*

58. "His Last Stand," *Stillwater Gazette,* 7.

59. *Bartlesville Independent*, April 2, 1915.

60. "Saying 'Howdy,'" *Kansas City Star*.

61. "Colonel Zach Mulhall Has A New One," *Guthrie Daily Leader*, October 16, 1923.

62. "Starr Failed as Bill Hart," *Los Angeles Times*, February 20, 1921.

63. Glenn Shirley, *West of Hell's Fringe: Crime, Criminals, and the Federal Peace Officer in Oklahoma Territory, 1889–1907* (University of Oklahoma Press, 1978), 427–29. John W. Morris, *Ghost Towns of Oklahoma* (University of Oklahoma Press, 1977), 100–102.

Notes for Reel Two

64. Shirley, *West of Hell's Fringe*, 156–63.

65. Arkansas Tom's scene at the top of the O.K. Hotel is part of the surviving reels of *The Passing of the Oklahoma Outlaws*, housed at the Library of Congress. DVD copies of the film can be ordered from the Lincoln County Museum of Pioneer History, 719 Manvel Ave, Chandler, OK 74834: http://www.okpioneermuseum.org. "*The Passing of the Oklahoma Outlaws*, Motion Picture Copyright Descriptions Collection. Class L, 1912–1977," *Library of Congress*, accessed June 6, 2024, https://www.loc.gov/item/s1229l06941.

66. "Gang of Outlaws Raided Two Banks at Stroud," *Chandler News-Publicist*. "Week's Doings," *Chandler News-Publicist*, April 30, 1915, 5.

67. "Saying 'Howdy,'" *Kansas City Star*.

68. "Hold Fifth Stroud Bank Robber," *Waurika (OK) News-Democrat*, April 16, 1915. "Five Outlaws in Jail," *Chandler News-Publicist*, April 16, 1915. "Estes to Peach on Pals; Henry Starr Will Plead Guilty," *Chandler News-Publicist*, July 16, 1915.

69. "Lige Higgins Last of Starr Gang," *Neodesha (OK) Daily Sun*, December 24, 1915. "Higgins Wanted at Chandler Now," *Tulsa Daily World*, December 18, 1915. "Get Last of Starr Gang," *Nowata (OK) Weekly Star Times*, March 17, 1916.

70. Thompson, *Wrecked Lives and Lost Souls*, 184. Tilghman, *Marshal of the Last Frontier*, 317–18.

71. "Estes Tells Story," *Chandler News-Publicist*. "Heard in the Post Office," *Chandler News-Publicist*, August 13, 1915. "Sawyer Gets Minimum," *Chandler News-Publicist*, August 13, 1915. "Starr Gangster on Stand," *Coffeyville Daily Journal*, August 4, 1915.

72. "Estes Implicates," *Osage Journal*. "Johnson Not Guilty," *Chandler News-Publicist*, August 13, 1915.

73. "Maxfield Making Efforts to Prove Alibi at Hearing," *Muskogee Daily Phoenix and Times-Democrat*, August 13, 1915. "Not Men Wanted," *Muskogee Times-Democrat*, April 8, 1915. "Bud Maxfield Is Found Guilty," *Stonewall (OK) Weekly News*, August 26, 1915. "Maxfield Guilty," *Chandler News-Publicist*, August 13, 1915.

74. "Estes Gets Five Years," *Chandler News-Publicist*, August 20, 1915.

75. "Henry Starr Enters Plea Of Guilt; Gets 25 Years," *Oklahoma City Times*, August 2, 1915. "Bandits Waive Preliminary," *Chandler News-Publicist*, June 4, 1915. "Another Member of the Starr Gang Convicted," *Topeka Daily Capital*, August 13, 1915. "Starr Enters Plea of Guilt," *Oklahoma City Times*. "Starr Given 25 Years," *Stroud Democrat*, August 6, 1915.

238   Notes for Reel Two

76. "Judge C. B. Wilson," *Chandler (OK) Tribune*, July 15, 1915.
77. "Starr Admits His Guilt," *Tulsa Daily World*. "Starr Given 25 Years," *Stroud Democrat*, August 6, 1915. "Sawyer Case Goes to Jury To-Night," *Chandler Tribune*, August 5, 1915.
78. "Starr Will Not Testify Against His Former Pals," *Southwest American* (Fort Smith, AR), August 3, 1915.
79. Irwin Hurst, "Starr Returns Gem He'd Stolen," *Daily Oklahoman*, May 17, 1959.
80. Letter from Starr to A. B. MacDonald, April 20, 1915, Box 7, A. B. MacDonald Papers, Library of Congress, Washington, DC.
81. "Trial of the Starr Gang Is Postponed," *Tulsa Daily World*, July 21, 1915, 2.
82. "The Week's Doings," *Chandler News-Publicist*, May 21, 1915.
83. "Henry Starr on Way to Begin Long Sentence," *Daily Oklahoman*.
84. "Paul Curry and Starr in Movies," *Muskogee Times-Democrat*, April 8, 1915. "Henry Starr Bank Robbery," *Stroud Messenger*, May 21, 1915.
85. "Notes," *Chandler News-Publicist*, April 23, 1915.
86. *Chandler News-Publicist*, August 20, 1915. "Bandits Are Safe Across State Line," *Daily Ardmoreite*, April 1, 1915.
87. "Reward for Each Robber," *Bartlesville Morning Examiner*, March 31, 1915. "Here and Everywhere," *Chandler Tribune*, October 21, 1915. "Paul Curry Gets $500," *Chandler News-Publicist*, October 22, 1915.
88. Wonderland Theatre Advertisement, "The Capture of Henry Starr," *Tulsa Daily World*, April 21, 1915.
89. "Wounded Outlaws Improving," *Chandler News-Publicist, Chandler Tribune*, April 8, 1915.
90. "The Week's Doings," *Chandler News-Publicist*, May 21, 1915. "This Week's Doings," *Chandler News-Publicist*, May 28, 1915. "Passing of the Oklahoma Outlaws," *Chandler Tribune*, May 20, 1915.
91. "Henry Starr Bank Robbery," *Stroud Messenger*. "Henry Starr on Way to Pen," *Chandler Tribune*.
92. Harper, "Oklahoma Oil Town," *Tulsa Tribune*.
93. "Henry Starr on Way," *Daily Oklahoman*.
94. Offender Ledger Extraction, Closed Records Unit. Oklahoma Department of Corrections, Oklahoma City.
95. "Gazettes," *Stillwater Gazette*, April 2, 1915.
    Epigraph. "About Filmack Studios," *Filmack Studios*, accessed June 17, 2024, http://www.filmack.com/about.html.

Notes for the Intermission

1. Matthew Kennedy, *Roadshow! The Fall of Film Musicals in the 1960s* (Oxford University Press, 2014), 4.
2. "'I'll Stick By Him' Says Starr's Pal," *Heavener (OK) Ledger*, May 11, 1916.
3. "Starr Offers Service," *State Sentinel* (Stigler, OK), May 25, 1916.
4. "Lots of Sob Stuff," *Tulsa Daily World*, June 27, 1916, 7.
5. "3 Million in US Army Within Six Weeks, Crowder Announces," *Washington (DC) Herald*, June 16, 1918, https://www.history.com/this-day-in-history/wilson-asks-for-declaration-of-war.
6. "Potted One Outlaw; Now Wants Kaiser," *Guthrie Daily Leader*, March 6, 1918. "State Briefs," *Tulsa Daily World*, March 5, 1918.
7. "In Starr Robbery," *Daily Oklahoman*, May 17, 1918.
8. "Henry Starr Wants to Fight for Uncle Sam," *Stroud Democrat*, May 10, 1918. "Famous Train Robber Seeks Chance at Huns," *El Paso Herald*, July 22, 1918. "Any Kind of Fireworks Would Suit Him," *Daily Oklahoman*, May 8, 1918.
9. *Bartlesville Examiner*, May 5, 1918, 2.
10. Letter from Starr to Governor Robertson, March 30, 1919, Governor Robertson Finding Aide Part One, Box #17, Folder #3, Record Group 8-D-1-1, Governor's Office Records, Oklahoma State Archives, Oklahoma Department of Libraries, Oklahoma City (hereafter cited as GOR).
11. "Wife Seeks Pardon That Husband May Fight," *Oklahoma City Times*, September 13, 1918.
12. "Theodore Roosevelt Dies Suddenly at Oyster Bay Home," *New York Times*, January 6, 1919.
13. Kevin Brownlow, *The West, the War, and the Wilderness* (Knopf Doubleday, 2013), xvi.
14. "Helping Henry Starr," *Vinita Daily Chieftain*, January 16, 1903. "Mother's Appeal Successful," *St. Louis Republic*. Nash, *Nash's Crime Chronology*, 10. Glenn Shirley, *Last of the Real Badmen: Henry Starr* (University of Nebraska Press, 1965), 144. "Henry Starr, Famous Outlaw Was Always Devoted Son, His Mother Declares," *Nowata (OK) Star*, September 15, 1926.
15. "Henry Starr Leads Roosevelt Giving," *Tulsa World*, October 25, 1919.
16. "No Pardoning in Wholesale Lots Says Robertson," *Tulsa Democrat*, March 19, 1919. "Starr's Parole Fills Promise, Says Governor," *Oklahoma City Times*, March 3, 1917.

240 Notes for Reel Three

17. "Starr Filled Engagement in 101 Ranch Show," *Ponca City (OK) News*, February 22, 1921.
18. "Territory Life Fresh in Memory," *Sunday Oklahoman* (Oklahoma City), March 18, 1979.
19. "Starr Off for Muskogee," *Daily Oklahoman*, March 19, 1919.
20. "A Parole to Henry Starr," *Chickasha (OK) Daily Express*, March 19, 1919.

Notes for Reel Three

1. "Henry Starr, 45, Starts All Over," *Muskogee Daily Phoenix and Times-Democrat*, March 21, 1919.
2. "Starr Pardoned by Governor," *Collinsville Star*, March 21, 1919.
3. "Henry Starr Will Make Tulsa Home," *Tulsa Democrat*, April 8, 1919. "Film or Farm Is Problem of Henry Starr," *Daily Oklahoman*, March 27, 1919.
4. "A Hint to Henry," *Oklahoman City Times*, March 28, 1919.
5. "Film or Farm," *Daily Oklahoman*.
6. "Last 'Send-Off' for 'Jim' Kidd," *Daily Times* (Los Angeles), December 18, 1916.
7. "Jennings Outlaw Film Winning Praise," *Moving Picture World*, January 4, 1919.
8. "London Wants Outlaw Film," *Moving Picture World*, January 11, 1919. Other productions included *Fugitives Who Came Back*, recounting the first time Jennings met the writer O. Henry, *The Unexpected Shot*, *The Tryout*, *The Frame-Up*, *Seeds of Dishonor*, *Fate's Mockery*, *Fate's Frame-Up*, *The Outlaw's Alibi*, and *A Fugitive's Life*. "Here and There," *Motion Picture News*, September 6, 1919.
9. Capitol Film Co. advertisement, *Motion Picture News*, November 8, 1919, 293.
10. *Motion Picture News*, September 13, 1919. "Al Jennings' Newest," *Motion Picture News*, September 27, 1919.
11. Mystic Theatre advertisement for the *Hatfield-McCoy Feud*, *Daily Republican* (Rushville, IN), January 17, 1916. The next evening featured three films: *The True Life and History of the Dalton Boys* (a new title for *Last Ride of the Dalton* Gang?), *Bold Emmett*, and *Luxurious Lew*.
12. *Fort Wayne (IN) Journal-Gazette*, January 9, 1916.
13. Southern Film Corporation advertisement, *Gastonia (NC) Gazette*, February 28, 1919.

Notes for Reel Three 241

14. "Notice," *Charlotte (NC) Observer*, March 31, 1918.
15. "Dalton Brothers' Exploits Furnish Subject for Film," *Moving Picture World*, November 2, 1918, 613.
16. "Beyond the Law," *Moving Picture World*, December 28, 1918, 1558.
17. "Actual Scene of Exploits Used in Dalton Product," *Moving Picture World*, December 14, 1918, 1241. "First Dalton Picture Is Now Ready for Release," *Moving Picture World*, November 30, 1918, 977.
18. "Beyond the Law," *Moving Picture World*, December 28, 1918, 1558.
19. "Critical Reviews & Comments, Beyond the Law," *Moving Picture World*, December 14, 1918.
20. "Dalton Reports Many Deals Closed," *Motion Picture News*, March 29, 1919.
21. "Foreign Rights Sold on 'Beyond the Law,'" *Moving Picture World*, February 15, 1919. "Emmett Dalton to Film Other Western Stories," *Moving Picture World*, January 11, 1919.
22. "Former Member of Dalton Gang Here," *Charlotte (NC) News*, March 2, 1919. Southern Film Corporation advertisement, *Gastonia Gazette*, February 28, 1919.
23. "Dalton Reports," *Motion Picture News*.
24. "Hazel Robertson Is Overcome in Court, Boy Clings to Story," *Tulsa Tribune*, January 17, 1917.
25. "Starr in 'Movies,'" *Muskogee Daily Phoenix*, April 16, 1919, 4. "State Charters," *Tulsa Tribune*, May 4, 1919, 6.
26. *Tulsa Daily World*, September 12, 1915.
27. "Sam Konkel's Take on the Al Jennings 'Fishy' Autobiography— Baca County History," *Baca County History*, September 11, 2018, https://plainsmanherald.com/2018/09/sam-konkels-take-on-the-al-jennings-fishy-autobiography/.
28. "In Pen with O. Henry," *Bartlesville (OK) Daily Express*, May 1, 1919.
29. "The Motion Picture Hall of Fame," *Motion Picture Magazine*, July 1918.
30. "William S. Hart Museum History," William S. Hart Museum, accessed April 10, 2025, https://hartmuseum.org/william-s-hart-museum-history.
31. Ronald L. Davis, *William S. Hart: Projecting the American West* (University of Oklahoma Press, 2003), xi.
32. Davis, *William S. Hart*, 7.
33. "Henry Starr Will Make," *Tulsa Democrat*.
34. "Tulsan to Produce Photoplay of Starr," *Tulsa Democrat*, April 14, 1919, 3.

35. "Of Outlawry Is Shown in Movie," *Muskogee Times-Democrat*, April 26, 1919.
36. "In Pen with O. Henry," *Bartlesville Daily Enterprise*, May 1, 1919.
37. *Tulsa Daily World*, July 9, 1919, 13.
38. *Beaver (OK) Herald*, July 24, 1919.
39. "'Blue Sky' Committee Sanctions Big Oil Co. with Ardmore Capital," *Daily Ardmoreite*, July 12, 1919. "Starr's Film Concern Can't Sell Stock, Blue-Sky Law Verdict," *Daily Ardmoreite*, July 26, 1919.
40. "Henry Starr's Company Gets 'Okeh,'" *Oklahoma City Times*, July 27, 1919. "Henry Starr Movie Concern Permitted to Sell Some Stock," *Daily Ardmoreite*, August 29, 1919.
41. "Don't Worry by W.W.M.," *Oklahoma City Times*, August 30, 1919.
42. "Starr Picture Director Here," *Tulsa Morning News*, July 18, 1919.
43. "Requisition for Starr to be Difficult," *Tulsa Morning News*, June 17, 1919, 5. "Of Outlawry," *Muskogee Times-Democrat*.
44. "Second 'As You Like It,' Excels First Performance," *Daily Illini*, June 6, 1916.
45. "Student Actor Appear As Stars In Photoplay," *Daily Illini* (Chicago), September 20, 1916. *Champaign (IL) Daily News*, Colonial Theatre advertisement for Pro Patria, August 19, 1916. "Colonial," *Champaign Daily News*, August 18, 1916. "At the Theatres," *Urbana (IL) Daily Courier*, August 5, 1916.
46. Edward Wagenknecht, *The Movies in the Age of Innocence*, 3rd ed. (McFarland, 2014), 48–49. Bowser, *Transformation of Cinema*, 25.
47. "Illini Photoplay Stars in Chicago," *Urbana Daily Courier*, August 17, 1917.
48. "Starr Picture Director Here," *Tulsa Morning News*. J. L. L. Kuhn, *List of Films, Reels and Views Examined* (1918). Copy in possession of the author.
49. Joseph P. Eckhardt, *The King of the Movies: Film Pioneer Siegmund Lubin* (Fairleigh Dickinson University Press, 1997), 1, 80–95. "Before Hollywood There Was Betzwood," *Libraries at Montgomery County Community College*, accessed April 10, 2025, https://library.mc3.edu/betzwood.
50. Eckhardt, *King of the Movies*, 225–26.
51. "Personals," *Urbana Daily Courier*, June 5, 1918, 5.
52. "Everywoman Contest," *Tulsa Daily World*, April 4, 1919.
53. "Starr Picture Director Here," *Tulsa Morning News*.
54. "Henry Starr to Be Movie Star," *Daily Oklahoman*, June 1, 1919.

Notes for Reel Three 243

55. "Henry Starr Asks Aid of His Pal in Movie Films," *Tulsa Daily World*, July 11, 1919. "Henry Starr Prepares for Reel Bandit Work," *Muskogee Daily Phoenix*, July 11, 1919.

56. Al Jennings, *Six-Shooters*, chap. 36 (unpublished, date unknown), Al Jennings Papers, Oklahoma Historical Society, Research Center, Oklahoma City. Copy in possession of the author.

57. "Starr and Mix Worked Together," *Tulsa Morning News*, June 23, 1919, 4.

58. "Son to 'Act' For Father as a Youth," *Tulsa Daily World*, July 12, 1919.

59. "The Starring of Henry Starr," *Daily Ardmoreite*, June 22, 1919.

60. "Movie of Bad Man Corrupts Youth Is Belief of Butz," *Muskogee Times-Democrat*, April 17, 1919.

61. "Of Outlawry," *Muskogee Times-Democrat*.

62. Letter from Starr to Governor Robertson, March 30, 1919, GOR. In the handwritten note, Starr writes, "Sir. I am here in Tulsa. I think I shall make this my home. A number of old-time friends including Bankers, Lawyers, oil-men and Businessmen assure me of their good will and support. The Sheriff is my friend, also the Chief of Police. I believe it's a good place to locate."

63. "Henry Starr Is in Jail for Crime of 27 Years Ago," *Collinsville Star*, June 20, 1919.

64. "Henry Starr Is Wanted," *Hooker (OK) Advance*, June 27, 1919. "Starr to Protest Extradition Plan," *Arkansas Democrat* (Little Rock), June 17, 1919.

65. "Requisition for Starr," *Tulsa Morning News*, 5.

66. "Henry Starr," *Tulsa Tribune*, June 16, 1919, 6.

67. Wallis, *Pretty Boy*, 45. A Sallisaw, Oklahoma, merchant, J. H. Harkrider remembered Starr was "in every way a perfect gentleman." "A Gentleman Bandit Was Starr, Now Prisoner in Oklahoma 'Pen,'" *Tulsa Daily World*, September 12, 1915.

68. Clara B. Kennan, "When Henry Starr Visited Bentonville," *Arkansas Democrat Magazine*, July 27, 1947.

69. Sutton and Macdonald, *Hands Up!*, 251.

70. Starr, *Thrilling Events*, 39–40.

71. "Outlaw Starr, the Captured Bandit Makes a Confession," *Arkansas Gazette*, July 11, 1893. Wilson was a farm boy from Emporia, Kansas. He was described as "a rather pleasant-faced little chap, 18 years old, five feet in height and bearing no earmarks of a desperado."

72. Sutton and Macdonald, *Hands Up!*, 255.

244   Notes for Reel Three

73. "Requisition for Starr," *Tulsa Morning News*, 5.
74. "Henry Starr Will Not Be Tried for Old Bank Robbery," *Miami (OK) Daily Record-Herald*, June 17, 1919.
75. "Requisition for Starr," *Tulsa Morning News*, 5.
76. "Congressmen Would Prohibit Interstate Commerce to Films with Crime Scenes," *Moving Picture World*, January 17, 1920. C. W. B. Hinds, "Oklahoma at Washington," *Harlow's Weekly*, January 21, 1920, 7.
77. "Would Stop Crime Films," *Moving Picture World*, January 24, 1920, 560.
78. "Law Would Stop Former Bandits Shown on Screen," *Muskogee Daily Phoenix and Times-Democrat*, January 8, 1920.
79. "Movie Men Will Bar Bandit Films," *Daily Oklahoman*, February 5, 1920. "Bar Bandit Pictures in O.C.," *Oklahoma News*, February 13, 1920.
80. Derek Jones, *Censorship: A World Encyclopedia* (Fitzroy Dearborn, 2001), 1447, 1627, 1703. Vicki Anderson, *The Dime Novel in Children's Literature* (McFarland, 2014), 84.
81. Anthony Comstock, *Traps for the Young* (Funk & Wagnalls, 1884), 28.
82. Anderson, *Dime Novel*, 91, 107.
83. "Due to Bad Novels," *Kansas City (MO) Journal*, January 17, 1898, 2.
84. Michael Denning, *Mechanic Accents: Dime Novels and Working-Class Culture in America* (Verso, 1987), 233.
85. Daryl Jones, *The Dime Novel Western* (Popular Press, Bowling Green State University, 1978), 79.
86. Jim Cullen, *The Art of Democracy: A Concise History of Popular Culture in the United States* (New York University Press, 2002), 144–45.
87. 236 US 230 (1915) Mutual Film Corporation v. Industrial Commission of Ohio.
88. "Letters from the People," *Muskogee County Democrat*, February 4, 1915.
89. "Bad Advertising from Bank Robbing," *Tulsa Democrat*, December 30, 1914.
90. "Mayor Is Censor of Movie Shows," *Muskogee Times-Democrat*, December 23, 1915, 2. "Pastors at Outs over Censorship," *Daily Oklahoman*, December 12, 1915, 16. "Churches Vote to Establish Censor," *Daily Oklahoman*, December 13, 1915, 12.
91. "Would Censor Crime Movies," *Oklahoma City Times*, February 2, 1915, 4.

Notes for Reel Three

92. "Movies Hold Sway in House Friday," *Tulsa Daily World*, February 6, 1915. J. R. Jones, "Progressive Legislation," *Moving Picture World*, February 20, 1915.

93. "Motion Pictures, the Newest Art," *Tulsa Daily World*, November 29, 1914.

94. "Moving Picture Bill Is Recommitted by House for Amendment After Being Debated," *Guthrie Daily Leader*, February 6, 1915. After the amendment, House Bill No. 161 written by Hargis, Barbee, and Nesbit was passed and sent to a committee in the senate but was not reported out. "Legislative Report," *Daily Oklahoman*, May 21, 1916, C-5.

95. Library of Congress, "Constitution Annotated," Congress.gov, 2018, https://constitution.congress.gov/.

96. Giebler, "Rubbernecking in Film Land," *Moving Picture World*, September 13, 1919, 1632.

97. "City Council Commends State Bar Association," *Marlow (OK) Review*, January 1, 1920. "Oklahoma Association Endorse Bill," *Moving Picture World*, February 7, 1920. "Bandit Films Barred," *Harlow's Weekly*, February 11, 1920, 19.

98. "Talbot Is President of Oklahomans," *Moving Picture World*, January 25, 1919, 466.

99. "Asks Drastic Motion Pictures Censorship," *News-Capital*, February 21, 1919, 6. "New Bills Before State Legislature," *News-Capital*, February 18, 1919, 2.

100. "Congressmen Would Prohibit," *Moving Picture World*.

101. "To Bar Outlaw Pictures," *Hominy (OK) News*, January 8, 1920.

102. "Would Stop Crime Films," *Moving Picture World*, January 24, 1920, 560.

103. *Dustin (OK) News*, January 23, 1920.

104. Marshall L. Smith, editor, "Censorship of Films," *Hominy News*, April 23, 1920.

105. "Bar Bandit Pictures in O.C.," *Oklahoma News*, February 13, 1920.

106. "Henry Starr and the Movies," *Daily Oklahoman*, April 6, 1919, 13-A.

107. "Movie Men Will Bar," *Daily Oklahoman*.

108. Edith C. Johnson, "Why We Have the 'Movie Mind,'" *Daily Oklahoman*, August 22, 1920, 8.

109. "Former Convicts Can Not Be Movie Stars," *Enid Daily News*, February 8, 1920, 3C.

110. "Henry Starr to Visit Stroud Again," *Stroud Democrat*, October 24, 1919.

246 Notes for Reel Three

111. *Investor* (Oklahoma City), August 1, 1920.

112. *Stroud Messenger*, October 31, 1919.

113. "Henry Starr Again Robs," *Tulsa Daily World.*

114. *Stroud Messenger*, February 28, 1919.

115. Glenn Shirley Papers, National Cowboy & Western Heritage Museum, Oklahoma City (hereafter cited as Shirley Papers). Copy of the photo in author's possession.

116. "Henry Starr Re-Enacts," *Daily Oklahoman*, November 16, 1919.

117. "Double-Header Topped Bank Robber's Career," *Daily Oklahoman*, April 5, 1959.

118. "Henry Starr Again Robs," *Tulsa Daily World.*

119. Glenn Shirley, *Purple Sage: The Exploits, Adventures, and Writings of Patrick Sylvester McGeeney* (Barbed Wire Press, 1989), 128.

120. Shirley, *Purple Sage*, 128.

121. Shirley, *Purple Sage*, 3–10. John Hudson, "Wichitan Recalls Attempt by Henry Starr to Rob Train," *Wichita (KS) Eagle*, June 28, 1931, 2A. "Eagle Reader Says He Foiled Starr's Attempted Holdup," *Wichita Eagle*, December 6, 1931, 25. Fred Gipson, *Fabulous Empire: Colonel Zack Miller's Story* (Houghton Mifflin, 1946), 134–40. One of the men being held at gunpoint was Zack Miller of the 101 Ranch, whom Starr would later attempt to partner with on his Claremore motion picture project.

122. Shirley, *Purple Sage*, ix.

123. Shirley, *Purple Sage*, 99.

124. Georges Méliès, "Le Voyage Dans La Lune (1902)," *YouTube*, April 9, 2018, https://youtu.be/ZNAHcMMOHE8?si=0ubcJ5BXA_KiFbjp.

125. Bowser, *Transformation of Cinema*, 23.

126. Bowser, *Transformation of Cinema*, 156.

127. Shirley, *Purple Sage*, 115, ix. Shamrock was a nod to McGeeney's heritage. He was born in Tyrone County, Ireland, in 1873, but his parents moved to Kansas when he was an infant.

128. Frank T. Thompson, *Texas Hollywood: Filmmaking in San Antonio Since 1910* (Maverick Publishing, 2002), 11–12. "Eight-Reel Photoplay Made on Texas Soil," *San Antonio Express*, January 25, 1918. "Work Starts On Rex Beach Movie," *San Antonio Express*, December 24, 1917, 7.

129. Shirley, *Purple Sage*, 128.

130. "Ft. Smith Letter," *Indian Chieftain* (Vinita, OK), September 9, 1895. "Henry Starr Guilty," *Tahlequah (OK) Arrow*, September 21, 1895, 4. "Detective Killed," *Arkansas Gazette*, December 14, 1892.

Notes for Reel Three   247

131. Examples of the three definitions: Hugh S. Fullerton, "New Jesse James! Here's Wild West Romance Of Today," *Tacoma (WA) Times*, April 7, 1915. Fullerton refers to Starr as a savage. "A Gentleman Bandit Was Starr, Now Prisoner in Oklahoma 'Pen,'" *Tulsa Daily World.* The headline speaks for itself. Jim Kearney (pseudonym for Oliver "Oll" Coomes), *Hank Starr at Pryor Creek, or, Old Jack Drew Heard From* (Street & Smith Log Cabin Library, 1893). The dime-novel is the first to imbue Starr with Robin Hood qualities.

132. Eric Hobsbawm, *Bandits* (New Press, 2000), 20.

133. Paul Kooistra, *Criminals as Heroes: Structure, Power & Identity* (Popular Press, Bowling Green State University, 1989), 32–33.

134. Kooistra, *Criminals as Heroes*, 11.

135. Kent Ladd Steckmesser, *Western Outlaws: The Good Badman in Fact, Film and Folklore* (Regina Books, 1983), 1–8.

136. Hobsbawm, *Bandits*, 168.

137. Hobsbawm, *Bandits*, 47.

138. Steckmesser, *Western Outlaws*, 141–45.

139. Steckmesser, *Western Outlaws*, 2.

140. "Overlooked," *St. Louis Weekly Gazette*, May 11, 1893, 7.

141. Kearney, *Hank Starr at Pryor Creek*.

142. Kearney, *Hank Starr at Pryor Creek*, 14.

143. Milt Hinkle, "Henry Starr and the Rough Ones," *Golden West Magazine*, March 1974.

144. "Starr Tossed Farmers' Debts into the River," *Guthrie Daily Leader*, April 3, 1915.

145. Al Sylvester, "Barber Recalls Comic Carney Bank Holdup," *Tulsa Daily World*, September 13, 1964. "Carney State Bank Robbed," *Meeker (OK) Herald*, January 1, 1915. "Reward for Each Robber," *Bartlesville Morning Examiner*, March 3, 1931. Harry Dobson told the same, consistent Herman Stump story on KSBI Radio, November 1964; Lincoln and Paine Historical Society Program, Living Legend Library, Oklahoma Christian College. Copy of audio in author's possession.

146. "Daylight Robbers Secure Big Sum," *Daily Oklahoman*, December 30, 1914, 10.

147. Kearney, *Hank Starr at Pryor Creek*, 5.

148. Starr, *Thrilling Events*, 76–78.

149. Steckmesser, *Western Outlaws*, 142.

150. Alexander Huling, interview, "One Escapade of the Noted Outlaw, Henry Starr," April 22, 1938, Indian-Pioneer Papers, vol. 45–8, Western History Collections, Oklahoma Libraries, University of

248   Notes for Reel Three

Oklahoma, Norman (hereafter cited as Indian-Pioneer Papers). https://repository.ou.edu/islandora/object/oku%3A10042?solr_nav%5Bid%5D=c603aba83bbab2166fac&solr_nav%5Bpage%5D=0&solr_nav%5Boffset%5D=1&search=Huling.

151. Steckmesser, *Western Outlaws*, 142–43.
152. Starr, *Thrilling Events*, 7.
153. "The Oklahoma Land Rush Begins," History.com, updated January 31, 2025, https://www.history.com/this-day-in-history/the-oklahoma-land-rush-begins
154. Starr, *Thrilling Events*, 9–10.
155. Steckmesser, *Western Outlaws*, 141.
156. Lewis Alvin Blackburn, interview, May 24, 1937, Indian-Pioneer Papers, vol. 8, https://repository.ou.edu/islandora/object/oku%3A13768?solr_nav%5Bid%5D=0b9c29adc01066f0ad27&solr_nav%5Bpage%5D=0&solr_nav%5Boffset%5D=2&search=Blackburn.
157. Hobsbawm, *Bandits*, 51.
158. Kearney, *Hank Starr at Pryor Creek*, 12.
159. Shirley, *Purple Sage*, 128.
160. Fred Harvey Harrington, *Hanging Judge* (University of Oklahoma Press, 1996), 86. Letter, Glenn Shirley to Ivan Tribe, January 11, 1961, Shirley Papers.
161. Harrington, *Hanging Judge*, 85.
162. *Starr v. United States*, US Supreme Court, May 14, 1894, No. 1080.
163. "Story of Life of Henry Starr as Told by Famous Bandit," *Wichita (KS) Daily Eagle*, March 3, 1921, 3.
164. "The witnesses agreed that Wilson fired the first shot, and also that, during the time he was riding up to Starr, Starr did not raise his gun, or make any effort to stop Wilson." *Starr v. United States*, May 14, 1894, No. 1080.
165. A Starr family friend, F. M. Allen, wrote that Sleepy Tuck, a buckskin horse with zebra markings, was not gun shy, and "I know that Henry would never have mounted some other horse and ridden off and left Sleepy Tuck. He loved that horse." *True West* 4, no. 2 (Nov-Dec 1956).
166. "Story of Life of Henry Starr as Told by Famous Bandit," *Wichita Daily Eagle*, March 3, 1921, 3.
167. P. S. McGeeney, Henry Starr short story, 8, Shirley Papers.
168. Evett Dumas Nix and Gordon Hines, *Oklahombres: Particularly the Wilder Ones* (Eden Publishing House, 1929), 265.
169. Shirley, *Purple Sage*, 132.

Notes for Reel Four 249

170. Starr, *Thrilling Events*, 35.
171. "Dan Cupid Forms 'Movie Company,'" *Muskogee Daily Phoenix*, August 24, 1920.
172. Bill Caldwell, "Carthage's Karl Hackett Classic Western Villain," *Joplin Globe* (St. Louis), October 20, 2023.
173. "Dan Cupid," *Muskogee Daily Phoenix*, August 24, 1920, 3.
174. Triangle Exchange advertisement, *Moving Picture World*, December 6, 1919.
175. Letter, Claude Smith to Glenn Shirley, October 11, 1965, Shirley Papers. Shirley. *Purple Sage*, 132.
176. Claude Smith, letter to Glenn Shirley, October 11, 1965.

Notes for Reel Four

1. *Stroud Messenger*, February 27, 1920. *Boynton (OK) Index*, March 12, 1920.
2. "San Antonian Reluctantly Parts with His Old-Time Winchester," *San Antonio Evening News*, January 10, 1939.
3. "In these early years, theaters were still running single-reel films, which came at a standard length of 1,000 feet, allowing for about 16 minutes of playing time." "8.2: The History of Movies," in *Understanding Media and Culture: An Introduction to Mass Communication*, 2016, https://pressbooks.ccconline.org/accintrotomedia/chapter/8-2-the-history-of-movies/.
4. Jack Spears, "Hollywood's Oklahoma," *Chronicles of Oklahoma* 67, no. 4 (Winter 1989–90): 347.
5. Shirley, *Purple Sage*, 132.
6. Wallis, *Real Wild West*, 383.
7. John Wooley, *Shot in Oklahoma: A Century of Sooner State Cinema* (University of Oklahoma Press, 2012), 50.
8. Richard Slotkin, letter to Mark Archuleta, 2021. Review of *Henry Starr*, email, May 17, 2021.
9. *A Debtor to the Law* at New Yale Theatre, *Muskogee Times-Democrat*, July 1, 1920.
10. Claude Smith, letter to Glenn Shirley, October 11, 1965, Shirley Papers.
11. Mary Kinnear, "There Is No Place Like Home," *Newton (KS) Journal*, May 29, 1925.
12. Starr, *Thrilling Events*, 27.
13. Shirley, *Purple Sage*, 129.
14. Shirley, *Purple Sage*, 130.

250 Notes for Reel Four

15. Circuit Court of the United States Western District of Arkansas, *United States vs. Crawford Goldsby, alias Cherokee Bill* (August 8–9, 1895), pp. 97–107, 114–18, 127–38, 146–49, 157–62, courtesy of the Fort Smith National Historic Site, US National Park Service, https://www.nps.gov/fosm/index.htm.

16. Harrington, *Hanging Judge*, 139.

17. Harrington, *Hanging Judge*, 139–40.

18. Rufus Buck Gang members Meome (Maoma) July, Sam Samson, and Louis Davis were full-blood Creek, Lucky Davis was Black, and Rufus Buck was African-Indian. Arthur T. Burton, *Black, Red, and Deadly: Black and Indian Gunfighters of the Indian Territory, 1870–1907* (Eakin Press, 1991), 88.

19. Glenn Shirley, *Marauders of the Indian Nations* (Barbed Wire Press, 1994), 68. "On Trial for His Life," *Arkansas Gazette*, February 26, 1895. Harrington, *Hanging Judge*, 144.

20. US Department of Justice, Grand Jury Report, August term 1896, GJ, Fort Smith (FOSM). See also Frank Strong to the Attorney General, November 4, 1893, Year Files, DOJ; Grand Jury Report, February 13, 1891, August term 1891, GJ, FOSM. Juliet L. Galonska, "Reforming the Hell on the Border Jail," *Fort Smith*, accessed June 4, 2024, https://www.nps.gov/fosm/learn/historyculture/reforming-the-hell-on-the-border-jail.htm.

21. "Murderous Bill," *Arkansas Gazette*, July 27, 1895. The original plan was for Cherokee Bill to disarm the two guards while Pierce ran for the jailer's office to grab two additional weapons. Harrington, *Hanging Judge*, 145.

22. "Henry Starr Arrested Again," *AHTA Weekly News*, June 26, 1919.

23. "Killed By Cherokee Bill," *Indian Chieftain*, July 27, 1895.

24. "Killed By Cherokee Bill," *Indian Chieftain*. "Murderous Bill," *Arkansas Gazette*, 2.

25. Starr, *Thrilling Events*, 58.

26. "Henry Starr Meets His Waterloo at Harrison," *Boone County Headlight* (Harrison, AR), February 24, 1921.

27. "The End of the Noted Outlaw Rapidly Drawing Near," *Southern Standard* (Arkadelphia, AR), March 6, 1896. "Died As He Lived," *Semi-Weekly Graphic* (Pine Bluff, AR), March 21, 1896.

28. Harrington, *Hanging Judge*, 150–54.

29. Nix and Hines, *Oklahombres*, 121. Harrington, *Hanging Judge*, 159.

30. "Three Men Hung at Fort Smith," *Brinkley (AR) Argus*, May 7, 1896.

Notes for Reel Four

31. "Five Men Hanged," *Muskogee Phoenix*, July 9, 1896.
32. Burton, *Black, Red, and Deadly*, 88–96. "Buck Gang Convicted," *Black Hills Union* (Rapid City, SD), October 4, 1895. "Indian Outlaws Taken," *San Francisco Call*, August 12, 1895.
33. Burton, *Black, Red, and Deadly*, 90.
34. "Five Men Hanged," *Muskogee Phoenix*.
35. "Larson Opens Offices," *Moving Picture World*, January 1, 1920. Majestic Theatre advertisement for the film *Shepherd of the Hills*, *Tulsa World*, July 13, 1919. Larson was the general manager of the Okla.-Ark. Attractions Company.
36. "Chattel Mortgages," *Tulsa Daily Legal News*, January 17, 1920.
37. "Drexel Building," *Tulsa World Online*, May 10, 2016, https://tulsaworld.com/drexel-building/image_2da2af57-d141-57f5-a3b5-6ec39ad1c9ae.html.
38. "A Debtor to the Law," *Peacock Productions* press book (Oklahoma City, OK), 1920, 1–4.
39. Olive Stokes Mix, *The Fabulous Tom Mix* (Hassell Street Press, 2021), 25. "Starr and Mix Worked Together," *Tulsa Morning News*.
40. "A Debtor to the Law," *Peacock Productions*, 1–4.
41. Starr, *Thrilling Events*, 56.
42. Jürgen Malitz, *Nero* (Proquest, 2005), 70–71.
43. Harrington, *Hanging Judge*, xii.
44. Starr, *Thrilling Events*, 58.
45. "Boy Bandit Hanged," *Atlanta Journal*, February 21, 1894.
46. Circuit Court of the United States Western District of Arkansas, *United States vs. Henry Starr, in forma pauperis* request, November 1895. Copy in possession of author.
47. Starr v. United States, 153 US 614 (1894), 844–45. Shirley, *Last of the Real Badmen*, 117.
48. Starr, *Thrilling Events*, 27.
49. "Henry Starr Convicted," *Topeka (KS) State Journal*, September 17, 1895.
50. Starr, *Thrilling Events*, 57.
51. Starr v. United States, 164 US 627 (1897), 164.
52. Harrington, *Hanging Judge*, 192–94.
53. Starr, *Thrilling Events*, 27.
54. Jamie Harrison, "What Is Whitewashing—and Why Is It So Harmful?" *MSN*, accessed April 4, 2024, https://www.msn.com/en-us/news/us/what-is-whitewashing-%E2%80%94-and-why-is-it-so-harmful/ar-AAQjYkZ.

55. Shirley, *Marauders*, 8.
56. David K. Fremon, *The Jim Crow Laws and Racism in United States History* (Enslow Publishers, 2015), 10.
57. C. Vann Woodward, *The Strange Career of Jim Crow* (Oxford University Press, 2001), 7.
58. Fremon, *Jim Crow Laws*, 18–19. History.com Editors, "Jim Crow Laws," *History*, February 28, 2018, https://www.history.com/topics/early-20th-century-us/jim-crow-laws
59. Donald Bogle, *Toms, Coons, Mulattoes, Mammies, and Bucks: An Interpretive History of Blacks in American Films* (Continuum, 1994), 6. Stephen Burge Johnson, ed., *Burnt Cork: Traditions and Legacies of Blackface Minstrelsy* (University of Massachusetts Press, 2012), 3.
60. Bogle, *Toms, Coons*, 17.
61. Johnson, *Burnt Cork*, 137.
62. Cameron McWhirter, *Red Summer: The Summer of 1919 and the Awakening of Black America* (Henry Holt, 2011), 12–13.
63. McWhirter, *Red Summer*, 15.
64. *A Debtor to the Law,* press book, author's collection, 2.
65. Starr, *Thrilling Events*, 7.
66. Starr, *Thrilling Events*, 79–80.
67. Alexander Huling, interview, "One Escapade," April 22, 1938, Indian-Pioneer Papers.
68. "In Pen with O. Henry," *Bartlesville Daily Enterprise*, May 1, 1919.
69. *A Debtor to the Law,* press book, author's collection, 2.
70. *A Debtor to the Law,* press book, author's collection, 4.
71. S. Lea, "Silent Film Makeup: What Was It Really Like?" *Silent-Ology*, February 22, 2016, https://silentology.wordpress.com/2016/02/22/silent-film-makeup-what-was-it-really-like/.
72. *A Debtor to the Law,* press book, author's collection, 4.
73. Andrew Brodie Smith, *Shooting Cowboys and Indians* (University of Colorado Press, 2003), 45.
74. Smith, *Shooting Cowboys and Indians*, 82–83.
75. Young Deer's Native American ancestry was "murky." On the 1900 US Census, he identified as Black. However, he came from a small mid-Atlantic mixed-race community of whites, Blacks, and Nanticoke Indians. Angela Alesis, "Who Was the Real James Young Deer?" *Bright Lights Film Journal*, no. 80 (May 2013): 3.
76. "The 'Bison 101' Headliners," *Moving Picture World*, April 27, 1912, 302.

Notes for Reel Four

77. "Story of Oklahoma's Early Days," *Moving Picture World*, June 19, 1920. "Lahoma, Seven-Reel Pathé Release Tells Vivid Story of Southwest, With Real Life as Basis," *Moving Picture World*, September 4, 1920. *Lahoma* poster, *Moving Picture World*, September 18, 1920.
78. Starr, *Thrilling Events*, 10.
79. Shirley Papers.
80. "Mrs. Wilson Adjudged Insane," *Muskogee Times-Democrat*, January 31, 1917.
81. "Floyd Wilson's Widow Dead Here," *Muskogee Times-Democrat*, April 1, 1920.
82. "Making Movies at Fair Likely," *Muskogee Times-Democrat*, April 13, 1920.
83. "Plans Building of Studio Here," *Muskogee Daily Phoenix*, April 16, 1920.
84. Starr, *Thrilling Events*, 23.
85. Max Alvarez, "The Origins of the Film Exchange," *Film History* 17, no. 4, (2005): 431.
86. Bowser, *Transformation of Cinema*, 2.
87. George Potamianos, "Movies at the Margins: The Distribution of Films to Theaters in Small-Town America," chap. 1 in *American Silent Film: Discovering Marginalized Voices*, ed. Gregg Bachman and Thomas J. Slater (Southern Illinois University Press, 2002), 16. *Moving Picture World*, August 5, 1911, 301.
88. Alvarez, "Origins of the Film Exchange," 457.
89. "Big Wheat Crops and Oil Wells Bring Prosperity to Southwest Exhibitors," *Moving Picture World*, March 6, 1920.
90. "Million Feet of Kisses Reel Through City in Day," *Oklahoma City Times*, August 6, 1920, 8.
91. "New Building For Vitagraph Company," *Oklahoma News,* (Oklahoma City), October 22, 1920, 14.
92. Tilghman, *Marshal of the Last Frontier*, 322–23.
93. *Stroud Messenger*, June 16, 1919.
94. "New Picture Show," *Stroud Messenger*, July 18, 1919.
95. *Stroud Messenger*, July 25, 1919.
96. *Stroud Messenger*, January 23, 1920.
97. *Stroud Messenger*, April 30, 1920. "Heart O' the Hills," *Mary Pickford Foundation*, accessed May 19, 2024, https://marypickford.org/filmography/heart-o-the-hills-feature/.

98. "Henry Starr in Motion Pictures at the Rialto," *Stroud Messenger*, April 30, 1920.

99. *Tulsa Daily World*, May 11, 1920.

100. *Stroud Democrat*, May 21, 1920. *Stroud Messenger*, August 1, 1919.

101. "Outlaw Pictures Would Be Taboo in Oklahoma," *Okemah (OK) Ledger*, March 18, 1920, 5.

102. "Special Picture Shown Small Audience," *Okemah Ledger*, May 20, 1920.

103. *Lincoln County Republican* (Chandler, OK), May 27, 1920. Joe Klein, *Woody Guthrie: A Life* (Delta Trade Paperbacks, 1999), 16.

104. "Committee Views Henry Starr Production," *Okfuskee County News* (Okemah, OK), May 5, 1920, 4.

105. "Woman and Boy Lynched," *Okemah (OK) Independent*, May 25, 1911. Klein, *Woody Guthrie*, 13. "Lynching of Laura and L. D. Nelson," accessed April 27, 2024, https://acrowdgathers.wordpress.com/wp-content/uploads/2012/01/bridge2899_03.jpg.

106. "Special Picture Shown Small Audience," *Okemah Ledger*.

107. "Committee Views Henry Starr Production," *Okfuskee County News*, 4. "Special Picture Shown Small Audience," *Okemah Ledger*.

108. *Fort Gibson (OK) New Era*, May 20, 1920.

109. *Dallas Express*, May 22, 1920.

110. *Henryetta (OK) Daily Freelance*, June 6, 1920. *Henryetta Daily Freelance*, May 24, 1920.

111. *Tulsa Daily World*, June 14, 1920.

112. *Guthrie Daily Leader*, June 15, 1920.

113. *Democrat-Herald* (Newkirk, OK), June 17, 1920.

114. *Lindsay (OK) News*, June 11, 1920.

115. *Ponca City News*, June 16, 1920.

116. *Lawton News*, June 19, 1920.

117. *Guthrie Daily Leader*, June 24, 1920.

118. *Hominy (OK) News Republican*, June 25, 1920.

119. *Drumright (OK) Weekly Derrick*, June 29, 1920.

120. "Debtor to the Law," *Muskogee Times-Democrat*, July 4, 1920. "First Movie Made Here o Be Shown," *Muskogee Times-Democrat*, June 28, 1920. "Starr Picture Starts Well," *Muskogee Times-Democrat*, June 30, 1920, 2.

121. *Jenks (OK) News*, July 9, 1920.

122. *McAlester (OK) News-Capital*, July 15, 1920.

123. *Bartlesville Examiner*, July 21, 1920.

Notes for Reel Four

124. *Marietta (OK) Monitor*, June 25, 1920.
125. *Stroud Democrat*, July 2, 1920.
126. "Starr Off The Movies," *Oklahoma News*, June 15, 1920.
127. "Mrs. Starr Asks Support for Boy," *News-Capital*, April 16, 1920.
128. "Starr Agrees to Help Son," *Tulsa Daily World*, April 24, 1920.
129. "Former Outlaw Married Again, Records Reveal," *Muskogee Daily Phoenix*, May 14, 1920.
130. "Wife of Henry Starr," *Muskogee Daily Phoenix*, May 13, 1920.
131. "Henry Starr Married Texas Woman While He Was Making Pictures," *Shawnee (OK) Morning News*, May 14, 1920. Henry Starr and Lucille Starr, Certificate of Marriage No. 55668, February 20, 1920, Bexar County, TX, copy in possession of author.
132. Hulda Lucille Sullivan, death certificate, April 27, 1932, file no. 20428, Department of Health, Austin, TX, copy in possession of the author. "John L. Sullivan Sued For Divorce," *Muskogee Daily Phoenix*, November 30, 1919.
133. "Former Outlaw Married," *Muskogee Daily Phoenix*.
134. "Kate Barnard Grieves for Henry Starr," *Daily Oklahoman*, February 22, 1921.
135. "Woman and the Ballot," *Custer County News* (Clinton, OK), March 27, 1909. "Kate on Mission," *Stillwater Gazette*, February 26, 1909. "Girl Chief of New State's Charities," *Brooklyn Citizen*, January 5, 1908.
136. "Nothing Serious," *Blackwell (OK) Daily News*, December 16, 1908. "She May Probe Further into Prison Horrors," *Muskogee Daily Phoenix*, December 20, 1908.
137. "A Juvenile Court," *Muskogee Daily Phoenix*, August 16, 1908, 2. Dr. J. H. Stolper, "The State and the Nation," *Wilburton (OK) News*, October 7, 1910, 2. Lynn Musslewhite and Suzanne Jones Crawford, *One Woman's Political Journey: Kate Barnard and Social Reform, 1875–1930* (University Of Oklahoma Press, 2003), 98–100.
138. "Kate Barnard's Denver Interview Startles Oklahomans," *Daily Ardmoreite*, July 28, 1914, 7. Musslewhite and Jones Crawford, *One Woman's Political Journey*, 165.
139. "Miss Kate to Publish Book," *Muskogee Times-Democrat*, January 31, 1917.
140. "Kate Barnard Grieves for Henry Starr," *Daily Oklahoman*.
141. "Starr Sought in Vain to Borrow Money Here," *Tulsa Tribune*, February 19, 1921.

142. *Cherokee (OK) Sentinel*, September 17, 1920. The film was titled *The Oklahoma Outlaw*.
143. *Chillicothe (MO) Constitution*, October 23, 1920.
144. "The Debtor to the Law," *Chillicothe Constitution*, October 23, 1920.
145. *Kansas City (MO) Post*, October 31, 1920.
146. *Grenola (KS) Gazette*, November 4, 1920. *Iola (KS) Register*, November 15, 1920.
147. "Notorious Oklahoma Bandit, Twice Freed from Prison, Fatally Wounded by Banker," *Bisbee (AZ) Daily Review*, February 19, 1921.
148. Tilghman, *Marshal of the Last Frontier*, 319.
149. Jennings, *Six-Shooters*, chap. 36.
150. "Henry Starr's Reformation," *Arkansas Gazette*, 7.
151. "List of California Governors," *Governors' Gallery*, accessed April 5, 2024, https://governors.library.ca.gov/list.html.
152. "A Film History of the Osage Tribe," *Hominy News Republican*, July 24, 1919.
153. "Muskogee Woman Scenario Writer," *Muskogee Daily Phoenix*, May 2, 1920. "Making Movies at Fair Likely," *Muskogee Times-Democrat*, April, 13, 1920.
154. Letter, Starr to Governor Robertson, March 30, 1919, Governor Robertson Finding Aide Part One, Box #17, Folder #3, Record Group 8-D-1-1, GOR.
155. "The amount of radium detected in Claremore's groundwater in the 1950s is about seventy-eight times the Environmental Protection Agency's acceptable limit of 5 x 1012 Curies (5 picocuries) per liter, which was set in 1976." Marjorie Malley, "Bygone Spas: The Rise and Decay of Oklahoma's Radium Water," *Chronicles of Oklahoma*, Winter 2002, p. 459, https://gateway.okhistory.org/ark:/67531/metadc2016875.
156. Austin Whittall, "Claremore, Route 66 Oklahoma," TheRoute-66.com, updated August 14, 2021, https://www.theroute-66.com/claremore.html. Larry Larkin, "Radium Town, the Smell of Success," Claremore Museum of History, accessed May 23, 2024, https://claremoremoh.org/radium-town-the-smell-of-success/.
157. "City of Healing Waters," *Tulsa Daily World*, April 20, 1919.
158. Dr. Andrew Lerskov, "Review of Radium Water," *Journal of the Oklahoma State Medical Association*, no. 5 (1913): 458–64.
159. Will Rogers, *Will Rogers' Weekly Articles*, ed. James Smallwood and Steven K. Gragert, vol. 1, *The Harding/Coolidge Years, 1922–1925* (Oklahoma State University Press, 1980), 240.

Notes for Reel Five 257

160. Holly Hayes, "Mendenhall's Bath House," *Go Historic*, accessed May 23, 2024, https://gohistoric.com/places/297597-mendenhalls-bath-house-claremore.
161. Lerskov, "Review of Radium Water," 560.
162. Malley, "Bygone Spas," 453.
163. "Henry Starr Is to Make Picture Here," *Claremore (OK) Progress*, December 16, 1920.
164. Smith, *Shooting Cowboys and Indians*, 166–71.
165. Smith, *Shooting Cowboys and Indians*, 168.
166. "Henry Starr Is to Make Picture Here," *Claremore Progress*.
167. E. E Woods, letter to Oklahoma Historical Society, October 3, 1960.
168. *Kansas City (MO) Times*, December 16, 1920.

Notes for Reel Five

1. *Tulsa Daily World*, December 20, 1920.
2. "Starr Filled Engagement in 101 Ranch Show," *Ponca City News*, February 22, 1921.
3. "Local News," *Sequoyah County Democrat*, July 30, 1920.
4. "Real Estate Transfers," *Sequoyah County Democrat*, August 27, 1920.
5. Al Jennings believed Starr had pledged Hulda's ranch as collateral, and when he defaulted, they lost their home. Jennings, *Six-Shooters*, chap. 36.
6. "Starr Sought in Vain to Borrow Money Here," *Tulsa Tribune*, February 19, 1921. "Henry Starr Needed Cash," *Blackwell (OK) Weekly Sun*, February 24, 1921.
7. "To Serve Three Years," *Vian (OK) Press*, April 15, 1921. "Helped Starr Given Three Years," *Muskogee Daily Phoenix*, April 2, 1921, 5. "Admits He Helped Starr," *Okmulgee (OK) Daily Times*, April 2, 1921, 2.
8. "Man of Lurid Career," *Tulsa Daily World*, February 26, 1921, 5.
9. "Sheriff's Bullet Brings End to Lockhart's Career," *Blackwell (OK) Morning Tribune*, March 27, 1924.
10. "Forced into Vault," *Pine Bluff (AR) Daily Graphic*, February 20, 1921.
11. *Attica (OK) Independent*, December 23, 1920.
12. *Springfield (MO) News Leader*, December 26, 1920.
13. "Starr Sought in Vain," *Tulsa Tribune*.
14. "At the Movies," *Fort Worth Star-Telegram*, January 9, 1921. *Fort Worth Star-Telegram*, January 11, 1921. *Fort Worth Star-Telegram*, January 17, 1921.
15. "Bandit's Funeral to Be Held at Dewey," *Sequoyah County Democrat*, February 25, 1921. "She Loves Starr," *Muskogee Daily Phoenix*.

16. Wallace C. Perry, "Starr's Bride Has Hope for State Parole," *Daily Oklahoman*, February 21, 1921.
17. "Henry Starr Meets His Waterloo at Harrison," *Boone County Headlight*, February 24, 1921.
18. Homer Croy, *Cole Younger: Last of the Great Outlaws* (University Of Nebraska Press, 1999), 5.
19. Croy, *Cole Younger*, 175.
20. Koblas, *Great Cole Younger*, 11.
21. Koblas, *Great Cole Younger*, 52.
22. Koblas, *Great Cole Younger*, 6, 45.
23. Koblas, *Great Cole Younger*, 54–56.
24. "Henry Starr Meets His Waterloo at Harrison," *Boone County Headlight*.
25. Matt Hinkle, "Henry Starr and the Rough Ones," *Golden West*, March 1974. Hinkle wrote that Starr said he was going to Fort Worth to pick up his brother Pony and Rufus Roland. Pony Starr was not a brother but a cousin who ran with Joe Davis and was not part of the Harrison bank robbery. Wallis, *Real Wild West*, 383–85.
26. "Had an Eye on Ponca City," *Tulsa Daily World*, March 4, 1921.
27. "Henry Starr Shot in Arkansas Robbery," *Claremore Progress*, February 24, 1921. "Loser in Claremore Poker Game, Starr Deserted the 'Straight' Path; Two Gamblers Reported Missing," *Tulsa Daily World*, February 19, 1921.
28. Letter, Starr to Governor Robertson, March 30, 1919, Governor Robertson Finding Aide Part One, Box #17, Folder #3, Record Group 8-D-1-1, GOR.
29. *Harlow's Weekly*, January 6, 1921.
30. "Would Put Ban on Showing Bad Pictures Here," *Ada (OK) Evening News*, February 14, 1921.
31. "Starr's Widow Says He Told Her," *Shawnee (OK) News-Star*, February 23, 1921.
32. *King Jack* (Commerce, OK), February 17, 1921.
33. "Came after Stolen Car," *Mountain Echo* (Yellville, AR), May 26, 1921. "Rowlens, Starr's Accomplice, Goes to Arkansas," *Ponca City News*, March 3, 1921.
34. "Henry Starr Dead," *Star Progress* (Berryville, AR), February 25, 1921.
35. Sarah Hartley, email message to Kathy Watson, November 2, 2005, regarding her grandmother Ethel Holman when Hartley served as a constituent services representative for Congressman John Boozman, Third District, Arkansas.

Notes for Reel Five

36. J. D. Eagle, "The Story of Henry Starr and the Harrison Holdup Recalled by Local Robbery," *Harrison (AR) Times*, March 1, 1961.

37. "Failure of Starr's Last Bank Robbery Attempt Blamed on Lack of Definite Plans," *Daily Oklahoman*, February 27, 1921, 2-B. Lynn Barron Sr., review of "Henry Starr, Oklahoma Outlaw," *National Outlaw Lawman Association Quarterly* (1981): 13.

38. "Henry Starr Shot in Raid at Harrison," *Daily Arkansas Gazette*, February 19, 1921.

39. "Henry Starr Meets His Waterloo," *Boone County Headlight*. "Henry Starr Shot in Arkansas Robbery," *Claremore Progress*, February 24, 1921. "Henry Starr Notorious Bandit Departs," *Baxter Bulletin* (Mountain Home, AR), March 18, 1921.

40. Robert Elman, *Fired in Anger: The Personal Handguns of American Heroes and Villains* (Doubleday, 1968), 259–60.

41. Barron, review of "Henry Starr," 13.

42. "Partner Of Henry Starr Sentenced," *Okfuskee County News*, April 14, 1921.

43. Barron, review of "Henry Starr," 13.

44. J. D. Eagle, "Story of Henry Starr."

45. David Holsted, "Woman Recalls Grandmother's Role in 1921 Henry Starr Killing," *Harrison (AR) Daily Times*, June 16, 2012. Naomi Moore's granddaughter Mona Garvin recounts the stories she was told of the bank robbery by her grandmother.

46. "Henry Starr Meets His Waterloo," *Boone County Headlight*.

47. Some accounts say his nickname was "Bug" or "Mug."

48. "Failure of Starr's," *Daily Oklahoman*.

49. Barron, review of "Henry Starr," 14.

50. "Failure of Starr's," *Daily Oklahoman*. "Henry Starr the Notorious Outlaw Is Shot at Harrison," *Baxter Bulletin*, February 25, 1921. "Henry Starr Meets His Waterloo," *Boone County Headlight*.

51. Barron, review of "Henry Starr," 14.

52. "Henry Starr Meets His Waterloo," *Boone County Headlight*.

53. Holsted, "Woman Recalls Grandmother's Role."

54. Barron, review of "Henry Starr," 14.

55. "Identifies Starr in Bank Robbery," *Cassville (MO) Republican*, February 24, 1921.

56. "Bandit Offered Gun to Old Man," *Tulsa Daily World*, February 20, 1921, 19.

57. "Other Days, from the Files of the Times," *Harrison Daily Times*, February 20, 1979.

260   Notes for Reel Five

58. "Henry Starr Meets His Waterloo," *Boone County Headlight*.
59. Historians Richard and Judy Dockery Young believe Starr's accomplices stole horses to escape, making the People's Bank robbery the last horseback robber of the Middle Border. Richard Young and Judy Dockrey Young, *Outlaw Tales: Legends, Myths, and Folklore from America's Middle Border* (August House, 1992), 181.
60. "Doctors Believe Henry Starr Will Die from Wounds," *Oklahoma City Times*, February 19, 1921, 16. Perry, "Starr's Bride Has Hope," *Daily Oklahoman*.
61. "Starr's Parole Should Have Been Revoked Before, Bill Tilghman Believes," *Oklahoma City Times*, February 19, 1921.
62. "Starr Tells on Pals; Asks for Divine Aid," *Tulsa Tribune*, February 21, 1921. The bullet was returned to Dr. Fowler, who kept it for years. It is now in the possession of the Boone County Heritage Museum in Harrison, Arkansas.
63. "Death May Claim Henry Starr's Life at Any Time Now," *Tulsa Daily World*, February 20, 1921. "Three Men Suspected Pals of Henry Starr," *Pine Bluff Graphic*, February 20, 1921.
64. "Failure of Starr's," *Daily Oklahoman*. "Henry Starr Meets His Waterloo," *Boone County Headlight*.
65. Letter, John S. Kuehner, Oklahoma Department of Corrections, Administrator, Offender Records to Robert Curry, March 4, 1986. "Arkansas Has Priority on Starr—Parole Revoked," *Tulsa Daily World*, February 20, 1920.
66. Barron, review of "Henry Starr," 15, 16.
67. Eagle, "Story of Henry Starr."
68. "Henry Starr Meets His Waterloo," *Boone County Headlight*.
69. "Failure of Starr's," *Daily Oklahoman*.
70. "Slayer of Starr Knows Firearms," *Arkansas Gazette*, February 27, 1921, 7.
71. James W. Loewen, *Sundown Towns: A Hidden Dimension of American Racism* (New Press, 2018), 424. In 2003 Harrison Mayor Bob Reynolds, acknowledging the town's dark and racist past, drew up a collective statement that read in part, "The perception that hangs over our city is the result of two factors: one, unique evils resulting from past events, and two, the silence of the general population toward those events from 1905 and 1909."
72. "Henry Starr the Notorious Outlaw," *Baxter Bulletin*. The phrase "whitest manner" is not a direct quote from Starr and may have been

Notes for Reel Five

how the reporter from the *Baxter Bulletin* editorialized the moment. When the paper reran parts of the original story the wording changed to "cleanest manner." "Henry Starr Notorious Bandit Departs," *Baxter Bulletin*.

73. "Henry Starr the Notorious Outlaw," *Baxter Bulletin*. In 1953 Coffman sold the .44 caliber New Service Colt (serial no. 250696) to a collector. Elman, *Fired in Anger*, 259–60. Starr's gun is now on display at the Ralph Foster Museum at College of the Ozarks, Point Lookout, MO.

74. Barron, review of "Henry Starr," 15.

75. "Henry Starr Meets His Waterloo," *Boone County Headlight*.

76. "Debt Drove Starr to Theft He Says, Spinal Cord Cut," *Muskogee Daily Phoenix*, February 19, 1921. "Henry Starr Needed Cash," *Blackwell Weekly Sun*. "Kate Barnard Grieves," *Daily Oklahoman*.

77. "She Love Starr at First Sight, Loves Him Still," *Daily Phoenix* (AZ), February 19, 1921.

78. Perry, "Starr's Bride Has Hope," *Daily Oklahoman*.

79. "Bride Is Speeding to Bed of Bandit Who 'Quit Robbing,'" *Muskogee Daily Phoenix*, February 19, 1921.

80. Perry, "Starr's Bride Has Hope," *Daily Oklahoman*.

81. "Identifies Starr in Bank Robbery," *Cassville Republican*, February 24, 1921.

82. "Perry, Starr's Bride Has Hope," *Daily Oklahoman*.

83. "Starr's Life a Lesson to His Boy, Son Says," Oklahoma City Times, February 19, 1921.

84. "Starr Will Die, Doctors Repeat; Suspects Freed," *Muskogee Daily Phoenix*, February 21, 1921.

85. Perry, "Starr's Bride Has Hope," *Daily Oklahoman*, 11.

86. "Kate Barnard Grieves," *Daily Oklahoman*.

87. "Bank Robber's Wife Visits Him in Cell," *Oklahoma City Times*, February 21, 1921.

88. "Starr's Body Taken to Dewey," *Monett (MO) Times*, February 25, 1921.

89. Barron, review of "Henry Starr," 16.

90. "Starr's Parole Should Have," *Oklahoma City Times*.

91. Sutton and Macdonald, *Hands Up!*, 243.

92. Perry, "Starr's Bride Has Hope," *Daily Oklahoman*, 11.

93. Young, *Outlaw Tales*, 183–84.

94. "Starr Tells on Pals," *Tulsa Tribune*.

95. The original note is in possession of the Boone County Heritage Museum, Harrison, AR.

96. "Henry Starr 'Squeals' on His Confederates.," *St. Louis Globe-Democrat*, February 22, 1921.

97. "Bandit Offered," *Tulsa Daily World*, 19.

98. Starr, *Thrilling Events*, 93.

99. "Starr Suffering as Death Nears," *Tulsa Daily World*, February 22, 1921.

100. "Famous Bandit Dies; Stoic to the Last," *Dresden Enterprise* (Gleason, TN), February 25, 1921.

101. "Starr Tells on Pals," *Tulsa Tribune*.

102. "Henry Starr Meets His Waterloo," *Boone County Headlight*.

103. Eagle, "Story of Henry Starr."

104. "Henry Starr, Bank Bandit, Is Dead," *Mena (AR) Weekly Star*, February 24, 1921. Henry George Starr, death certificate, February 22, 1921, file no. 73, State of Arkansas Board of Health, copy in possession of the author.

105. "Henry Starr, Noted Outlaw Is Dead," *El Reno (OK) Daily Democrat*, United Press, February 22, 1921.

106. *Ocala (FL) Evening Star*, February 23, 1921.

107. "Bandit Offered," *Tulsa Daily World*.

108. Young, *Outlaw Tales*, 184.

109. Young, *Outlaw Tales*, 182.

110. "Henry Starr Meets His Waterloo," *Boone County Headlight*.

111. "Myers Threatened," *Tulsa Tribune*, March 3, 1921.

112. "Starr Died at Jail Tuesday At 1:25 P.M.," *Ozark Daily Times* (Harrison, AR), February 21, 1921.

113. "Bandit's Body Is Taken to Oklahoma," *Daily Arkansas Gazette*, February 24, 1921. *Star Progress*, February 25, 1921.

114. "Starr's Body Through Cherryvale," *Coffeyville Daily Journal*, February 24, 1921.

115. "Starr's Body Taken," *Monett Times*.

116. "Dewey News," *Bartlesville Daily Enterprise*, February 26, 1921, 6. "Gadabout," *Bartlesville Daily Enterprise*, February 25, 1921, 7.

117. Lucy J. Auldridge Oklahoma Federation of Labor Collection, Western History Collections, University of Oklahoma, Norman.

118. "Dewey News," *Bartlesville Daily Enterprise*, February 26, 1921, 6.

119. Wallis, *Real Wild West*, 384.

120. Barron, review of "Henry Starr," 16.

Notes for Reel Six 263

121. "I Loved Him," *Daily Oklahoman*.
122. "Starr Died at Jail," *Ozark Daily Times*.
123. "Quitter and Parasite Is Real Henry Starr," *Daily Oklahoman*, February 22, 1921, 6.
124. Kenneth Carter, *Buzz! Inside the Minds of Thrill-Seekers, Daredevils, and Adrenaline Junkies* (Cambridge University Press, 2019), 5.
125. Fred William Allsopp, *Folklore of Romantic Arkansas*, vol. 1 (Grolier Society, 1931), 329.
126. Harper, "Life in an Oklahoma Oil Town," *Tulsa Tribune*.
127. "Life of Henry Starr," *Durant (OK) Weekly News*, March 4, 1921.
128. "Tuesday Last Day Senators Get Full Pay, Some Bills Murdered; Others Just Go to Sleep," *Oklahoma City Times*, March 12, 1921.

Notes for Reel Six

1. *Creek County Democrat* (Shamrock, OK), February 25, 1921.
2. *Wetumka (OK) Gazette*, February 25, 1921.
3. *Mena Weekly Star*, March 3, 1921
4. "Henry Starr Still Alive 'Was in Debt,'" *Fayetteville (AR) Daily Democrat*, February 19, 1921.
5. "Sat on Jury Which Tried Henry Starr," *Arkansas Democrat*, February 21, 1921.
6. "Henry Starr at Princess," *Daily Arkansas Gazette*, March 4, 1921.
7. "Tell of Need of Restoring Peace," *Daily Arkansas Gazette*, April 4, 1921.
8. "Wop," *Merriam-Webster*, accessed April 22, 2024, https://www.merriam-webster.com/dictionary/wop. "Wop" is a pejorative term for Italians or people of Italian descent.
9. "Hiding Place Revealed by Trip of Wife," *Tulsa Tribune*, February 26, 1921. "Arrest Man In Connection With Starr Robbery," *Ponca City News*, February 26, 1921. "Admits He Helped Starr," *Okmulgee Daily Times*, April 2, 1921. "Partner of Henry Starr Sentenced," *Okfuskee County News*, April 14, 1921.
10. "Trio Who Held Up Locust Grove Bank Captured," *Miami Record*, April 29, 1921.
11. "Sheriff's Bullet Brings End to Lockhart's Career," *Blackwell Morning Tribune*. "Bandit Slain at Farmhouse Near Sperry," *Tulsa Tribune*, March 26, 1924. "Lockhart Known As Last of 'Big Three' of State's Outlaws," *Muskogee County Democrat*, March 3, 1927.

12. Thompson, *Wrecked Lives*, 217–18.

13. Shirley, *West of Hell's Fringe*, 429.

14. Victor Luckerson, "The Promise of Oklahoma: How the Push for Statehood Led a Beacon of Racial Progress to Oppression and Violence," *Smithsonian Magazine*, March 17, 2021. https://www.smithsonianmag.com/history/unrealized-promise-oklahoma-180977174/.

15. "W." Oklahoma Law Enforcement Memorial, accessed June 2, 2024, http://www.oklemem.com/w.html.

16. David Holsted, "Woman Recalls Grandmother's Role in 1921 Henry Starr Killing," *Harrison Daily*, June 16, 2012.

17. Victor Emmanuel Harlow, *Makers of Government in Oklahoma: A Descriptive Roster of Oklahomans Whose Influence and Activity Make Them Significant in the Course of Public Events in Their State* (Harlow Publishing Company, 1930), 455.

18. Harlow, *Makers of Government in Oklahoma*, 464.

19. "Kate Barnard Heart Victim," *Oklahoma News* (Oklahoma City, OK), February 24, 1930, 3.

20. "Miss Barnard Gives Estate to Aid Poor," *Oklahoma News*, February 26, 1930. "Kate Barnard Will Gives Funds to Establish Home," *Tulsa Daily World*, February 27, 1930, 5.

21. "Probate of Oklahoma Woman's Estate Denied," *Granite (OK) Enterprise*, November 14, 1930.

22. "Oklahoma State Capitol Art Collection," *Oklahoma Arts Council*, accessed May 29, 2024, https://www.arts.ok.gov/Art_at_the_Capitol/Capitol_Collection.php?c=cac&awid=43.

23. "Patrick Sylvester McGeeney," *IMDb*, accessed June 2, 2024, https://www.imdb.com/name/nm0569153. "Karl Hackett - Carl Ellsworth Germain," B-Westerns.com, accessed June 2, 2024, https://www.b-westerns.com/villan55.htm.

24. Tilghman, *Marshal of the Last Frontier*, 350–66. Samuelson, *Shoot from the Lip*, 119–26.

25. "Henry Starr's Son Held Here Suspect," *Little Rock Daily News*, July 29, 1921. "Suspects in Bauxite Robbery Are Released," *Arkansas Democrat*, July 30, 1921.

26. "Loretta Wilkins Austin (1888–1980)," *Find a Grave*, accessed June 3, 2024, https://www.findagrave.com/memorial/45197931/loretta-austin.

27. "Between Reels," *Wichita Eagle*, October 7, 1921, 14.

28. "Suits Filed in District Court," *Sequoyah Democrat*, April 29, 1921.

Notes for Reel Six

29. "Widow of Henry Starr Arrested in El Paso," *Waco (TX) News-Tribune*, October 22, 1925.

30. Hulda Lucille Sullivan, death certificate, April 27, 1932, file no. 20428, Texas State Department of Health, copy in possession of author.

31. Petition for Letters of Administration, State of Oklahoma, County of Rogers, March 10, 1921, copy in possession of the author.

32. Final Report of Administration, State of Oklahoma, Rogers County, May 20, 1924, copy in possession of author.

33. "Mrs. Henry Starr Weds Grocery Man," *Daily Oklahoman*, January 22, 1922.

34. "Heart Attack in US Office Fatal for Clerk," *Daily Oklahoman*, November 24, 1951, 16. "Olive F. 'Ollie' Griffin Starr (1882–1951)," *Find a Grave*, accessed May 29, 2024, https://www.findagrave.com/memorial/69646047/olive-f-starr.

35. "1LT Theodore Q. (Roosevelt) 'Ted' Starr," *Find a Grave*, accessed May 29, 2024, https://www.findagrave.com/memorial/5817995/theodore-q_.

36. "Mary Ellen Scott Gordon (1847–1938)," *Find a Grave*, accessed May 29, 2024, https://www.findagrave.com/memorial/20164605/mary_ellen_gordon.

37. "Rapid Sales Reported by Great Western," *Motion Picture News*, March 27, 1920, 2929. "Al Jennings and Emmett Dalton Meet in West," *Ada Weekly News*, November 13, 1919.

38. Rex H. Lampman, "When Hell Broke Loose In Coffeyville," *Pasadena (CA) Post*, January 31, 1931, 19.

39. "The Last of the Daltons Returns to Coffeyville and Points Out the Scenes of Their Last Bank Raid," *Kansas City Star*, May 10, 1931, Section C. "Dalton Here Once One of Bandit Gang," *Miami (FL) Herald*, February 22, 1917, section 2, p. 9.

40. "Dalton Loses Suit Asserting Story Pirating," *Los Angeles Times*, May 2, 1936, Part I. "Dalton Loses Suit on Film Title," *Hollywood Citizen News*, May 1, 1936.

41. "Last of Daltons to be Buried Near Brother Slain in Coffeyville," *Oklahoma News*, July 14, 1937, 5.

42. George Marshall, dir., *When the Daltons Rode*, *IMDb*, August 23, 1940. https://www.imdb.com/title/tt0033254/?ref_=nv_sr_srsg_0_tt_7_nm_0_q_When%2520the%2520Daltons%2520Rode.

43. "Dalton Raid Is Reenacted," *Parsons (KS) Sun*, June 19, 1940, 6.

44. "Al Jennings, Ex-Bandit, Former Outlaw, Incorporates Motion Picture Company," *Los Angeles Times*, January 12, 1921, 10.
45. Al Jennings, *Through the Shadows with O. Henry: The Unlikely Friendship of Al Jennings and William Sydney Porter* (Skyhorse, 2016).
46. "Al Jennings and O. Henry, Fugitives Who Came Back," *Moving Picture World*, October 4, 1919.
47. *The Oklahoma Kid* (1939), *IMDb*, accessed June 4, 2024, https://www.imdb.com/title/tt0031747/fullcredits/.
48. "Al Jennings Sues Radio," *Los Angeles Times*, September 27, 1945, 2.
49. Hedda Hopper, "Dan Duryea to Star in Al Jennings Role," *Los Angeles Times*, March 29, 1950, Part III, p. 6.
50. *Al Jennings of Oklahoma*, *IMDb*, January 17, 1951, https://www.imdb.com/title/tt0043272/?ref_=nv_sr_srsg_0_tt_1_nm_0_q_Al%2520Jennings%2520of%2520Oklahoma.
51. "TV Series on Life of Al Jennings," *Los Angeles Evening Citizen News*, January 6, 1960.
52. "He's Dead, but Legend Lives," *Record Searchlight* (Redding, CA), December 27, 1961.
53. Jennings, *Six-Shooters*, Chapter 36.
54. "Al Jennings (1863–1961)," *Find a Grave*, accessed June 4, 2024, https://www.findagrave.com/memorial/8036563/al-jennings.

Notes for the Epilogue

1. "Stroud to Re-enact Cattle Drive, Robbery," *Sunday Oklahoman*, August 9, 1992.
2. Author met with City Manager Robert Pearman in October 2022.
3. Jack Moyer, CORE Marketing Spokesperson, "CORE hears proposal to bring back Henry Starr," *Staff Report*, September 28, 2009.
4. OK Corral, Tombstone, AZ, https://www.ok-corral.com/#attractions.
5. *The Harder They Fall*, *IMDb*, November 3, 2021, https://www.imdb.com/title/tt10696784/?ref_=nm_flmg_t_15_act.
6. *You Know My Name*, *IMDb*, August 22, 1999, https://www.imdb.com/title/tt0163913/?ref_=nv_sr_srsg_2_tt_8_nm_0_q_They%2520Know%2520my%2520Na.
7. "The Wild Bunch Film Festival," *The Wild Bunch Film Festival*, accessed June 4, 2024, https://www.thewildbunchfilmfestival.com/.

Bibliography

Archives

A. B. MacDonald Papers. Library of Congress, Washington, DC.

Bartlesville Area History Museum, Bartlesville, Oklahoma.

Bexar County, Texas.

Boone County Heritage Museum, Harrison, Arkansas.

Department of Health, Austin, Texas.

Dewey Cemetery, Dewey, Oklahoma.

Dickinson Research Center, National Cowboy and Western Heritage Museum, Oklahoma City.
>Glenn D. Shirley Western Americana Collection
>Glenn Shirley Papers.

Dime Novel and Popular Literature Collection. Digital Library at Villanova University, Villanova, Pennsylvania.

Fort Smith National Historic Site, Fort Smith, Arkansas.

Governor's Office Records. Oklahoma State Archives, Oklahoma Department of Libraries, Oklahoma City, OK.

Greenwood Rising, Tulsa, Oklahoma.

Huntington Library, San Marino, California.

Jim and Theresa Earle Collection.

Kansas Historical Society, Topeka.

Key Wing Education Center & Historic Hawkins House. Rogers Historical Museum, Rogers, Arkansas.

Lincoln and Paine Historical Society Program. Living Legend Library, Oklahoma Christian College, Oklahoma City.

Museum of Colorado Prisons.

Museum of Pioneer History. Lincoln County Historical Society, Chandler, Oklahoma.

National Archives, Washington, DC
>Eastern Cherokee Applications of the US Court of Claims, 1906–1909
>Dawes Packets

National Archives at Kansas City, Missouri.

National Board of Review of Motion Pictures Records. Manuscripts and Archives Division, New York Public Library, New York.

Offender Ledger Extraction, Closed Records Unit. Oklahoma Department of Corrections, Oklahoma City.

Ohio Penitentiary Prisoners Register, 1829–1973, State Archives Series 1536. Ohio History Connection, Columbus.

Oklahoma Historical Society, Research Center, Oklahoma City.

Al Jennings Papers

Frank Harrah Collection

Fred J. Acton Collection

Fred S. Barde Papers

Grant Foreman Papers

Pawnee Bill Ranch and Museum

Oral History Program, University of California, Los Angeles.

Petition for Letters of Administration, Rogers County, Oklahoma.

Princeton University Library.

Ralph Foster Museum. College of the Ozarks, Point Lookout, Missouri.

State Board of Health Bureau of Vital Statistics. Arkansas Department of Health, Little Rock.

University of Arkansas Libraries, Fayetteville.

University of Illinois, Chicago.

Western History Collections. University Libraries, University of Oklahoma, Norman.

Lucy J. Auldridge Oklahoma Federation of Labor Collection

Indian-Pioneer Papers

N. H. Rose Photo Collection

William S. Hart Museum, Newhall, California.

Books

Aleiss, Angela. *Making the White Man's Indian: Native Americans and Hollywood Movies.* Praeger, 2009.

Allsopp, Fred William. *Folklore of Romantic Arkansas.* Vol. 1. Grolier Society, 1931.

Anderson, Vicki. *The Dime Novel in Children's Literature.* McFarland, 2014.

Bibliography

Benedict, John Downing. *Muskogee and Northeastern Oklahoma: Including the Counties of Muskogee, McIntosh, Wagoner, Cherokee, Sequoyah, Adair, Delaware, Mayes, Rogers, Washington, Nowata, Craig, and Ottawa.* S. J. Clarke Publishing, 1922.

Betz, Ava, Virginia Downing, Dixie Munro, and Florence Dolsen. *A Prowers County History.* Prowers County Historical Society, 1986.

Bogle, Donald. *Toms, Coons, Mulattoes, Mammies, and Bucks: An Interpretive History of Blacks in American Films.* Continuum, 1994.

Bowser, Eileen. *The Transformation of Cinema, 1907–1915.* University of California Press, 1994.

Brooks, Kent. *Old Boston: As Wild as They Come.* Lonesome Prairie Publications, 2018.

Brownlow, Kevin. *The West, the War, and the Wilderness.* Knopf Doubleday, 2013.

Burton, Arthur T. *Black, Red, and Deadly: Black and Indian Gunfighters of the Indian Territory, 1870–1907.* Eakin Press, 1991.

Cain, James Mallahan. *The Postman Always Rings Twice.* Grosset & Dunlap, 1934.

Carter, Kenneth. *Buzz! Inside the Minds of Thrill-Seekers, Daredevils, and Adrenaline Junkies.* Cambridge University Press, 2019.

Comstock, Anthony. *Traps for the Young.* Funk & Wagnalls, 1884.

Croy, Homer. *Cole Younger: Last of the Great Outlaws.* University Of Nebraska Press, 1999.

Cullen, Jim. *The Art of Democracy: A Concise History of Popular Culture in the United States.* New York University Press, 2002.

Davis, Ronald L. *William S. Hart: Projecting the American West.* University of Oklahoma Press, 2003.

Denning, Michael. *Mechanic Accents: Dime Novels and Working-Class Culture in America.* Verso, 1987.

Eckhardt, Joseph P. *The King of the Movies: Film Pioneer Siegmund Lubin.* Fairleigh Dickinson University Press, 1997.

Elman, Robert. *Fired in Anger: The Personal Handguns of American Heroes and Villains.* Doubleday, 1968

Fitzgerald, F. Scott. *The Great Gatsby.* Charles Scribner's Sons, 1925.

Foreman, Grant. *The Five Civilized Tribes: Cherokee, Chickasaw, Choctaw, Creek, Seminole.* University of Oklahoma Press, 1934.

270   Bibliography

Fremon, David K. *The Jim Crow Laws and Racism in United States History.* Enslow Publishers, 2015.

Gipson, Fred. *Fabulous Empire: Colonel Zack Miller's Story.* Houghton Mifflin, 1946.

Guinn, Jeff. *Go Down Together.* Simon and Schuster, 2012.

Harlow, Victor Emmanuel. *Makers of Government in Oklahoma: A Descriptive Roster of Oklahomans Whose Influence and Activity Make Them Significant in the Course of Public Events in Their State.* Harlow Publishing Company, 1930.

Harrington, Fred Harvey. *Hanging Judge.* University of Oklahoma Press, 1996.

Haven, Lisa Stein. *The Early Years of Charlie Chaplin: Final Shorts and First Features.* Pen and Sword, 2023.

Girardin, G. Russell, and William J. Helmer, with the assistance of Rick Mattix. *Dillinger: The Untold Story.* Indiana University Press, 2004.

Haven, Lisa Stein. *The Early Years of Charlie Chaplin: Final Shorts and First Features.* Pen and Sword, 2023.

Henry, O. *Sixes and Sevens.* Doubleday, Page, 1911.

Hightower, Michael J. *Banking in Oklahoma, 1907–2000.* University of Oklahoma Press, 2014.

Hobsbawm, Eric J. *Bandits.* New Press, 2000.

Hough, Emerson. *The Story of the Outlaw.* Curtis Publishing, 1907.

Jennings, Al, and Will Irwin. *Beating Back.* D. Appleton, 1915.

Jennings, Al. *Through the Shadows with O. Henry: The Unlikely Friendship of Al Jennings and William Sydney Porter.* Skyhorse, 2016.

Johnson, Stephen Burge, ed. *Burnt Cork: Traditions and Legacies of Blackface Minstrelsy.* University of Massachusetts Press, 2012.

Jones, Daryl. *The Dime Novel Western.* Popular Press, Bowling Green State University, 1978.

Jones, Derek. *Censorship: A World Encyclopedia.* Fitzroy Dearborn, 2001.

Kearney, Jim [Oliver "Oll" Coomes]. *Hank Starr at Pryor Creek, or, Old Jack Drew Heard From.* Street & Smith Log Cabin Library, 1893.

Kennedy, Matthew. *Roadshow! The Fall of Film Musicals in the 1960s.* Oxford University Press, 2014.

Klein, Joe. *Woody Guthrie: A Life.* Delta Trade Paperbacks, 1999.

Bibliography

Koblas, John J. *The Great Cole Younger and Frank James Historical Wild West Show.* North Star Press of St. Cloud, 2002.

Kooistra, Paul. *Criminals as Heroes: Structure, Power & Identity.* Popular Press, Bowling Green State University, 1989.

Koszarski, Richard. *An Evening's Entertainment: The Age of the Silent Feature Picture, 1915–1928.* University of California Press, 1994.

Kuhn, J. L. L. *List of Films, Reels, and Views Examined.* Published by the author, 1918.

Lahue, Kalton C., and Terry Brewer. *Kops and Custards: The Legend of the Keystone Films: A Book.* University of Oklahoma Press, 1972.

Lawrence, David Herbert. *Studies in Classic American Literature.* Thomas Seltzer, 1923.

Loewen, James W. *Sundown Towns: A Hidden Dimension of American Racism.* New Press, 2018.

Malitz, Jürgen. *Nero.* Proquest, 2005.

Matera, Dary. *John Dillinger.* Hachette Books, 2005.

McWhirter, Cameron. *Red Summer: The Summer of 1919 and the Awakening of Black America.* Henry Holt, 2011.

Mix, Olive Stokes. *The Fabulous Tom Mix.* Hassell Street Press, 2021.

Morris, John W. *Ghost Towns of Oklahoma.* University of Oklahoma Press, 1977.

Musslewhite, Lynn, and Suzanne Jones Crawford. *One Woman's Political Journey: Kate Barnard and Social Reform, 1875–1930.* University Of Oklahoma Press, 2003.

Nash, Jay Robert. *Bloodletters and Badmen.* Warner Books, 1975.

Nash, Jay Robert. *Encyclopedia of Western Lawmen & Outlaws.* Da Capo Press, 2010.

Nash, Jay Robert. *Jay Robert Nash's Crime Chronology: A Worldwide Record, 1900–1983.* Facts on File Publications, 1984.

Neibaur, James L., and Terri Niemi. *Buster Keaton's Silent Shorts, 1920–1923.* Scarecrow Press, 2013.

Newman, Victoria R. *Prisons of Cañon City.* Arcadia, 2008.

Nix, Evett Dumas, and Gordon Hines. *Oklahombres: Particularly the Wilder Ones.* Eden Publishing House, 1929.

Nolan, Jeannette Covert, and Hamilton Greene. *O. Henry: The Story of William Sydney Porter.* Messner, 1945.

Rogers, Will. *Will Rogers' Weekly Articles*. Edited by James Smallwood and Steven K. Gragert. Vol. 1, *The Harding/Coolidge Years, 1922–1925*. Oklahoma State University Press, 1980.

Samuelson, Nancy B. *The Dalton Gang Story: Lawmen to Outlaws*. Shooting Star Press, 1992.

Samuelson, Nancy B. *Shoot from the Lip: The Lives, Legends, and Lies of the Three Guardsmen of Oklahoma and US Marshal Nix*. Shooting Star Press, 1998.

Shirley, Glenn. *Belle Starr and Her Times: The Literature, the Facts, and the Legends*. University of Oklahoma Press, 1982.

Shirley, Glenn. *Last of the Real Badmen: Henry Starr*. University of Nebraska Press, 1965.

Shirley, Glenn. *Marauders of the Indian Nations*. Barbed Wire Press, 1994.

Shirley, Glenn. *Purple Sage: The Exploits, Adventures, and Writings of Patrick Sylvester McGeeney*. Barbed Wire Press, 1989.

Shirley, Glenn. *Temple Houston: Lawyer with a Gun*. University of Oklahoma Press, 2010.

Shirley, Glenn. *West of Hell's Fringe: Crime, Criminals, and the Federal Peace Officer in Oklahoma Territory, 1889–1907*. University of Oklahoma Press, 1978.

Slotkin, Richard. *The Return of Henry Starr*. Atheneum, 1988.

Smith, Andrew Brodie. *Shooting Cowboys and Indians*. University of Colorado Press, 2003.

Solomon, Matthew. *Fantastic Voyages of the Cinematic Imagination: Georges Méliès's Trip to the Moon*. State University of New York Press, 2011.

Starr, Henry. *Thrilling Events: Life of Henry Starr, by Himself*. R. D. Gordon Publishing, 1914.

Steckmesser, Kent Ladd. *Western Outlaws: The Good Badman in Fact, Film and Folklore*. Regina Books, 1983.

Sutton, Fred Ellsworth, and A. B. Macdonald. *Hands Up! Stories of the Six-Gun Fighters of the Old Wild West*. Bobbs-Merrill, 1927.

Thompson, Frank T. *Texas Hollywood: Filmmaking in San Antonio Since 1910*. Maverick Publishing, 2002.

Thompson, Jerry. *Wrecked Lives and Lost Souls: Joe Lynch Davis and the Last of the Oklahoma Outlaws*. University of Oklahoma Press, 2019

Tilghman, Zoe A. *Marshal of the Last Frontier: Life and Services of William Matthew (Bill) Tilghman, for 50 Years One of the Greatest Peace of the West.* Arthur H. Clark, 1949.

Treherne, John. *The Strange History of Bonnie and Clyde.* Cooper Square Press, 2000.

Wagenknecht, Edward. *The Movies in the Age of Innocence.* 3rd ed. McFarland, 2014.

Wallis, Michael. *Oil Man: The Story of Frank Phillips and the Birth of Phillips Petroleum.* University of Oklahoma Press, 2014.

Wallis, Michael. *Pretty Boy: The Life and Times of Charles Arthur Floyd.* W. W. Norton, 2011.

Wallis, Michael. *The Real Wild West: The 101 Ranch and the Creation of the American West.* St. Martin's Press, 2000.

Woodward, C. Vann. *The Strange Career of Jim Crow.* Oxford University Press. 2001.

Wooley, John. *Shot in Oklahoma: A Century of Sooner State Cinema.* University of Oklahoma Press, 2012.

Young, Richard, and Judy Dockrey Young. *Outlaw Tales: Legends, Myths, and Folklore from America's Middle Border.* August House, 1992.

Articles and Chapters

Alesis, Angela. "Who Was the Real James Young Deer?" *Bright Lights Film Journal,* no. 80 (May 2013): 1–10.

Alvarez, Max. "The Origins of the Film Exchange." *Film History* 17, no. 4 (2005): 431–65.

Barron, Lynn, Sr. Review of "Henry Starr, Oklahoma Outlaw." *National Outlaw Lawman Association Quarterly* (1981): 13.

Hinkle, Matt. "Henry Starr and the Rough Ones." *Golden West,* March 1974.

Kennan, Clara B. "When Henry Starr Robbed the Bentonville Bank: 1893." *Arkansas Historical Quarterly* 7, no. 1 (Spring 1948): 68–80.

L'Engle, Henry A. "Prison Reform in Colorado." *La Follette's Weekly Magazine* 4, no. 2 (January 13, 1912): 7–8.

Lerskov, Dr. Andrew. "Review of Radium Water." *Journal of the Oklahoma State Medical Association,* no. 5 (1913): 458–64.

Parker, Alison M. "New York Society for the Suppression of Vice." In Jones, *Censorship.*

274 Bibliography

Potamianos, George. "Movies at the Margins, The Distribution of Films to Theaters in Small-Town America." Chap. 1 in *American Silent Film: Discovering Marginalized Voices,* edited by Gregg Bachman and Thomas J. Slater. Southern Illinois University Press, 2002.

Spears, Jack. "Hollywood's Oklahoma." *Chronicles of Oklahoma* 67, no. 4 (Winter 1989–90): 340–81.

Newspapers and Magazines

Abilene (KS) Daily Chronicle
Ada (OK) Evening News
AHTA Weekly News (St. Paul, KS)
American-Democrat (Anadarko, OK),
Arizona Republican (Phoenix)
Arkansas City (KS) Daily Traveler
Arkansas Daily Gazette (Little Rock)
Arkansas Democrat (Little Rock)
Arkansas Democrat Magazine
Arkansas Gazette (Little Rock)
Atlanta Journal
Attica (OK) Independent
Bakersfield Californian
Bartlesville (OK) Daily Enterprise
Bartlesville (OK) Daily Express
Bartlesville (OK) Examiner
Bartlesville (OK) Morning Examiner
Bartlesville (OK) Weekly Examiner
Baxter Bulletin (Mountain Home, AR)
Beaver (OK) Herald
Bisbee (AZ) Daily Review
Black Hills Union (Rapid City, SD)
Blackwell (OK) Daily News
Blackwell (OK) Journal-Tribune
Blackwell (OK) Morning Tribune
Blackwell (OK) Weekly Sun

Boone County Headlight (Harrison, AR)
Boone County Historian (Harrison, AR)
Boynton (OK) Index
Brinkley (AR) Argus
Bristow (OK) Daily Record
Brooklyn Citizen
Butler (MO) Weekly Times
Cameron Missouri Sun
Cañon City (CO) Record
Cassville (MO) Republican
Champaign (IL) Daily News
Chandler (OK) News-Publicist
Chandler (OK) Tribune
Charlotte (NC) News
Charlotte (NC) Observer
Cherokee (OK) Sentinel
Cherryvale (KS) Republican
Chickasha (OK) Daily Express
Chillicothe (MO) Constitution
Choctaw Herald (Hugo, OK)
Chronicle (Scottburg, IN)
Chronicles of Oklahoma
Claremore (OK) Progress
Coalgate (OK) Record-Register

Bibliography

Coffeyville (KS) Daily Journal
Coffeyville (KS) Journal
Collinsville (OK) Star
Columbus (KS) Daily Advocate
Columbus (KS) Weekly Advocate
Creek County Democrat (Shamrock, OK)
Cushing (OK) Independent
Custer County News (Clinton, OK)
Daily Ardmoreite (Ardmore, OK)
Daily Arkansas Gazette (Little Rock)
Daily Chieftain (Vinita, OK)
Daily Durant (OK) Democrat
Daily Illini (Chicago)
Daily Oklahoman (Oklahoma City)
Daily Phoenix (AZ)
Daily Republican (Rushville, IN)
Daily Sentinel (Grand Junction, CO)
Daily Times (Los Angeles)
Dallas Express
Democrat-Herald (Newkirk, OK)
Dresden Enterprise (Gleason, TN)
Drumright (OK) Weekly Derrick
Durant (OK) Weekly News
Dustin (OK) News
Ebony
El Paso Herald
El Reno (OK) Daily American
El Reno (OK) Daily Democrat
Enid (OK) Daily News
Evening Star (Independence, KS)
Fayetteville (AR) Daily Democrat
Fort Smith (AR) Times
Fort Wayne (IN) Journal-Gazette

Fort Gibson (OK) New Era
Fort Worth Record and Register
Fort Worth Star-Telegram
Franklin County Tribune (Union, MO)
Frontier Times
Gastonia (NC) Gazette
Golden West Magazine
Granite (OK) Enterprise
Grenola (KS) Gazette
Guthrie (OK) Daily Leader
Harlow's Weekly
Harrison (AR) Daily Times
Harrison (AR) Times
Heavener (OK) Ledger
Henryetta (OK) Daily Freelance
Hollywood Citizen News
Hominy (OK) News
Hominy (OK) News Republican
Hooker (OK) Advance
Hughes County Tribune (Holdenville, OK)
Independence (KS) Daily Reporter
Indian Chieftain (Vinita, OK)
Indian Citizen (Atoka, OK)
Investor (Oklahoma City)
Iola (KS) Register
Jasper County (MO) News
Jenks (OK) News
Jet (OK) Visitor
Joplin Globe (St. Louis)
Kansan (Jamestown, KS)
Kansas City (MO) Journal
Kansas City News Service
Kansas City (MO) Post

Kansas City (MO) Star

Kansas City (MO) Times

King Jack (Commerce, OK)

LaJunta (CO) Tribune

Lamar Register (Prowers County, CO)

Lamont (OK) Valley News

Lawton (OK) News

Lincoln County Republican (Chandler, OK)

Lindsay (OK) News

Little Rock Daily News

Los Angeles Evening Citizen News

Los Angeles Times

Marietta (OK) Monitor

Marlow (OK) Review

Maysville (OK) News

McAlester (OK) News-Capital

Meeker (OK) Herald

Mena (AR) Weekly Star

Miami (FL) Herald

Miami (OK) Daily Record-Herald

Miami (OK) Record

Monett (MO) Times

Morning Examiner (Bartlesville, OK)

Morning Oregonian (Portland, OR)

Motion Picture Magazine

Motion Picture News

Mountain Echo (Yellville, AR)

Moving Picture World

Muskogee (OK) Daily Phoenix

Muskogee (OK) Times-Democrat

Neodesha (OK) Daily Sun

News-Capital (McAlester, OK)

Newton (KS) Journal

New York Times

Northwest Arkansas Democrat-Gazette (Fayetteville)

Nowata (OK) Star

Nowata (OK) Weekly Star Times

Ocala (FL) Evening Star

Okemah (OK) Independent

Okemah (OK) Ledger

Okfuskee County News (Okemah, OK)

Oklahoma City Times

Oklahoma Farmer and Laborer (Sapulpa)

Oklahoma News (Oklahoma City)

Oklahoma State Capital (Guthrie)

Oklahoma Today

Okmulgee (OK) Daily Times

Osage Journal (Pawhuska, OK)

Ozark Daily Times (Harrison, AR)

Paint, Oil, and Drug Review (Chicago)

Palmyra (MO) Spectator

Parsons (KS) Sun

Pasadena (CA) Post

Pawnee (OK) County Journal

Perry (OK) Republican

Pine Bluff (AR) Daily Graphic

Ponca City (OK) News

Prague (OK) Times-Herald

Queen City Times (Agra, OK)

Quinlan (OK) Mirror

Record Searchlight (Redding, CA)

Rushville (IN) Republican

San Antonio Evening News

San Antonio Express

San Francisco Call

Bibliography

San Mateo (CA) Times

Santa Cruz (CA) Evening News

Sapulpa (OK) Herald

Saturday Evening Post

Sedan (KS) Times-Star

Semi-Weekly Graphic (Pine Bluff, AR)

Sequoyah County Democrat (Sallisaw, OK)

Shawnee (OK) Daily News-Herald

Shawnee (OK) Morning News

Shawnee (OK) News-Star

Silver Blade (Rathdrum, ID)

Smithsonian magazine

Southern Standard (Arkadelphia, AR)

Southwest American (Fort Smith, AR)

Springfield (MO) Democrat-Herald

Springfield (MO) News Leader

St. Louis Globe-Democrat

St. Louis Republic

St. Louis Weekly Gazette

St. Paul Pioneer Press

Star Progress (Berryville, AR)

State Sentinel (Stigler, OK)

Stillwater (OK) Gazette

Stonewall (OK) Weekly News

Stroud (OK) Democrat

Stroud (OK) Messenger

Sunday Oklahoman (Oklahoma City)

Tacoma (WA) Times

Tahlequah (OK) Arrow

Times-Democrat (Pawnee, OK)

Topeka (KS) Daily Capital

Topeka (KS) State Journal

True West Magazine

Tulsa Daily Legal News

Tulsa Daily World

Tulsa Democrat

Tulsa Morning News

Tulsa Post

Tulsa Tribune

Tulsa World News

Tulsa World Online

Urbana (IL) Daily Courier

Vernon (TX) Record

Vian (OK) Press

Vinita (OK) Daily Chieftain

Waco (TX) News-Tribune

Washington (DC) Herald

Washington (DC) Times

Washington County Sentinel (Bartlesville, OK)

Watonga (OK) Republican

Waurika (OK) News-Democrat

Wetumka (OK) Gazette

Wichita (KS) Beacon

Wichita (KS) Daily Eagle

Wichita (KS) Eagle

Wid's Daily

Wilburton (OK) News

Winfield (KS) Daily Free Press

Index

101 Ranch, 26, 88, 141, 158, 181, 183, 188, 209, 215

A

American Robin Hoods, 122
Amerman, Anna Lee, 115
Amity, CO, 4, 9, 140
anti-Starr legislation, 189
Arkansas Bankers' Association, 212
Arnold, George (Lincoln County sheriff), 69, 80
Aryan, The (film), 182

B

Bandits (book), 120, 122
Bank Robber Bill, 38–39
Bank Robbery (film), 26, 65
Barbee, L. N. (Oklahoma state representative), 109
Barnard, Kate, 176–77, 202–3, 214
Barrow, Clyde. *See* Bonnie and Clyde
Bartlesville, OK, 3, 36, 89, 121, 174
bathhouses, 179–80
Battle of Ingalls, 66, 69–70, 72
Beach, Rex, 110
Beating Back (book), 24, 27, 65, 94, 218
Beating Back (film), 28, 65, 108
Beating Back Bill, 109–10
Benge, Adna, 206–7
Bentonville, AR, 3, 44, 100–105, 140, 198
Bentonville Sun (newspaper), 103–5
Berry, J. D (captain, Fort Smith prison), 146
Betzwood Studio, PA, 98–99
Beyond the Law (film), 37, 92, 217
Birth of a Nation (film), 97, 161, 163
Black Codes, 161
blackface, 161, 163
Blaine, George (Tulsa Police captain), 185
Blue-Sky Commission, OK, 96
Bonnie and Clyde, x, 122
Boone County Jail, AR, 195, 197–200, 202–3

279

280   Index

Bouse, AZ, 4, 173
Boynton, OK, 139
Brackett, Charles, 184, 190–91, 193–95, 197, 201, 205, 213
Breeding, Homer, 47, 49, 84
Broadwell, Dick, 29–30, 33, 35, 40
Brown, Kelley (Oklahoma state representative), 109
Brownlow, Kevin, 85
Buck, Rufus, 122, 130, 146, 154–55, 222
Butz, Warren (Muskogee Police commissioner), 100

C

C. M. Condon and Company Bank (Coffeyville, KS), 30–32, 36, 217
Callicott, Darley, 197
Captain Scott, 130
Capture of Henry Starr (film), 78–79
Carlisle Indian Industrial School, PA, 7
Cassville, MO, 184–85
Cattle Annie, 27, 66
censorship, 106–13, 189, 210
Chandler, OK, 26, 59, 64–65, 67–70, 72–75, 77, 79–80, 213
Charlton, Defense Attorney J. R., 74
Cherokee (Native Americans), ix–xi, 6–8, 12, 14, 17, 19–20, 86–87, 126,
    128, 130, 142, 144–47, 149–55, 159–65, 175
Cherokee Bill, 87, 93, 122, 128, 130, 142, 144–47, 149–55, 160–63, 199,
    222. *See also* Goldsby, Crawford
Cherokee Civil War, 14
Cherokee Nation, xi, 17
Claremore, OK, 179–81, 184, 188–89, 196, 202, 204
Claremore Commercial Club (CCC), 180–83, 189
Clark, P. J (president, Pan-American Motion Picture Corporation), 93–95, 97,
    99–101, 111–13, 116–17, 120, 130, 135–36, 156, 163, 167–70, 174, 179
Clifton, Dan "Dynamite Dick," 71
Coffeyville Commercial Club (KS), 30, 35
Coffman, Cleve, 191–94, 196–97, 201
Colorado State Penitentiary, Cañon City, ix, 1, 4, 140
Community Organization for Reorganization and Enhancement (CORE)
    (Harrison, AR), 221
Comstock, Anthony (US postal inspector), 107–8
Cook, Bill, 146–47
Coomes, Oliver "Oll" (a.k.a. Jim Kearney), 124–25
Cove Bank (Cove, AR), 17
Cromwell, OK, 215, 222
    Chamber of Commerce, 214

Index   281

Crump, George (US marshal), 146–47, 150–53, 198–99
Cumplin, Link, 103–5
Curnutt, Carter, 197
Curry, Paul, 46, 52–53, 55–56, 62–64, 73, 78–80, 84, 114, 140

D

Dalton, Bill, 29, 35, 40, 70–71, 122, 128, 130
Dalton, Bob, 23, 29–30, 32, 34–35, 40, 71, 92, 122, 130, 217
Dalton, Emmett, x, 23, 27, 29–37, 71, 81, 90–91, 112, 217
Dalton, Grat, 23, 29–30, 34–35, 40, 92
Dalton, Julia, 217
Dalton Gang, ix, 23, 29–30, 34–37, 40, 57, 92, 122, 128, 130, 217
Daly, William Robert, 161
Daugherty, Roy, 66, 70. *See also* Jones, Arkansas Tom
Davis, Joe, 16–19, 42–43, 45–47, 49, 52–54, 56–58, 72, 94–95, 193, 213
Death Alley (Coffeyville, KS), 31–34
Death Row (Fort Smith Prison), 146. *See also* Murderers Row
Debtor to the Law, A (film), ix–x, 128, 132–33, 139–46, 156–57, 160–61,
    163–76, 178–79, 183, 185–87, 189, 214, 216
DeMille, Cecil B., 166
Dempsey, Jack, 174
Department of Impure Literature (WCTU), 108, 110
Diaz, Porfirio (Mexico president), 119
Dickerson, J. T. (Oklahoma state representative), 109
Dickey, Detective Henry, 131–34, 142, 159–60, 173
Dillinger, John, x, 43, 122
Dodge, Arthur, 6, 8, 131
Dodge City, KS, 64, 66
Dodrill, Isaac (deputy sheriff), 54
Doolin, Bill, 66, 69–71, 80, 118, 130
Doolin-Dalton Gang, 69–70
Draper, Lauron, 136, 142
Drumright, OK, 59, 70, 174
Duncan, Johnny, 218
Duryea, Dan, 218

E

Eagle, J. D. "Bud," 194, 205
Eagle Film Company, 66, 78. *See also* Nix-Tilghman Anti-Outlaw
    Movie Company
Earp, Wyatt, 64, 219
Eaton, Charles, 12–13, 159, 179
Edison, Thomas, 119

Eighteenth Amendment of 1919, 110. *See also* Prohibition
Elba, Idris, 222
Eldridge, Reverend James, 208
Elliot, Sam, 222
Elwick, Guy, 10, 20, 68, 215
Elwick, Loretta "Retta," 10–11, 20–23, 60, 68, 72, 76–77, 83, 88, 90, 215
Enloe, B. A (US marshal), 39
Eoff, Turnkey R. C., 147, 149–50
Essanay Studios, 97
Estes, Lewis, 41–47, 56–61, 63–64, 67–68, 72–74, 78, 80, 140–41
Evans, Dr. J. J., 60–61, 63
Exendine, Jasper (US marshal), 13

F

Fairbanks, Douglas, ix, 90, 136, 158
Farnum, George Henry, 171–72
Fenton, S. W., 4
Fitzgerald, F. Scott, 10
Floyd, Charles Arthur "Pretty Boy," x, 122
Fowler, Dr. Tildon P., 196–97, 200, 204
Fuller, Chief Justice Melville Weston, 159
Fullerton, Hugh S., 39

G

Gable, Clark, x
generosity (rubric), 123, 126
gentleman bandit, 17, 102, 120–21, 126, 130
Germain, Carl E., 136. *See also* Hackett, William Karl
Gilstrap, Captain H. B., 59
Glasco Usury Bill, 59
Glazier, Al, 118
Godfrey, Thomas Hamer, 50
Goldsby, Crawford, 145, 151, 161–62. *See also* Cherokee Bill
Goldwyn, Samuel, 120
Goldwyn Pictures Corporation, 120
"good" badman, 127, 129, 182
Gordon, Mary, 6, 68, 72, 77, 85–87, 177, 189, 202–3, 206–7, 217
Gordon, Raymond D (detective, Tulsa Police), 12, 177
Gore, Senator Thomas, 106–7, 111–13
Gore-Harreld Bill, 106, 111–13
Grace Methodist Episcopal Church (Tulsa), 21
Granada, CO, 6–8

Index 283

Great Dalton Raid, The (film), 36
Great Depression, The, 122
Great Gatsby, The (book), 10
Great War, The. *See* World War I
Grecian, O. E., 47, 49, 56
Greenshaw, Karl, 204
Griffith, D. W., 97, 136, 161, 163
Guild, Charles, 54, 63
Gunter Hotel (San Antonio, TX), 136, 141
Guthrie, OK, 2–3, 172
Guthrie, Woodrow Wilson "Woody," 171

H

Hackett, William Karl, 57, 136, 139–42, 170, 173, 214
Hackett, William Karl. *See also* Germain, Carl E.
Hammett, Cora D., 108–9
Hank Starr at Pryor Creek (book), 107, 124–25, 127, 129
Happy Jack (film), 102–3
Harder They Fall, The (film), 222
Hargis, Sam (Oklahoma representative), 109
Harreld, John (Oklahoma representative), 106–7, 111, 113
Harrison, AR, ix, 184, 186, 190, 192, 197, 199–200, 204–8, 210, 212, 221
Harrison, President Benjamin, 128
Harrison, Louis Reeves, 166
Harrison, Luther (Oklahoma state senator), 111
Harrison, W. B., 38, 108
Hart, William S., 93–95, 114, 136, 158, 166, 181–82
Haskell, Charles (Oklahoma governor), 3, 106
Hastings, William, 85, 106–7
Hatfield, "Devil" Anse, 91
Hatfield-McCoy Feud (film), 91
Heart of the Sunset (film), 120
Higgins, Elijah "Lige," 18–19, 42–43, 45–47, 52, 54, 56, 58, 72
Hinkle, Matt, 188
Hixon, John (deputy marshal), 71
Hobsbawm, Eric, 120, 122, 129
Hoch, E. W (Kansas governor), 35
Hoffman, Colonel Roy, 84–85, 177, 203
Holly, CO, 8–11, 20
Hollywood, CA, xi, 72, 91, 94–95, 120, 179, 181, 213–14, 217
Houston, Lea Temple, 24–25
Hueston, Thomas (deputy marshal), 71

284 Index

Hughes, Lorene, 49–51, 114–15, 128
Huling, Alexander, 127–28, 164
Hunter, Lewis (Oklahoma state representative), 109

I

Ince, Thomas, 95, 136
Indian Territory, x, 6–7, 43, 86, 128, 143
Irwin, Will, 24, 26
Isham Hardware (Coffeyville, KS), 31, 34

J

James, Frank, x, 14, 107, 122, 158
James, Jesse, ix, 14, 40, 57, 107, 122, 125, 158, 219
James–Younger Gang, 95, 186
Jennings, Alphonso "Al," x, 23–27, 65–66, 90, 93–95, 99, 107–9, 112, 171–72, 179, 184, 189, 217–19
Jim Crow laws, 161, 163, 166
Johnson, Charles, 42, 46, 72, 74
Johnson, Dr. J. J., 198–99
Jones, Arkansas Tom, 27, 66, 69–72, 213. *See also* Daugherty, Roy

K

Kaiser, Hose, 84, 124, 126
Kansas State Penitentiary, 29
Kearney, Jim, 124–25
Keating, Lawrence, 147, 149–50
Keaton, Buster, 24
Kent, James "Bennie," 26–27, 36, 65; 67–68, 77
kinetograph, 119
King of Bank Robbers, ix, 21, 67, 93–95, 158
Kirby, Dr. Frank, 196, 206
Kloehr, John, 33–34
Knox, Philander (US attorney general), 87
Kooistra, Paul, 122

L

Lady of the Dugout (film), 90
Lahoma (film), 166
Lamar, CO, 4
land rush, 76, 122, 128, 166
Larson, T. E., 156
Last Ride of the Dalton Gang (film), 217
Last Stand of the Dalton Boys at Coffeyville Kansas (film), 36–37

Index 285

Lawson, George, 150
Lee-Huckins Hotel (Oklahoma City), 99, 111, 113
Lenapah, OK, 147
Lipsey, Elizabeth "Lizzie," 131, 139
Little Breeches, 27, 66
Little Caney River, 127
Lockhart, Dave Edward, 184, 190–91, 195, 197, 204–6, 212–13
Log Cabin Library (book series), 107, 124–25
Lone Ranger lawsuit, 218
Love, Sheriff Jack, 25
Lubin, Sigmund, 97–99
Lubinville, 98–99
Lucas, Sam, 161
Lumière brothers, 85
Lycan, Marshal A. W., 44–45, 54–55
"Lytell Geste of Robyn Hode, The," 124

M

MacDonald, A. B., 16, 62, 77, 92
Maledon, George, 153–54
Man and the Law, The, 112. See also *A Debtor to the Law*
Manhattan Melodrama (film), x
Mason Hotel (Claremore, OK), 180
Maxfield, Bud, 42, 44–46, 50, 56–58, 72, 74
McAlester, OK, 74, 80, 83, 99, 174, 176–77
McClellan, George B., Jr., 108
McConnell, William "Uncle Bill," 150
McGeeney, Patrick Sylvester (P. S.), 57, 117–20, 130, 132–33, 135–37, 139–44, 173, 187, 214
McKinley, President William, 25
Méliès, Gaston, 119
Méliès, George, 1
Méliès Manufacturing Company (Fort Lee, NJ, and San Antonio, TX), 119
Melton, Ernest, 147
Mendenhall Hotel and Bath House (Claremore, OK), 180
Miller, Colonel Joseph C., 56, 183, 188
Miller, Zack, 188
Miller brothers 101 Ranch. *See* 101 Ranch
Milum, Bill Jim, 198
Minnesota Board of Pardons, 186
Minnesota Territorial Prison, 186
Mitchell, Tony, 77
Mix, Tom, 158, 166, 215

286 Index

Moore, Bob (deputy sheriff), 38–39, 193–96, 214
Moore, Naomi, 191–92, 196, 213
Morrison, May, 13, 135, 140
Mosher, A. A., 123–24
Motion Picture Patents Company (MPPC), 119
Mulhall, Colonel Zach, 69–70, 72
Muller, Alix, 187
Murderers Row (Fort Smith Prison), 144, 146–47, 152. *See also* Death Row
Mutual Film Corporation vs. Industrial Commission of Ohio (1915), 108
Myers, William J. "Bill," 191, 193–95, 197, 199–200, 206, 212

N

Nash, J. Robert, 21, 23, 39, 190–92, 195, 197, 206
Native Americans, 128, 164, 166, 177, 182
  as violent threat on film, 164, 166
Natural Mutoscene Company, 26, 36, 65
Nelson, Laura, 171–72
Newcomb, George "Bitter Creek," 71, 118
Nichols, W. B (Oklahoma City chief of police), 80
Nix, Evett "E. D." Dumas (US marshal), 65–66, 70, 72, 80, 135, 209
Nix-Tilghman Anti-Outlaw Movie Company, 66. *See also* Eagle Film Company
noble robber, 122–23, 129
Northfield, MN, 186
Nowata, OK, 12–13, 131, 168
Nowata Depot Train Robbery, 131, 142

O

Ohio State Penitentiary, ix, 1–2, 23, 25–26, 94, 160, 172, 174, 219
OK Corral (Tombstone, AZ), 221
OK Hotel (Ingalls, OK), 71–72
Okemah City Council (Okemah, OK), 170
Oklahoma Bankers Association (OBA), 38, 59
Oklahoma Board of Review, 111
Oklahoma City, 57, 77–78, 80, 99, 109, 112–13, 169, 214, 216
Oklahoma City Board of Commissioners, 112
Oklahoma Kid, The (film), 218
Oklahoma National Guard, 84–85
Oklahoma Press Association (OPA), 111–12
Oklahoma State Bar Association (OSBA), 110–11
Oklahoma State Medical Board, 180
Oklahoma State Pardon and Parole Office, 178
Oklahoma State Penitentiary, ix, 2, 74, 76, 80, 87, 93, 95, 99, 176–79, 212, 215

Index   287

Oklahoma statehood, 109, 128
Old Bliss, OK, 26
Old Gray Mare, 4
Old Ponca Depot, 124

P

Pacific Express Company, 130–31, 142
Pan-American Motion Picture Corporation, 93, 95–96, 100–101, 105, 112–14, 116, 120, 160–61, 164, 166–67, 177
Parker, Bonnie. *See* Bonnie and Clyde
Parker, Brass, 150
Parker, Judge Isaac, 131, 159
Parks, J. M., 41, 45, 47–48, 60
Passing of the Oklahoma Outlaws, The (film), 65–66, 69–70, 75, 78–80, 88, 106, 109, 114, 169, 178, 212–13
Pathé (Native Americans), 119, 164, 166, 168–69
Patrick, Lee, 48, 61, 76
Peacock Productions, 156, 164, 166, 186
Peck, George Dewey, 169–72, 174, 214
People's Bank (Bentonville, AR), 3, 102–5, 127, 140
People's Bank (Harrison, AR), xiii, 186, 190–97, 213, 219, 221
Pershing, John "Blackjack" (US Army general), 84
Phillips, Frank, 41
Phillips, L. E., 41
Phillips, Waite, 41
Pierce, George, 146, 149–50, 154
Pierce, John, 146, 154
Pindall, Xenopon (Arkansas acting governor), 3
Ponca Agency, 119
Porter, William S., 161
Porter, William Sydney. *See* Henry, O.
Porum Range War, 17
Postman Always Rings Twice, The (book), 10
Power, Bill, 29–35, 40, 122
Pratt, Lt. Richard Henry, 7
Pro Patria (film), 97–98
Prohibition, 110. *See also* Eighteenth Amendment of 1919
Pryor Creek, OK, 123–24
Purple Sage, The (book), 141

Q

Quay, Matthew (Pennsylvania senator), 87

R

R. D. Cline Furniture and Undertaking Company, 206–8
Ransom's Saloon (Ingalls, OK), 71
Red Buck, 71
Red Wing, Lillian (a.k.a. Lillian St. Cyr), 164
Reehm, George E., 97
Reehm, Lilian Gaynor, 136, 139–40
Return of Henry Starr, The (book), 141
Rice, Thomas, 161
Robertson, J. B. A (Oklahoma governor), 85, 87–88, 101, 105–6, 177, 179, 189
Robin Hood, 120–23, 127, 129, 135
Rogers, Ance, 88
Rogers, Will, 180
Rollens, Rufus, 184, 190–95, 197, 201, 205, 212
Roosevelt, President Theodore, ix, 1–3, 25–27, 41, 85, 87, 216
Rufus Buck Gang, 122, 130, 146, 155
Rutherford, Lew (Claremore night chief of police), 189

S

Sabinas, Mexico, 137
San Antonio, TX, 117, 119–20, 136–37, 141, 145, 175, 187
San Luis Potosi, Mexico, 119
Santa Paula, CA, 119
Sawyer, Claud, 42–43, 45–47, 49, 56–58, 72, 74, 99
Selective Service Act, 84
Shadley, Lafayette (deputy marshal), 71
Shamrock Photoplay Corporation (a.k.a. Shamrock Studios) (San Antonio, TX), 117, 120
Shelley, Ed, 147
Slaughter Kid, 71
Slosson's Drug Store (Coffeyville, KS), 34
Smith, Claude, 136, 141
social bandits, 120, 129
socialism, 19, 187–88
socialist, 19, 187–88
Southern Feature Film Corporation (SFFC), 91–92
Speakman, Streeter (Lincoln County attorney), 59, 74, 87
Speed, Dick (deputy marshal), 71
Spurrier, John R. "Buffalo Ray," 180–81, 184
St. Cyr, Lillian. *See* Red Wing, Lillian
Star Cafe (Holly, CO), 9–10
Star Films, 119

Index

289

Starr, Baby, 4
Starr, Belle, 14, 95
Starr, George, 8, 16, 67, 69, 76, 86, 105, 115, 118, 149, 164
Starr, Hulda "Lucille," 175–76, 184, 186, 189, 196, 201–3, 206, 208–9, 215–16
Starr, Olive "Ollie," 1–4, 78, 88–89, 100, 175, 202–3, 208–9, 216
Starr, Theodore (Teddy) Quay Roosevelt, 1–4, 6, 77, 88, 99, 143, 175, 201–3, 206, 208, 216
Starr, Tom, 10, 14, 16, 27, 158, 213, 215
Starr, Toney, 203–4, 207, 209, 215–16
Steckmesser, Kent Ladd, 122–23, 127–29
stereopticon, 23, 212
Stockton, Arch, 150
Street & Smith, 107–8, 124
Stroud National Bank, 40, 43, 45–47, 55, 61, 84, 115, 221
Stump, Herman, 126–27
Suedekum, Carl, 10

T

Tackett, John, 30, 34–36, 40
Tahlequah Male Seminary, 7–8
Talbot, Ralph (president of TOMA), 113
Terlton, OK, 38
Thanhouser Film Corporation, 27, 65
Theatre Owners and Managers Association (TOMA), 113, 168, 171
Thistlewaite, Edith, 191–92, 196
Thomas, Heck (US marshal), 117
Thrilling Events (book), ix–xi, 12, 15–16, 127–28, 135, 142, 152, 164, 166, 205
Tilghman, William "Bill" (US deputy marshal), 26–27, 64–68, 70, 72, 75, 77–78, 80, 87–88, 90, 178, 213–15, 222
Tousey, Frank, 107–8
Traps for the Young (book), 107
Trojan horse, 71
Tulsa Jack, 71
Tulsa Race Massacre, x, 156, 163, 213
Tynan, Thomas J (Colorado State Penitentiary warden), 4

U

Uncle Tom's Cabin (play, film), 161
Unto Him Who Transgresses, 97, 106, 113, 116. *See also* A Debtor to the Law
US marshal system, 129
US marshal system, corrupt, 12, 128

US Postal Service, 106, 111
US Supreme Court, 108

V

Villa, Francisco "Pancho," 84, 97, 177
Voyage dans la lune, Le (film), 1, 119

W

Wagley, Marvin J. (People's Bank president), 191–93, 195–96
Wheeler, Commissioner Stephen, 131
whitewashing, x, 160, 164–66, 182
Willard, Frances, 108
Williams, R. L. (Oklahoma governor), 21, 39, 63, 78
Wilson, Bridget, 167
Wilson, Charles B. (Oklahoma District Court judge), 72, 74, 76, 87
Wilson, Floyd, 120, 130–35, 139–40, 142, 159–60, 167, 173, 212
Wilson, George B., 10
Wilson, John "Kid," 3–4, 9, 103, 135, 140
Wilson, President Woodrow, 84
Wilson, Ruth, 190–95
Wilson, W. H., 199
Wolf Hunt, The (film), 26, 85
Women's Christian Temperance Union (WCTU), 108, 110
Wood, Maggie, 103–5
Woodcock Kay, Vivian, x, 97–98, 179
Woods, E. E. (Oklahoma state senator), 109, 182, 189
Woolley, James (Tulsa County sheriff), 21–22, 100–101, 213
World War I, 99, 163, 177, 184
Wynn, Bud, 198, 201, 205

X

XU ranch, 131, 133

Y

Yocum, Bob, 71
Yoes, Jacob (US marshal), 131
You Know My Name (film), 222
Young Deer, James, 164, 166
Younger, Bob, 14, 122
Younger, Cole, x, 14, 122, 186
Younger, Jim, 14, 122, 186, 188
Younger, Scout, 30, 36